THE CARIBBEAN COURT OF JUSTICE

Closing the Circle of Independence

THE CARIBBEAN COURT OF JUSTICE

Closing the Circle of Independence

Duke E. Pollard

Kingston

First published in Jamaica 2004 by
The Caribbean Law Publishing Company Ltd
Box 686
11 Cunningham Avenue
Kingston 6

Set in Sabon 11 pt
Book and cover design by Allison Brown

Printed and bound in the USA

National Library of Jamaica Cataloguing in Publication Data

Pollard Duke,
The Caribbean Court of Justice: closing the circle of independence/ Duke Pollard

p. ; cm

ISBN 976-8167-41-6

1. Appellate courts- Caribbean Area 2. Court administration- Caribbean
3. Caribbean Courts of Appeal
I. Title

347.03509729 dc 21

Dedicated to
Roy Augier and Elsa Goveia

CONTENTS

TABLE OF CASES

FOREWORD & ACKNOWLEDGEMENTS

The signing by ten Heads of Government of the Caribbean Community[1] on February 14, 2001 of the Agreement Establishing the Caribbean Court of Justice in Bridgetown, Barbados, must be perceived as the imminent denouement of a protracted, intensive, regional debate among the principal stakeholders of the Caribbean Court of Justice concerning delinking from the Judicial Committee of the Privy Council. This debate was punctuated, on the one hand, with vigorous asseverations about the imperatives of public accessibility to the Court, the normative relevance of the law to be applied, political and judicial autonomy of decision-making, and, on the other, with persistent, and oftentimes, genuine reservations about the diabolical intentions of the regional political directorate, the normative maturity of our indigenous legal system, the desired legal erudition of regional candidates for the Bench of the Court, their judicial integrity and independence, and the financial sustainability of the Court.[2]

The genesis of this controversy goes back to 1901 when the Jamaican Gleaner Newspaper, in an editorial comment, surmised that the Judicial Committee of the Privy Council might be out of joint with the times and serious consideration must be given to establishing a replacement, a regional court of last resort.[3] However, enthusiasm for the idea of an indigenous regional court of last resort did not enjoy widespread support at the time and the idea remained in a state of dormancy for almost another 50 years. In 1947 however, colonial governors of the Commonwealth Caribbean, meeting in Bridgetown, Barbados, resuscitated the idea of a regional court of last resort, but once again, the idea did not commend itself generally to competent decision-makers. A state of dormancy once again appeared to have overtaken the idea which was not revived until 1970 at the Sixth Heads of Government Conference in Kingston, Jamaica, where the Jamaican delegation tabled a proposal for the establishment of a Caribbean Court of Appeal.[4]

By this time, the Commonwealth Caribbean had already produced a remarkable constellation of brilliant, articulate professionals who were not averse to indulging intellectual forays into innovative forms of governmental institutions and constitutional development. The issue attracted the attention of the Organisation of Commonwealth Caribbean Bar Associations (OCCBA) which established a Representative Committee to consider and report on the establishment of a Caribbean Court of Appeal in substitution for the Judicial Committee of the Privy Council. The Representative Committee of OCCBA, which presented its report in 1972, did not only recommend the establishment of a Caribbean Court of Appeal in substitution for the Judicial Committee of the Privy Council, but also recommended that 'the Court be vested with original jurisdiction in respect of matters referred to it by agreement between the Caribbean States or any two or more of them arising out of such original treaties as the CARIFTA Agreement or by the Council of the Area or such matters as the interpretation of the Agreement'.[5]

Unable to sustain the initial fervour generated by the resurgence of the idea, competent decision-makers allowed it to subside only to be revived again two decades later when the West Indian Commission, established by the Heads of Government at their Tenth Meeting in Grand Anse, Grenada in 1989, succeeded in injecting political adrenalin into the ruminating veins of competent decision-makers by reference to the changing political and economic landscape in Europe and the wider world, with the bleak prospects for the regional economic integration movement, and plausible expectations for regional immiseration, unless drastic improvements were introduced into the relevant institutional arrangements to take the Caribbean Community into the new millennium.

The history of developments following *Time for Action*, the Report of the West Indian Commission in 1992, is very well known. The Judicial Committee of the Privy Council, commencing with its landmark decision in *Pratt and Morgan v. Attorney General of Jamaica*[6] delivered a spate of decisions on the application of the ultimate sanction in the Caribbean Community Member States which, juridically, were expressed to have emasculated the hallowed common law doctrine of precedent as it was generally understood in common law jurisdictions, and, by allegedly turning on their heads numerous decisions of the Judicial Committee of the Privy Council of long standing, introduced unacceptable levels of instability and uncertainty in the administration of criminal justice in the sub-region.[7] Employing the clairvoyance of hindsight, it is easy to discern that competent decision-makers did not, at the material time, respond to what might have been considered judicial heresy on the part of the Judicial Committee of the Privy Council in a dispassionate, measured, calm and collected way. Tempers were allowed to run high; reaction was swift and accusatorial; emotionalism was substituted for careful reflection and rational response, with the result that the impression was created that drastic measures were being contemplated by the regional political directorate to reassert the power of the executive over the judiciary. In this regional maelstrom of claim and counter-claim, any responsible initiative by the regional executive to implement the West Indian Commission's recommendations on the institutional arrangements perceived to be required to take the Community into the new millennium was taken out of context and accorded the status of an invidious, retaliatory remedial response. However, to the credit of the regional political directorate, sobriety and sound, informed, rational judgment were restored to the decision-making process resulting in the elaboration of a surfeit of international instruments which both deepened and widened the regional economic integration movement[8] to reflect some of the most far-reaching, insightful recommendations of the West Indian Commission. The Agreement Establishing the Caribbean Court of Justice was one such instrument and an attempt will be made in this book to present a reasoned, informed, balanced and dispassionate analysis of the essential thrust of its provisions with a view to evaluating the prospects of success of this innovative international judicial institution.

This book does not presume to be a comprehensive, much less an exhaustive, inimitable treatise on the Caribbean Court of Justice. Nor does it presume to divine how the Caribbean Court of Justice will or ought to perform its functions, either as a court of last resort, or as a court of first instance. This, in the present submission, would be an insensitive and untimely attempt to preempt determinations more appropriately reserved for the Court. However, by perusing and drawing attention to its constituent instruments, which, apparently, many members of the regional legal fraternity stoutly continue to resist reading, it is hoped that more inquisitive stakeholders, especially those other than members of the regional legal profession, will seek to be enlightened about the composition, functions and administration of the Court, whose determinations may be expected to impact importantly on their daily lives. Nevertheless, it was considered prudent and appropriate to draw attention to some critical issues which may need to be addressed at an early date by the Court in the exercise of its appellate and original jurisdictions without presuming to pontificate the manner of their resolution. It is the author's sincere hope that the discussion of various legal issues which follows was not so abstruse as to escape the grasp of the average stakeholder.

As one intimately involved in the elaboration of the constituent and supporting instruments of the Caribbean Court of Justice, I am disposed to believe that I am eminently well placed to write authoritatively on the orientation of these instruments. However, it is my fervent desire that no inarticulate biases on my part have operated to warp the perspectives set out herein or to distort the analysis and representation of events associated with this historic initiative.

For those irredeemable interlocutors persistently entertaining reservations about the capacity of CARICOM Member States to establish, man and sustain a Caribbean Court of Justice, let me resort to a submission of Sir Shridath Ramphal, a reassuring beacon of enlightenment in an otherwise depressingly dismal dimension of jurisprudential opaqueness:

> As a people, we are among the most literate and articulate in the developing world, and have been so for a long time now. We are a Region of democratic societies that live by the rule of law, not flawlessly, but in fundamental ways.[9]

ACKNOWLEDGEMENTS

The preparation of the manuscript for this book would not have been possible without the enthusiastic and unqualified endeavours of several persons. Among these are Ms. Indrowty Dianand who typed the manuscript, Ms. Jean Kennedy, Ms. Amrita Hall, Ms. Shola Bishop and Ms. Arlene Frank. My sincere appreciation and thanks must go to the CARICOM Secretariat for allowing me to reproduce, as sections of this book, several articles on the original jurisdiction of the CCJ and to Michele Walker for allowing me to utilise her research on the constitutional provisions of various Member States regarding delinking from the Judicial Committee of the Privy Council. Deepest appreciation must also be recorded for the generous permission of the Commonwealth Secretariat to utilise information provided on the current status of the Judicial Committee of the Privy Council and the Privileges and Immunities of the Caribbean Court of Justice and Commission. The gracious consent of the University of the West Indies in permitting reproduction of articles appearing in various publications is also deeply appreciated.

My thanks and deepest appreciation to my dear wife, Donna, must also be recorded. Her patience, forbearing and understanding allowed me to devote the time required for this effort, time which should have been devoted to her and our three children.

NOTES

1. The Heads of Government who signed the Agreement Establishing the Caribbean Court of Justice, hereinafter 'the Agreement' came from Antigua and Barbuda, Barbados, Belize, Grenada, Guyana, Jamaica, St. Kitts and Nevis, Saint Lucia, Suriname, and Trinidad and Tobago.
2. See Hugh Rawlins, 'The Caribbean Court of Justice: The History and Analysis of the Debate', CARICOM Secretariat, 2000. pp.34ff.
3. Coincidentally, debate about a court of last resort in Australia also dates back to 1901. See *Australia's Experience in Abolishing Privy Council Appeals* Paper prepared by the Commonwealth of Australia and presented to the Commonwealth Expert Group Meeting on Replacement of Appeals to the Privy Council, London, 10-13 June 2003, p.10.
4. See Rawlins, 'The Caribbean Court of Justice' p.5.
5. See Recommendation No. 16 of the 'Summary of Recommendations' set out in Appendix V of the Report at p.66.
6. (1993) 43 WIR 340.
7. Other judgments in this line of cases were *Guerra v. Baptiste* (1994) 45 WIR 400; *Reckley v. Minister of Public Safety* (No. 2) (1995) 47 WIR 9; *Henfield v. Attorney General* (1996) 47 WIR 1; *Fisher v. Ministry of Public Safety and Immigration (No.1)* (1997) 52 WIR 1; *Ministry of Public Safety and Immigration (No.2)* (1998) 53 WIR 27; *Thomas v. Baptiste* (1999) 54 WIR 387; *Neville Lewis et al v. Attorney General of Jamaica* (2000) 57 WIR 275.
8. See, for example, the Agreement establishing the Association of Caribbean States which was signed in Cartagena on July 24, 1994. The author was the principal draftsman of this instrument. Also, the Charter of Civil Society adopted by Heads of Government of the Caribbean Community by Resolution dated February 19, 1997. The Charter is not a legally binding instrument but has considerable persuasive influence.

9. K.O. Hall and Denis Benn, eds., *Governance in the Age of Globalisation: Caribbean Perspectives*, (Kingston: Ian Randle Publishers, 2003) 23.

CHAPTER ONE

The Preparatory Phase of the Court

GENESIS AND METAMORPHOSIS OF THE CARIBBEAN COURT OF JUSTICE

Hugh Rawlins in his publication, *The Caribbean Court of Justice: The History and Analysis of the Debate*,[1] discerned different periods in the evolution of an acrimonious debate on the establishment of a court of last resort for the English speaking Member States of the Caribbean Community. Commencing with a period of intense intellectuality, the regional debate on the establishment of the Court traversed interrupted periods of sober rationalisation and introspection, comprehended periods of excessive emotionalism and chauvinism and culminated in a period of careful premeditation and bold, innovative, imaginative decision making. Without challenging the accuracy or credibility of these perceptions, the reality is that the elaboration of the Court's constituent instrument did not appear to have been influenced significantly by its operational environment. In fact, the general contours of jurisdictional competence contemplated for the Court appear to have been devised independently of perceived changes in the relevant environment and remained largely unaffected in their essential attributes. However, important adjustments were required to be made in the supportive institutional arrangements for the achievement of the strategic objective – establishment of an independent Caribbean Court of Justice on a financially sustainable basis.

Thus, as early as 1972, the Representative Committee of the Organisation of Commonwealth Caribbean Bar Associations (OCCBA) set up to examine and report on the establishment of a Caribbean Court of Appeal in substitution for the Judicial Committee of the Privy Council, recommended the establishment of a Caribbean Court of Appeal. The Representative Committee also recommended that the Court of Appeal should be vested with an original jurisdiction in respect of the interpretation and application of international instruments like the CARIFTA Agreement.[2] And this is essentially the jurisdictional configuration of the Court as it exists today. Some important modifications have been made to the institutional arrangements contemplated for the Court, designed in large measure to address persuasively espoused legitimate concerns about its structure and operation in order to devise an institution which would command the public confidence and support of stakeholders, including the regional private Bar. Whether competent decision-makers have succeeded in this endeavour only history will judge. But the purpose of this chapter is to delineate the genesis and development of the Court's principal constituent instrument which is the Agreement Establishing the Caribbean Court of Justice, hereinafter called 'the Agreement' and to focus on the attributes which particularise it as a unique judicial institution in the development of international institutions.[3]

At its Eighth Meeting, the Conference of Heads of Government considered Paper HGC 87/8/13 which contained a 'proposal by the delegation of Trinidad and Tobago for the establishment of a Caribbean Court of Appeal as a final appellate Court for Member States of the Caribbean Community ... in place of the Judicial Committee of the Privy Council.'[4] Interestingly enough, the Paper maintained, *inter alia*,

> that in the field of law, Caribbean jurists have long ago attained the maturity, competence and distinction to man a Caribbean Court of appeal with honour. *In addition, there was the direction in which the development of English law and institutions have been pointing which must compel the Region to take charge of its jurisprudential destiny and move towards a West Indian*

> *jurisprudence, bearing in mind the existence of the regional University, which was preparing young lawyers to carry on a legal tradition that had not been indigenised.*[5] (emphasis supplied).

The Paper also submitted

> that the presence and activities of a Caribbean Court of Appeal in the Region would not only give a significant thrust to cementing the integration of the Region, but it would serve as well as a reliable instrument for forging and moulding its most precious asset, *viz.* its peoples' strong and steadfast attachment to law, liberty and justice.[5]

At the termination of the consideration of the proposal of Trinidad and Tobago, Conference:

> Agreed that –
>
> (i) Attorneys-General of Member States be mandated to undertake further study of the matter and make recommendations to the Conference of Heads of Government;
>
> (ii) the Attorneys-General should consult with the judiciary and bodies representative of the legal profession;
>
> (iii) the Attorneys-General should also consider the feasibility of providing a mechanism for adjudicating and settling disputes between Member States arising out of Treaty obligations relating to CARICOM arrangements between Member States.[6]

It would appear that the CARICOM Secretariat prepared a draft Inter-Governmental Agreement in response to the determination of Conference reached at its Tenth Meeting for consideration by the Sub-Committee of Attorneys General established by the Standing Committee of Ministers responsible for Legal Affairs (SCMLA). This draft Inter-Governmental Agreement on the Caribbean Court of Appeal, which was examined and approved by the Sub-Committee of Attorneys General, provided, *inter alia*, for the appointment of the President of the Court by the Conference of Heads of Government and for the establishment of a Regional Judicial Service Commission to appoint the other Justices of Appeal of the Caribbean Court of Appeal. This draft Inter-Governmental Agreement was considered by the Conference of Heads of Government at its Eleventh Meeting which convened in Kingston, Jamaica, from July 31 to August 2, 1991 where:

> The Conference:
>
> *Considered* a Report on progress made in the implementation of the proposal to establish the Caribbean Court of Appeal as the final Appellate Court for appeals from the Courts of Member States of the Caribbean Community.
>
> *Noted* that the Inter-Governmental Agreement to establish the Court had engaged the attention of a Sub-Committee of Attorneys-General; and
>
> *Approved* the following proposals from the Sub-Committee as modifications to the arrangements previously agreed for the establishment of the Court:
>
> (i) that, because not all Member States of the Caribbean Community are expected to participate in the Court initially, the President of the Court should be appointed by the Heads of Government of the Contracting Parties to the Inter-Governmental Agreement after appropriate consultations instead of by the Conference, as had been originally decided;
>
> (ii) appointment of the Registrar and Other Staff – that the proposed Regional Judicial Service Commission be responsible for the appointment of the Registrar and other staff of the Court instead of the President of the Court as was originally decided;
>
> (iii) membership of the Regional Judicial Service Commission – the appointment of a distinguished jurist as a member of the Commission should be made by the President, after consultation with the Dean of the Faculty of Law of the University of the West Indies and the Chairman of the Council of Legal Education (instead of the Principals of the regional Law Schools);
>
> (iv) ...
>
> (v) ...
>
> (vi) ....[7]

Thus, it is clear that the Proposal of the Delegation of Trinidad and Tobago at the Eighth Meeting of Conference provided the catalyst for the draft Inter-Governmental Agreement which was the basis of the present Agreement Establishing the Caribbean Court of Justice.

The earliest draft of the Agreement establishing the Court was prepared in response to a decision of the Heads of Government of the Caribbean Community reached at its Tenth Meeting, revised by the Sub-Committee of Attorneys-General along lines determined by the Conference at its Eleventh Meeting and considered again at its Twelfth Meeting.[8] The nomenclature of this institution, the Caribbean Court of Appeal, accurately reflected its institutional configuration – a court of last resort in respect of civil and criminal appeals from municipal jurisdictions of participating Member States of the Caribbean Community. As such, the earliest drafts of the Agreement did not reflect the recommendation of the Representative Committee of OCCBA to vest the Court with an original jurisdiction in addition to an appellate jurisdiction as a replacement for the Judicial Committee of the Privy Council. Had this recommendation commended itself to the competent decision-makers, the Sub-Committee of Attorneys-General could not have appropriately designated the institution the Caribbean Court of Appeal.

This circumstance, however, was not overlooked by the West Indian Commission (WIC) which was established by the Heads of Government at Grand Anse, Grenada, in 1989. And, after making an extremely persuasive case for an original jurisdiction of the Court, the WIC avoided the juridical malapropism of the Representative Committee of OCCBA by designating the institution the Caribbean Supreme Court, that is, an institution of final appeal but one which could also exercise an original jurisdiction in interpreting and applying the Revised Treaty of Chaguaramas and even the proposed Charter of Civil Society.[9] In the characterisation of the West Indian Commission:

> But there is now another reason for establishing a court of high authority in the Region and that is the process of integration itself. Integration in its broadest economic sense – involving a Single CARICOM Market, monetary union, the movement of capital and labour and goods, and functional cooperation in a multiplicity of fields – must have the underpinning of Community Law. Integration rests on rights and duties; it requires the support of the rule of law applied regionally and uniformly. A CARICOM Supreme Court interpreting the Treaty

> of Chaguaramas, resolving disputes arising under it, including disputes between Governments parties to the Treaty, declaring and enforcing Community law, interpreting the Charter of Civil Society – all by way of the exercise of an original jurisdiction – is absolutely essential to the integration process. It represents in our recommendations one of the pillars of the CARICOM structures of unity.
>
> Essentially, our recommendation is that the Court should have an original jurisdiction in matters arising under the Treaty of Chaguaramas (as revised) and that any CARICOM citizen (individual or corporate) and any Government of a Member State of the Community or the CARICOM Commission itself, should have the competence to apply for a ruling of the Court in a matter arising under the Treaty. This will include, perhaps prominently so, matters in dispute between Member States in relation to obligations under the Treaty, particularly under the Single Market regime, but it will also provide for the clarification of Community law as it develops pursuant to decisions taken within the CARICOM process...[10]

In this context, however, it is important to point out that the term 'Community Law' must not be construed in the same sense as regulations, directives and decisions issuing from the constituent institutions of the European Union like the Council and the Commission and the determinations of the European Court of Justice and the European Court of First Instance, all of which contribute to the body of Community Law. In the submission of the European Court of Justice:

> By contrast with ordinary international treaties, the EEC treaty has created its own legal system which became an integral part of the legal systems of the Member States and which their courts are bound to apply.[11] By creating a Community of unlimited duration, having its own institutions, its own personality, its own legal capacity and capacity of representation on the international plane and, more particularly, real powers stemming from a limitation of sovereignty or a transfer of powers from the States to the Community, the Member States have limited their sovereign rights and have thus created a body of law which binds both nationals and themselves. The transfer by the States from their legal systems to the Community's legal system of rights and obligations arising under the Treaty, carries with it a permanent limitation of their sovereign rights against which a subsequent unilateral act incompatible with the concept of the Community cannot prevail.[12]

In the present submission, the term 'Community Law' as employed by the European Court of Justice, refers to a corpus of norms separate and distinct from the municipal law of the Member States of the European Union and from the body of norms constituting international law. Community Law, in this context derives its being and uniqueness as a discrete corpus of norms from the status of the European Union as a supranational entity. In sharp contradistinction, however, the Caribbean Community, despite its misleading nomenclature, is and was always intended to be, an association of sovereign states. In fact, for depressingly sound historical reasons, any other status for this collectivity of states appears to be politically unacceptable even though not juridically infeasible.[13] In the premises, the term Community Law as employed by the West Indian Commission appears to be juridically misconceived.[14] Unless, of course, it is intended to signify no more than the norms to be applied by the Caribbean Court of Justice in interpreting and applying the Revised Treaty establishing the Caribbean Community including the CARICOM Single Market and Economy, and rules set out in international instruments, and in municipal law instruments elaborated to implement the Revised Treaty, as well as valid decisions of competent Community organs and the determination of their legal incidence by the Court for public and private entities.[15]

Consistently with its determination reached at its Nineteenth Meeting in Castries, Saint Lucia, to vest the Court with an original jurisdiction in accordance with the recommendations of the West Indian Commission, the Heads of Government of the Caribbean Community changed the designation of the institution to the Caribbean Court of Justice. Vesting the Court with original jurisdiction to reflect the recommendation of the West Indian Commission required far-reaching amendments to the Draft Inter-Governmental Agreement. Consider in this context the nomenclature 'Caribbean Court of Appeal' employed in the earliest draft of the agreement establishing the Court.[16]

The relevant determinations of the Conference of Heads of Government read as follows:

THE CONFERENCE:

Adopted, in principle, the Agreement establishing the Caribbean Supreme Court.

Recognised, however, that constitutional requirements would constrain some Member States from subscribing to the Appellate Jurisdiction of the Court initially;

Endorsed the change in appellation of the Court to the Caribbean Court of Justice;

Agreed to –

(i) invest the Caribbean Court of Justice with original jurisdiction in respect of the interpretation and application of the Treaty;

(ii) extend the notification period for withdrawal from the Court to three years;

Also agreed to establish a Working Group to consider and make recommendations on accommodating the differences of the legal systems of Member States for the effective functioning of the Court;

Noted the offer, and continued willingness, of the Government of Trinidad and Tobago to host the seat of the Court and the undertaking of that Government to withdraw its offer in the event of its inability to secure the required Parliamentary approval for full participation of Trinidad and Tobago in the Court;

Also recognised the need for some Member States, particularly those of the OECS sub-grouping, to conduct a programme of public education and consultations on participation in the Court;

Further recognised the need for the OECS States to take a collective approach to participating in the Court;

Mandated the CARICOM Secretariat to prepare estimates of costs for the efficient administration and functioning of the Court for submission to the Legal Affairs Committee at its next Ordinary Meeting;

Further agreed that the Legal Affairs Committee would consult with competent Ministries in Member States in order to arrive at a suitable budget for submission to the Conference at its Tenth Inter-Sessional Meeting;

Instructed the CARICOM Secretariat to take all necessary steps to ensure that the Conference will be in a position to make a final determination on the establishment of the Court at its Tenth Inter-Sessional Meeting;

> *Also noted* that the Government of The Bahamas was not in a position at this time to give a commitment on its participation in the Court.

Thus, Article III of the Agreement was drafted to expressly provide for two jurisdictions of the Court, an original jurisdiction and an appellate jurisdiction.[17] Consequential amendments were also made to Article IV in order to provide that at least three judges of the CCJ must 'possess expertise in international law including international trade law'.[18] The original jurisdiction of the Court was set out in Part II of the penultimate draft which consists of new Articles IX(a) to IX(n). In the Agreement, these provisions were renumbered and appear as Articles XII to XXIV. The significance of several of these provisions which constitute important innovations in traditional international law is discussed in chapter 6. Article IV (1) of the Agreement provides for a President and nine other judges compared to a President and five justices of appeal in one of the earliest drafts of the Inter-Governmental Agreement.[19] No provision was made for judges possessing expertise in international law in the earliest draft Inter-Governmental Agreement.

The provisions of the Agreement addressing the independence of the judges of the Caribbean Court of Justice attracted much attention by regional Attorneys General, if only to allay the fears of the general public and the apprehensions of the regional private Bar that the regional political directorate were engaged in some dark, invidious conspiracy to control or influence the judiciary thereby compromising that delicate balance of powers between the executive, legislative and judiciary which is generally acknowledged as the basis of good governance and best evidences the operation of the democratic principle in modern societies. In this context, regional Attorneys General were constrained to resist the temptation to view the regional private Bar as the only legitimate stakeholder in the process of establishing regional judicial institutional arrangements. Consequently, after considerable deliberation and soul searching, it was determined that civil society, as important stakeholders, need to be represented in any institution devised for the selection of judges of the Court – a determination reflected in the amendment to Article V of the Agreement Establishing the CCJ[20] as set out in Revision 7 of the Compendium of Instruments Establishing the CCJ produced by the CARICOM Secretariat. In order to insulate the selection of judges from political influence or control, appropriate amendments were made to provisions in the draft text of the Inter-Governmental Agreement addressing the appointment of judges and their removal from office.[21]

Amendments were also made to the draft text concerning the qualifications of persons to be appointed to the bench.[22] In this regard, attorneys were required to have at least 15 years standing at the bar of a participating Member State rather than 20 years as was earlier agreed. In the case of sitting judges, it was assumed that it would have taken approximately 10 years to become a judge of a court of unlimited jurisdiction in civil and criminal matters – hence a period or periods of service on the bench amounting in the aggregate to not less than five years. It was also decided to open the candidatures for the position of judge to teachers of law of 15 years standing, if, in the opinion of the Commission, such persons had distinguished themselves in the legal profession. In both cases, candidates for appointment were required to have 'high moral character, intellectual and analytical ability, sound judgment, integrity and understanding of people and society.'[23] Prior to making appointments to the position of judge, the Regional Judicial and Legal Services Commission had the power to consult with associations representative of the legal profession and with other bodies and individuals that it considered appropriate.[24] The age limit of judges was reduced from 75 years to 72 years.[25] In this context, it is interesting to note that the age of retirement for judges of the Supreme Court of Canada is 75 years, and 70 years for the High Court of Australia. However, acting on a proposal from the Heads of Judiciary of Member States of the Caribbean Community, regional Attorneys General have recommended to Heads of Government that the retiring age of judges be restored to 75 years.

In determining the composition of the Regional Judicial and Legal Services Commission, the regional Attorneys General agonised over the class of stakeholders to be represented. There was, however, an emerging consensus among the Heads of Government of the Caribbean Community that the CCJ was not intended to be a lawyer's institution and, consequently, stakeholders other than representatives of the regional private Bar should be included in its membership. In this context, it was agreed to empower the Secretary-General of the Community and the Director General of the OECS to nominate two members of civil society for positions on the Commission and to remove the Secretary General or his Deputy from the Commission in order to correct the perception of indirect political control or influence in this quarter. Provision was also made, at the insistence of the representative of Suriname, to have civil jurisdictions represented on the Commission. In the process of selection, the overriding concern of the regional Attorneys General was to preempt criticism about attempts by the regional political executive to control or influence the judiciary and to compose a structure which was seen to be relatively free from political influence. With what success this objective was achieved only the future can tell. Despite these commendable efforts by the regional political directorate, skepticism persists in some quarters about the independence of the Commission from political direction.[26]

Another important issue the regional Attorneys General were required to address with extreme care and circumspection was the appointment and removal of the President. But here again, the overriding concern was the establishment of procedures to generate public confidence that no invidious attempts were being made by the regional political executive to control the judiciary. In the earliest draft Inter-Governmental Agreement, it was decided that the President must be appointed by the Conference of Heads of Government of the Caribbean Community. However, at its Eleventh Meeting, the Conference decided that the President should be appointed by the Heads of Government of the Contracting Parties since not all Member States were expected to participate in the relevant regime initially. In this context, careful consideration was given to the proposal that the President should be elected by the judges of the Court in much the same way as the Presidents of the International Court of Justice, the European Court of Justice and the European Court of First Instance.[27] This proposal was rejected after careful consideration on the basis that the Heads of Government were entitled to have some say in the appointment of the President even though this role was not required to be determinative. In the case of the International Court of Justice, the European Court of First Instance and the European Court of Justice, the political directorate would already have had an important say in the appointment of the Presidents since Members of the Court were appointed by political representatives or Ministers of Government.[28] In the premises, it was agreed that the President should be appointed by the Contracting Parties[29] on the recommendation of the Regional Judicial and Legal Services Commission. The Contracting Parties, however, were not perceived to be competent to reject a nomination of the Commission and to substitute a candidate of their own choice, but were required to act, in every case, on the recommendation of the Commission. And, in making this determination, the vote required was a three-quarters majority of the Contracting Parties, since there were lingering memories of the impasse over the appointment of the Chief Justice of the OECS Court of Appeal. As such, the requirement of unanimity ordinarily established for reaching decisions of the Conference, was dispensed with in appointing the President of the Court.[30]

The position of the regional political directorate on the appointment of the President of the Court changed drastically from that in 1992 when the earliest draft Inter-Governmental Agreement[31] emerged. Article IX (5) of this instrument expressly required the President to be appointed by the unanimous vote of the Heads of Government of the Contracting Parties after such consultations with such persons or bodies of persons or organisations and in such manner as the Heads of Government of the Contracting Parties deem fit, including consultations with the Heads of the Judiciary and other members of the legal profession in the Member States of the Caribbean Community. The corresponding provisions of the Agreement lack the specificity set out in the Article above, which, however, should give the Regional Judicial and Legal Services Commission some guidance on the approach that may be adopted in arriving at a recommendation to the Contracting Parties on the appointment of the President. In this connection, it is of some significance that the consultations envisaged in the earliest draft Inter-Governmental Agreement were not restricted to the stakeholders of the Contracting Parties and that consultations with the regional judiciary appeared to bulk large in the required consultative process. It does appear to be a drafting oversight that the Agreement provides for the appointment of the President by the Contracting Parties and not the Heads of Government of the Contracting Parties.

Of equal importance for the independence of the judges were the institutional arrangements agreed for financing the operations of the CCJ and the payment of their salaries and emoluments. Consistently with the practice current in common law jurisdictions of the Commonwealth, it was originally agreed that expenses associated with the establishment and operations of the CCJ, including the remuneration and allowances of judges and officials of the Court, should be a charge on the consolidated fund of the Contracting Parties and paid in such proportions as agreed by them.[32] Subject to the approval of Conference and the Agreement, the Commission was charged with responsibility for determining the terms and conditions and other benefits of the President and other judges of the CCJ.[33] Further, the salaries and allowances and terms and conditions of service of the President and other judges of the Court could not be altered to their disadvantage during their tenure of office.[34] However, these arrangements were not perceived by the political directorate of the Community as addressing two legitimate and persistent concerns of the stakeholders relating to the ability of the regional political directorate to influence the determinations of the Court through control of the purse. Furthermore, the appalling record of some Member States of the Caribbean Community in discharging their financial obligations to regional institutions was indisputable and a source of considerable embarrassment for the Region.

In order to address those concerns the Conference, at its Twenty-first Meeting in Port-of-Spain, Trinidad and Tobago in 2000 mandated the Ministers of Finance to 'make provision in their national budgets for adequate funding of the cost of setting up the Court and the Regional Judicial and Legal Services Commission.'[35] The Draft Financial Protocol would have committed Member States participating in the regime establishing the CCJ to make provision in their national budgets 'for adequate funding of the cost of setting up the Court and the Regional Judicial and Legal Services Commission as well as recurrent expenditure for the first five years of their existence'.[36] Contracting Parties were also required to post a bond in an amount equivalent to five years of their assessed contributions which could be forfeited for failure to honour obligations to pay their assessed contributions.[37] The money so raised was to be lodged in a special account to be managed by the President and the Registrar. Non-payment of contributions would have been sanctioned by the inability of the defaulting Contracting Party to initiate proceedings in the CCJ while its contributions remained in arrears.[38] These provisions, however, did not preclude the establishment of a trust fund to be administered by the Caribbean Development Bank (CDB) or other agreed institution for the purpose of sustaining the operations of the Court.[39] However, as the situation now stands, the Draft Financial Protocol appears to have been superseded since credible arrangements have been made to set up a Trust Fund to finance the operations of the CCJ on a sustainable basis. In this connection, attention may be drawn to the Agreement Establishing the Caribbean Court of Justice Trust Fund.[40]

At its Twenty-first Meeting, the Conference of Heads of Government agreed to various amendments to the Draft

Agreement Establishing the Caribbean Court of Justice. These amendments which were partially informed by expressed concerns of the regional private Bar related to the appointment of judges trained in international law (Article IV); the duration of the term of office of the President (Article IV (5)); the composition of the Regional Judicial and Legal Services Commission and the conditions of service of its members (Article V); the first appointment of the President and members of the Commission (Article V *bis*); the oath of office of judges of the Court (Article IX); financial provisions (Article XIII) and conditions of withdrawal (Article XX). Despite these amendments, representatives of the Bar Associations of Member States of the Caribbean Community still ventilated serious misgivings about the Court, its composition and arrangements for its financing.

The financial proposals contemplated for the CCJ in the Draft Financial Protocol did not commend themselves to competent decision-makers. For one thing, they did not address the issue of sustaining the CCJ after the first five years. Secondly, they did not address the legitimate concerns of stakeholders that Governments would still be in a position to influence the determinations of the CCJ by virtue of the power of the purse. In the premises, the political directorate determined to avail themselves of the option of establishing a Trust Fund to address the legitimate concerns of stakeholders in terms of financing the operations of the Court on a sustainable basis. In this connection, the CDB was authorised by the Conference of Heads of Government to raise US$100 million in international capital markets to be on-lent to the Contracting Parties.[41] Before undertaking this task, the President of the CDB insisted, successfully, on the conclusion of appropriate loan agreements between the CDB and the Contracting Parties as well as the elaboration and conclusion of an Agreement establishing the CCJ Trust Fund. Further, an appropriate vesting deed had to be negotiated and agreed.[42] The Trustees of the CCJ Trust Fund assumed their offices on August 22, 2003.

The Trustees of the Fund were determined, independently, by the CARICOM Secretariat from institutions in the private sector and civil society and their activities are governed by the Agreement establishing the CCJ Trust Fund, the Vesting Deed of the CCJ Trust Fund and the relevant laws of Trinidad and Tobago, where the Trust Fund is to be located. The Trust Fund will have an executive director and a professional fund manager.[43] Detailed information about the structure of the Trust Fund and its operations may be gleaned from the relevant instruments appended hereto. As such, the regional political directorate appear to have adopted a principled, hands-off approach in respect of the financing of the establishment and operations of the CCJ. The CDB conservatively estimated that the yield from the resources of the Trust Fund could finance the operations of the CCJ on a sustainable basis. The financial arrangements for operations of the CCJ were also designed to give the President administrative control of its operations. The issue of accountability of judges of the Court, however, does not appear to have been adequately addressed by competent decision-makers.

Concern was also expressed by the Jamaican Bar Association about the provisions for withdrawal from the CCJ, which, in their view, could impact negatively on perceptions of security of tenure by prospective judges of the Court. In their submission, these provisions should be deleted and Contracting Parties should be required to entrench the CCJ in their national constitutions. This proposal from the Jamaican Bar Council appears to merit serious consideration given the applicable rules of international law. Article 54 of the Vienna Convention on the Law of Treaties provides that a party may withdraw from a treaty in conformity with its provisions or at any time after consulting and securing the consent of all parties and consultation with other contracting states. Where there is no provision in the instrument for withdrawal, as is not the case with the Caribbean Court of Justice, a party may only denounce or withdraw from a treaty if it can be established that withdrawal or denunciation was within the contemplation of the parties or that the right of withdrawal or denunciation may be implied from the nature of the treaty.

If the parties to the Agreement Establishing the Caribbean Court of Justice were to amend it now in order to provide for no withdrawal provisions, states wishing to withdraw would be hard put to establish such an intention from the conduct of the parties or the nature of the Agreement. In the premises, a state wishing to withdraw would be caught by the provisions of Article 54 of the Vienna Convention on the Law of Treaties. In any event, a party wishing to withdraw from a treaty must give at least twelve month notice of its intention to withdraw.[44] However, the withdrawal provisions set out in the Agreement are considerably more restrictive.[45]

A Member State withdrawing from the Agreement Establishing the Caribbean Court of Justice is required to withdraw from the Agreement Establishing the CCJ Trust Fund by notice in writing to the Secretary-General and is required to discharge all outstanding obligations. Presumably, such a Member State would also be entitled to a refund of a proportionate amount from the Trust Fund with the concurrence of the other Contracting Parties and the Trustees of the Fund

Among the most important Articles in the Agreement Establishing the Caribbean Court of Justice is Article XXXIX which provides that a reservation may be entered to Article XXV of the Agreement with the consent of the Contracting Parties. This provision was an attempt to address and come to grips with two intractable issues. The first related to the entrenchment of the Judicial Committee of the Privy Council in some national constitutions by a referendum and the diffidence of some Member States about educating their populations on the Caribbean Court of Justice to facilitate a positive outcome in any referendum to be conducted.[46] The second issue related to the fact that participation by Member States in the Caribbean Court of Justice in the exercise of its original jurisdiction was perceived to be a peremptory requirement from which no derogation was permissible. In the premises, caution and good sense advised facilitating acceptance of the CCJ in its original jurisdiction alone, giving Member States the option to continue with the Judicial Committee of the Privy Council for appellate matters.

One intractable issue to be resolved in respect of Member States not delinking from the Privy Council, but submitting to the Caribbean Court of Justice in the exercise of its original jurisdiction, is the manner of treating with a case which involves, *inter alia*, an issue relating to the interpretation and application of the Treaty and on which the CCJ has ruled in accordance with Article 214 of the Revised Treaty. If that case were appealed to the Judicial Committee of the Privy Council for a determination on other issues ruled on by the court below, would the Privy Council, by way of judicial comity, decline to rule on the issue determined by the CCJ, or would it pronounce on that issue as well? For the Member States delinking from the Privy Council, the latter course of action by that body would be politically unacceptable and could lead to some very curious results. The above scenario appears, therefore, to argue for all Member States of the Caribbean Community delinking from the Judicial Committee of the Privy Council.

DEVELOPING THE RULES OF THE COURT : APPELLATE AND ORIGINAL JURISDICTIONS

Given that the Caribbean Court of Justice is in the nature of a *sui generis* international judicial institution, being vested with both an appellate jurisdiction as a court of last resort in respect of civil and criminal matters determined by superior courts in the jurisdictions of Contracting Parties, and an original jurisdiction in respect of the interpretation and application of the Revised Treaty of Chaguaramas, establishing the Rules of Court posed certain problems for competent decision-makers. One such problem was whether to have two discrete instruments addressing the Court's dual jurisdictions or one instrument addressing the Rules of Court in both the appellate and original jurisdictions. The drafters did not appear to have received much guidance on this issue from the constituent instrument of the Court. In this context Article XXI of the Agreement addressing the original jurisdiction of the Court provides:

> 1. The President shall, in consultation with five other Judges of the Court selected by him, establish rules for the exercise of the original jurisdiction of the Court.
>
> 2. Without prejudice to the generality of the preceding sub-paragraph, Rules of Court may be made for all or any of the following purposes –
>
> (a) regulating the sittings of the Court, the selection of Judges for any purpose, and the period to be observed as a vacation in the Court and the transaction of business during any such vacation;
>
> (b) regulating the pleading, practice, procedure, execution of the process of the Court and the duties of the officers of the Court;
>
> (c) regulating matters relating to practice in the Court by Attorneys-at-Law, Legal Practitioners or advocates and the representation of persons concerned in any proceedings in the Court;
>
> (d) providing for the summary determination of any matter which appears to the Court to be frivolous or vexatious or to be brought for the purpose of delay;
>
> (e) regulating matters relating to the costs and the taxation thereof, of proceedings in the Court;
>
> (f) providing for the delivery of judgments in an expeditious manner;
>
> (g) prescribing forms and fees in respect of proceedings in the Court;
>
> (h) prescribing the time within which any requirement of the rules of Court is to be complied with;
>
> (i) regulating or prescribing or doing any other thing which may be regulated, prescribed or done by rules of Court.

The provisions of Article XXV (7) which address the Rules of Court relating to the appellate jurisdiction read as follows:

> 1. The President shall, in consultation with five other Judges of the Court selected by him, make Rules of Court for regulating the practice and procedure of the Court in exercise of the

appellate jurisdiction conferred on the Court and, in relation to appeals brought before the Court, the practice and procedure of any court in respect of such appeals.

2. Without prejudice to the generality of the preceding sub-paragraph, Rules of Court may be made for all or any of the following purposes –

(a) regulating the sittings of the Court, the selection of Judges for any purpose, and the period to be observed as a vacation in the Court and the transaction of business during any such vacation;

(b) regulating the pleading, practice, procedure, execution of the process of the Court and the duties of the officers of the Court;

(c) regulating matters relating to practice in the Court by Attorneys-at-Law or Legal Practitioners and the representation of persons concerned in any proceedings in the Court;

(d) prescribing the cases in which, and the conditions upon which an appellant in a criminal appeal to the Court shall be entitled to be present at the hearing of the appeal;

(e) providing for the summary determination of any appeal which appears to the Court to be frivolous or vexatious or to be brought for the purpose of delay;

(f) regulating matters relating to the costs and the taxation thereof, of proceedings in the Court;

(g) providing for the delivery of judgments in an expeditious manner;

(h) prescribing forms and fees in respect of proceedings in the Court;

(i) prescribing the time within which any requirement of the rules of Court is to be complied with;

(j) regulating or prescribing or doing any other thing which may be regulated, prescribed or done by rules of Court.

Several matters appear to be clear from a perusal of the foregoing provisions. Firstly, the Agreement imposes on the President of the Court the duty to establish the Rules of Court for both its original and appellate jurisdictions, and, in so doing he is obliged to consult with five other judges of the Court.[47] One compelling inference from the language of commitment of those provision is that, initially, the Court cannot consist of less than six judges, including the President despite contrary perceptions of the Regional Judicial and Legal Services Commission concerning the workload of the Court in the early days of its existence. It also appears from the language of commitment of the relevant provisions that the remit of the President is much wider in establishing the Rules of Court for the appellate jurisdiction than that in respect of the original jurisdiction. In this regard, it is interesting to note that the President, in establishing Rules of Court for the appellate jurisdiction, is required to make rules 'in relation to appeals brought before the Court for the regulation of the practice and procedure of any court in respect of such appeals.'[48]

Despite the fact that the Agreement imposes on the President the obligation to establish the Rules of Court, competent decision-makers mandated the CARICOM Secretariat to prepare draft Rules of Court to be utilised by the President as he sees fit. In this context, the Secretariat, in collaboration with Supreme Court Registrars and Chief Parliamentary Counsel of the Region, prepared draft Rules of Court for the appellate and original jurisdictions in two discrete instruments. After careful consideration, based on submissions issuing from the Solicitor General of Jamaica, however, it was decided to have one integrated instrument in three parts – a general part and two parts addressing the appellate and original jurisdiction separately. The draft Rules of Court (Appellate Jurisdiction) in the interest of continuity, were based largely on the Rules of Court of the Judicial Committee of the Privy Council. These are, however, being refined to take account of current developments in court procedures in the Community.

In developing the draft Rules of Court (Original Jurisdiction), competent decision-makers were constrained to bear several considerations in mind. Firstly, that in the exercise of its original jurisdiction, the Court was in fact discharging the functions of an international tribunal. Consequently, the emerging consensus was that the Rules of Court (Original Jurisdiction) should be elaborated along the lines of those employed in international tribunals. In the premises, the draft Rules of Court (Original Jurisdiction) relied heavily on precedents from the International Court of Justice and, to a lesser extent, the European Court of Justice. However, on a careful balance of probabilities, it does appear that the Rules of Court of the Court of First Instance of the European Union[49] may provide a more useful precedent, given that this tribunal is largely concerned with commercial disputes arising in connection with the interpretation and application of the Rome Treaty (1957) as amended by the Treaty of Maastricht (1992).

Competent decision-makers were also conscious of the fact that new ground had to be broken in establishing the Rules of Court (Original Jurisdiction). In this regard, it was important to bear in mind that the Court, as an international tribunal, was required to apply rules of international law in interpreting and applying the Revised Treaty.[50] These rules, in the present submission, are both substantive and adjectival. Competent decision-makers were also required to come to terms with the fact that legal practitioners in the Community did not have many opportunities to practise international law and inclined to the view that the Rules of Court (Original Jurisdiction) should exhibit some features familiar to the municipal law practitioners of the Community, while largely respecting the practice and procedures of international tribunals. At the same time, it would be difficult to ignore the fact that in the exercise of its original jurisdiction, the Court will have to be guided by the practice and procedures of superior courts of first instance in the Community where complex issues of law and fact have to be determined, a situation likely to be replicated in the Court in exercising its original jurisdiction.

In the final analysis, however, all these issues will have to be addressed and determined by the President in consultation with his colleagues. The President will be constrained to pay very careful attention to the provisions of the Agreement Establishing the Caribbean Court of Justice and the Revised Treaty, addressing the original jurisdiction of the Court. In this regard, it appears that due to a typographical error in formatting (Article XII(1) of the Agreement), the jurisdiction of the Court appears to be narrower under the first instrument than under the second. On closer scrutiny, however, it is clear that the jurisdiction of the Court set out in Article XII(1) of the Agreement is made subject to the Treaty. Article 211 of the Revised Treaty will be determinative in establishing the Rules of the original jurisdiction of the Court.

In developing the Rules of Court (Original Jurisdiction) it would be useful to bear in mind that the objective sought to be achieved is justice and that excessive formalism is likely to defeat its attainment. Thus, although as in international tribunals the principal litigants are States which will be espousing the claims of private entities aggrieved, the principal beneficiaries are nationals of States in their normal commercial interface with one another. Consequently, the procedures to be employed should focus on expedition of claims if economic activities in the CSME are not to be stymied. In this context, time for filing of pleadings and making oral submissions should be as brief as perceived to be consistent with efficiency and expedition. Consideration may be given, too, to joining all preliminary objections to the merits of the case to prevent litigants from benefiting financially from protracted proceedings which are likely to have a negative impact on efficiency in the delivery of services.

An important issue falling to be determined in developing the Rules of Court (Original Jurisdiction) is the treatment of non-appearance by a party. Should the Rules be developed along the lines similar to municipal rules in common law jurisdictions or should the practice of the International Court of Justice be employed, bearing in mind that the Court in the exercise of its original jurisdiction is an international tribunal while not forgetting that litigation is likely to be driven by disputes in relation to commercial and economic activities. In the practice of the International Court of Justice, non-appearance does not prevent the proceedings from taking their normal course where an affirmative finding for jurisdiction is made. In order to determine whether the claim brought by the applicant is well founded in fact and law, written and oral proceedings follow in the normal manner in accordance with the Statute and the principle of equality of states. Delivery of judgment is done in the normal way. Non-appearance may occur at every stage of the proceedings,[51] or only during certain stages.[52] Or should the Court deliver judgment in favour of the applicant in default of appearance or defence as is provided for in the Rules of Court of the European Court of First Instance?[53]

Article XIX of the Agreement empowers the Court to *prescribe* provisional measures or interim measures in order to preserve the interests of the parties pending the outcome of litigation. In the practice of the International Court of Justice this may take the form of proscribing any action likely to jeopardise the effectiveness of a decision delivered by the International Court of Justice.[54] In such a case the Court is expected to accord priority over other cases in order to ascertain the views of the litigants and deliver speedy judgment. Decisions of the International Court of Justice (ICJ) are set out in Orders. The Caribbean Court of Justice is competent to prescribe interim measures and may also decline to prescribe interim measures if it is satisfied that the interest of justice advises such a course of action. This appears to be the position in both municipal and international fora[55] where the court has a discretion in the matter. In the practice of the ICJ, chambers of the Court may also indicate provisional measures and it may be assumed that Divisions of the CCJ would have a similar competence.

The Rules of Court (Original Jurisdiction) may also be expected to provide for the joinder of proceedings where parties to separate proceedings are submitting identical arguments in respect of a common defendant in relation to the same issue and to deliver a single judgment. The Caribbean Court of Justice should also be allowed to direct common action in respect of any aspect of proceedings without effecting a formal joinder or may conduct proceedings in parallel and deliver similar judgments. Similarly, the Caribbean Court of Justice is required to allow third party intervention in a case if it is satisfied that the third party has an interest of a legal nature in the case and which may be affected by the judgment. Thus, the ICJ has allowed third party interventions in several cases.[56]

In the final analysis, however, it is the President of the Court, in consultation with his colleagues, who is required to establish the Rules of Court for both jurisdictions of the CCJ. The CARICOM Secretariat has prepared draft Rules of Court to assist the President with whom, ultimately, lies the manner of their disposition or employment. But it might be useful to bear in mind the need for innovation in respect of the Court's original jurisdiction especially where there is no precedent to serve as a guide.

THE PREPARATORY COMMITTEE : CONSTITUTION AND REMIT

Having taken a firm decision at its Nineteenth Meeting in Castries, Saint Lucia, in 1998 to establish the Caribbean Court of Justice with an original jurisdiction to interpret and apply the Revised Treaty of Chaguaramas, and an appellate jurisdiction in substitution for the Judicial Committee of the Privy Council, the Conference of Heads of Government at their Twentieth Meeting held in Port-of-Spain, Trinidad and Tobago from July 4-7, 1999:

> Established a Preparatory Committee under the Chairmanship of Barbados comprising the Attorneys-General of Barbados, Guyana, Jamaica, St. Kitts and Nevis, Saint Lucia, and Trinidad and Tobago, assisted by Chief Parliamentary Counsel and Supreme Court Registrars, as appropriate, and representatives of the Council of Legal Education and the Caribbean Community Secretariat with the following Terms of Reference:
>
> (i) determine and implement arrangements for the inauguration of the Caribbean Court of Justice prior to the establishment of the Caribbean Single Market and Economy, including –
>
> (a) the development and implementation of a programme of public education within the Community;

(b) assisting in the preparation of briefs for Member States for use in parliamentary debates and public discussions on the structure and functions of the Caribbean Court of Justice;

(c) assisting Member States in taking such steps as may be necessary to enable them to subscribe to the Caribbean Court of Justice in its appellate and original jurisdictions;

(d) proposing dates for the signing and ratification of the Agreement Establishing the Caribbean Court of Justice and related instruments;

(e) making arrangements for the functioning of the Caribbean Court of Justice, including:

    (i) the appointment and remuneration of the Members of the Regional Judicial and Legal Services Commission;

    (ii) the appointment and remuneration of the President, Judges and Officials of the Court;

(f) making the necessary arrangements for an appropriate inaugural ceremony.

The enumeration of activities identified for the Preparatory Committee and their placement speaks volumes about the perceptions of the Heads of Government in respect of priority needs in terms of establishing the CCJ. In this connection, it is not without considerable significance that uppermost on the list of activities is 'the development and implementation of a programme of public education within the Community'. In the perception of competent decision-makers the target audience was all the important public, including the regional private Bar whose awareness of the salient issues arguing persuasively for the establishment of the Caribbean Court of Justice allegedly leaves much to be desired. In respect of the appellate jurisdiction of the Court, the private Bar expressed legitimate concerns regarding the independence of the Court and its financial sustainability based on their own experience. Other concerns regarding the social proximity of judges of the Court to persons likely to appear before it, the questionable legal erudition of candidates for the Bench of the Court, the vulnerability of regional judges to political manipulation in contrast to the Olympian dispassionateness of Privy Councillors which distance can and does generate, coupled with public confidence were, at best inane, uninformed perceptions and, at worst, a perplexing and depressing exhibition of negative self-worth.

It was believed that a well-conceived and efficiently executed public education programme was indispensable for a basic, sensible appreciation of the purpose and functions of the Court in the exercise of its appellate jurisdiction. Even more important was the need to apprise the regional private Bar of the importance of the CSME in a world that was becoming extremely competitive and where the twin phenomena of globalisation and liberalisation were generally regarded as touchstones of national economic development and sustainability. In this evolving paradigm of economic development, the building of critical mass through the pooling of exiguous resources of individual political entities of the Caribbean Community appeared to offer the only plausible assurance of economic survival for its Member States. And for this experiment in regional institution building and regional integration to have any viable prospects of success, the Caribbean Court of Justice in its original jurisdiction must be seen as the institutional centrepiece of the CARICOM Single Market and Economy. That the regional private Bar was egregiously uninformed about global economic developments and their probable negative impact on Member States of the Community, could be discerned from various utterances of its leadership in opposition to the Court. The terms of reference of the Preparatory Committee would also appear to support the inference that even members of the regional political directorate needed to be educated about the proposed structure and functions of the Caribbean Court of Justice.

Under the skilful chairmanship of David Simmonds, Attorney General of Barbados, the Preparatory Committee set about to do its work with commendable vigour and dispatch. The immediate and overriding concern of the Preparatory Committee was getting the word out about the CCJ so that the targeted public could develop informed opinions about this international judicial body and challenge the negative perceptions emanating from the private Bar about the Court. As a first step, it was decided to engage the services of a consultant to trace the history and development of the regional debate about the court of last resort to replace the Judicial Committee of the Privy Council. This determination was made at the very first meeting of the Preparatory Committee[57] which took place in Christ Church, Barbados, on August 13, 1999. The Preparatory Committee also decided:

> that a report on the cost of the Caribbean Court of Justice in respect of its capital and relevant expenses should be ready at the end of September 1999 . . . (and) an assessment of the information technology for the Court should be done and that the report of the Ministers of Finance Meeting in September could be incorporated in the Committee's report along with an assessment of the salaries of the Judges of the Court.

At its second meeting held in Port-of-Spain[58] also under the chairmanship of David Simmons, the Preparatory Committee agreed, in principle, on a public information campaign in 'order to sensitise' civil society and various regional publics on the role and functions of the CCJ. At its third meeting held in Kingston, Jamaica[59] on December 6, 1999, the Preparatory Committee approved a report of the CARICOM Secretariat on a public education programme and noted the decision of the Government of Trinidad and Tobago to refurbish NIPDEC House in Port-of-Spain to be the temporary headquarters of the Court, pending more long-term arrangements to provide accommodation for the Seat of the Court to reflect its importance in the regional scheme of things. At its fourth meeting the Preparatory Committee addressed the intractable issue of financing the Court on a reliable, sustainable basis and took note that the Draft Financial Protocol which was being elaborated at the instance of the Council on Finance and Planning, had provision for the establishment of a Trust Fund which would eliminate the need for contributions by Member States to the budget of the Court on a regular basis. It was also agreed to publish the draft instruments relating to the

Court for information and to approach the IDB and OAS for funding for the 'Public Education Programme'.[60]

At its fifth meeting held in St. Michael, Barbados, on May 26, 2000, the Preparatory Committee 'agreed that appreciation should be shown of the concerns of the Council of the Jamaican Bar which was an important stakeholder'.[61] The Preparatory Committee also 'determined that a second set of documents should be prepared and sent out to Member States addressing those concerns expressed by the Council of the Jamaican Bar Association after the Fifth Special Meeting of the Legal Affairs Committee to be held in Kingston, Jamaica, June 19-21, 2000'.[62]

At its seventh meeting the Preparatory Committee agreed *inter alia* that 'the Legal Affairs Committee should meet in January 2001 to approve the final draft of the Agreement Establishing the Caribbean Court of Justice before commending it for signature by Heads of Government of the Caribbean Community at their Twelfth Inter-Sessional Meeting'[63] and that 'the final draft of the Agreement Establishing the Caribbean Court of Justice should be discussed with the prime minister of Saint Lucia, Dr. Kenny D. Anthony, before submission to the other Heads of Government for signature'.[64] From the foregoing it would be clear that the competent decision-makers of the Caribbean Community were ready to address and accommodate the legitimate concerns of stakeholders in elaborating the Agreement Establishing the Court. In fact it is alleged that approximately 80 per cent of the proposals of the Jamaican Bar Council were addressed and accommodated in the text of the Agreement. If some were rejected this may be attributed to the consensus approach adopted for the exercise. For, in the ultimate analysis, the Agreement was intended to be a regional instrument reflecting a regional consensus and not a Jamaican agreement designed exclusively for Jamaican stakeholders.

The elevation of Sir David Simmons to the Barbados Bench as Chief Justice paved the way for Mia Mottley, the Barbados Attorney General, to be appointed the chairperson of the Preparatory Committee. Ms. Mottley brought her usual brilliance and no-nonsense approach to the work of the Preparatory Committee which moved quickly to hold discussions with the CDB about the capital and recurrent costs of the CCJ and the capitalisation of the Trust Fund to yield the required income. The CDB also adopted a very conservative approach to estimating the yield of the Trust Fund which was presented to Dr. Kenny Anthony who is charged with the portfolio of Justice and Governance in the quasi-Cabinet of the Caribbean Community. The statesmanship and commitment to regional economic integration by Prime Minister Anthony were not only responsible for his colleagues Heads of Government agreeing to capitalise the Trust Fund in the amount of US$100 million but also for persuading the OECS Heads of Government to sign on to the Court.

The decision to establish the Trust Fund to be capitalised in the amount of US$100 million was reached in Georgetown, Guyana at the Twenty-third Meeting of the Conference of Heads of Government in July 2002. This was followed by the entry into force of the Agreement Establishing the Caribbean Court of Justice on July 23, 2003 with the deposit of the third instrument of ratification of this instrument by Guyana. At its Twenty-fourth Meeting, the Conference of Heads of Government established a High Level Task Force to plan for the inauguration of the Court. This was followed by the swearing-in of the members of the Regional Judicial and Legal Services Commission on August 21, 2003 and by the swearing in of the Trustees of the Trust Fund on August 22, 2003.

With these developments it appears that the ball is now in the court of the CCJ's erstwhile dissenters, some of whom, paradoxically, have succeeded in securing membership of the Commission and the Board of Trustees of the CCJ Trust Fund. To a large extent success of the Caribbean Court of Justice will depend on the quality of judges selected by the Commission and on the efficient management of the resources of the Fund to ensure an adequate, reliable source of finance for the capital and recurrent expenses of the Court – a burden which the Heads of

Government of the Caribbean Community have adroitly avoided and shifted to some of the CCJ's most vociferous, unrelenting detractors.

NOTES

1. Commissioned by the Caribbean Community Secretariat, 2000.
2. See chapter 4 *infra* at p. 90.
3. Compare in this context the composition and jurisdiction of the International Court of Justice (ICJ), the European Court of Justice (ECJ), the European Court of First Instance (CFI), the Court of Justice of COMESA (CJC), the Central American Court of Justice (CAJ), the Andean Court of Justice (ACJ); also the International Tribunal on the Law of the Sea (ITLOS) and the Court of Justice of the European Free Trade Area (CJEFTA).
4. See the Report of the Eighth Meeting of the Conference of Heads of Government of the Caribbean Community which convened in Castries, Saint Lucia from June 30 to July 3, 1987 – contained in Document REP.87/8/50 HGC dated January 27, 1988, at p.34.
5. *Ibid.*, 36.
6. *Ibid.*, 37.
7. See Report of the Eleventh Meeting of the Conference of Heads of Government of the Caribbean Community contained in the document REP/91/11/28 HGC dated July 15, 1991, 82-83.
8. See the Draft Inter-Governmental Agreement Establishing the Caribbean Court of Appeal circulated to Member States of the Caribbean Community under cover of Savingram No. 97/1992 dated May 20, 1992. At its Tenth Meeting 'the Conference agreed that an Inter-Governmental Agreement providing for the establishment and functioning of the Court based on principles and guidelines approved by the Conference should be prepared by the Secretariat . . . .' See document HGC 90/11/28 dated July 17, 1990, 1.
9. Contrary to the expectations of the West Indian Commission (WIC), the Heads of Government did not accord the Charter of Civil Society the status of a treaty. The Charter was adopted by Resolution and constitutes no more than recommendations to Member States of the Community. However, several provisions of the Charter are reflected in the written constitutions of some Member States of the Caribbean Community.

10. See *Time for Action: Report of the West Indian Commission*, 1992, Black Rock, Barbados, at p. 500 ff. Significantly enough, the Articles of the CCJ on original jurisdiction did not confer on private entities, legal and natural, a right to espouse a claim in proceedings of the Court. *Locus standi* is accorded only with the leave of the Court.
11. See Articles 189-92 of the Rome Treaty.
12. See *Costa v. ENEL* No. 6/64, 1964 CMLR 425. The implications of this ruling of the European Court of Justice for the British constitutional doctrine of Parliamentary supremacy need to be addressed.
13. For example, it is not without considerable significance that the recommendations of the Gonsalves Report which was prepared in response to a decision of Conference at its meeting in Trinidad and Tobago (2003) begins by acknowledging the Caribbean Community as an association of sovereign states. See, *Recommendation 1a of Regional Integration: Carrying the Process Forward – Report of the Expert Group of Heads of Government* (June 2003)
14. See, for example, D.E. Pollard, 'The Caribbean Court of Justice: Challenge and Response', *CARICOM Perspective*, Vol.1, 1999, p.28.
15. For a discussion of Community Law, see S.A. McDonald, 'Signposts to the Development of Judicial Institutions in the Caribbean Community'. *Issues and Perspectives*, Vol. 1, CARICOM Secretariat, 2001, pp.25ff.
16. See, for example, the Draft Inter-Governmental Agreement Establishing the Caribbean Court of Appeal circulated to Member States of the Caribbean Community under cover of Savingram No. 97/1992 dated May 20, 1992. This draft was prepared by Jeremy Pope of the Commonwealth Secretariat, London and refined by BTI Polland, SC, General Counsel of CARICOM.
17. The provisions of Articles III and IV are set out in Appendix 1 of this book. Contrast, however, the provisions of the draft instrument set out in the Compendium of CCJ instruments, Revision No. 7, prepared by the CARICOM Secretariat (2000), and the draft instrument mentioned in footnote no. 4.
18. See Article IV (1) of the Agreement.
19. See the Draft Agreement Establishing the Caribbean Court of Appeal circulated to Member States of the Caribbean Community under cover of Savingram No. 97/1992 dated May 20, 1992.
20. Article V (1) (e) of the Agreement reads as follows: 'Two persons from civil society nominated jointly by the Secretary General of the

Community and the Director General of the OECS for a period of three years following consultations with regional non-governmental organizations.'

21. See Article VIII of the Agreement.
22. See Article IV (10) of the Agreement as compared to Article IV (a) of the draft set out in the Compendium of Instruments of the CCJ, prepared by the CARICOM Secretariat, Revision 7, dated June 3, 1999.
23. These requirements were insisted on by the Attorney General of Trinidad and Tobago, the Hon. Ramesh Maharaj. See Article IV (11) of the Agreement.
24. See Article IV (12) of the Agreement.
25. This was done at the Twenty-First Meeting of the Conference of Heads of Government in Canouan on a proposal by the Prime Minister of Saint Lucia. In the earliest draft Inter-Governmental Agreement the retiring age of judges was 70 years as is the case of Australia's highest court of appeal.
26. See Bernice Lake, 'Public Confidence and the Role of the Media', paper delivered at the Fifth Annual Caribbean Media Conference in St. John's, Antigua, dated May 16, 2002.
27. See, for example, Article 7 (2) (6) of the Rules of the Court of First Instance; see also Article 21 of the Statute of the International Court of Justice.
28. See Article 167 of the Rome Treaty or Article 223 of the Treaty of Maastricht; and Article 4 of the Statute of the International Court of Justice.
29. Despite the language of commitment employed in the text of the Agreement, it is very likely that the President will be appointed by no lesser persons than the Heads of Government of the Contracting Parties as originally agreed in an earlier draft Inter-Governmental Agreement.
30. Compare in this context the provision of Article 28(1) of the Treaty of Chaguaramas establishing the Caribbean Community, Chaguaramas, July 4, 1973
31. See the Draft Agreement Establishing the Caribbean Court of Appeal circulated to Member States of the Caribbean Community under cover of Savingram No. 97/1992 dated May 20, 1992.
32. See Article XIII (1) of the Agreement in the Caribbean Court of Justice Draft Instruments prepared by Barbados, 2000. Compare

Article XIII (1) of the earliest draft Inter-Governmental Agreement mentioned at Note 8 *supra.*

33. See Article XIII (2)(1) of the Agreement in the Caribbean Court of Justice Draft Instruments prepared by Barbados, 2000
34. See Article XIII (3) of the Agreement in the Caribbean Court of Justice Draft Instruments prepared by Barbados, 2000. Compare Article XIII (1) of the earliest draft Agreement mentioned at Note 4 *supra* and Article IX (1) of the Agreement.
35. See Article 1 of the Draft Financial Protocol.
36. See Article 1 of the Draft Financial Protocol.
37. See Article 1 of the Draft Financial Protocol.
38. See Article 7 of the Draft Financial Protocol.
39. See Article 8 of the Draft Financial Protocol.
40. See Appendix VI at p. 322 below for the full text of the Agreement Establishing the Caribbean Court of Justice Trust Fund.
41. Before this figure was arrived at the CDB engaged the services of a consultant to work with the Secretariat to determine the amount required on an annual basis to cover the expenses of the Court in addition to capital costs. When the matter was raised by the Chairman of the Preparatory Committee with Prime Minister Anthony of Saint Lucia, he suggested rounding of the amount at US$100 million. The Prime Minister probably played a critical role in gaining the concurrence of his OECS colleagues in the establishment of a Trust Fund and in contributing thereto in the agreed amounts. The idea of establishing a Trust Fund and authorising the CDB to raise the amount in international capital markets was a shrewd and workable one. For one thing, the CDB has a triple A rating and repayment of the loans to the CDB was not onerous. More important, the money raised by the CDB was to be placed directly into the Trust Fund and omission to repay invited its own peculiar sanctions without jeopardising the financial sustainability of the Court.
42. The legal officers of the CDB have proposed to incorporate the provisions of the Vesting Deed in the Regulations of the CCJ Trust Fund. Consequently, the Vesting Deed is likely to lose its status as a separate legal instrument.
43. See Article VII (1) (d) and (f) of the Agreement Establishing the Caribbean Court of Justice Trust Fund set out in Appendix VI.
44. See Article 56 (2) of the Vienna Convention on the Law of Treaties.
45. See Article XXXVIII of the Agreement.

46. The Member states requiring a referendum to delink from the Privy Council are Antigua and Barbuda, The Bahamas, Grenada and St. Vincent and the Grenadines.
47. See Article XXV (7) (1) and Article XXI (1) of the Agreement.
48. See Article XXV (7) (1) of the Agreement.
49. <http://www.curia.eu.int/en/instit/txdocfr/txtsenvigueur/tx7.pdf>.
50. See Article 217 (1) of the Revised Treaty and Article XXII (1) of the Agreement.
51. See, for example, the proceedings in *the North Atlantic Coast Fisheries Case* (1910), 11 RIAA and the *Nuclear Test Cases*, ICJ 1974.
52. See, for example, the proceedings in the *Corfu Channel Case*, ICJ 1949, 4 *Nottebohm (Preliminary Objection) Case*, ICJ 1955.
53. See Rule 94 of the Rules of Court of the European Court of First Instance. See also Rule 85 of the Rules of Court of the Court of Justice of COMESA.
54. See, for example, the *Anglo-Iranian Oil Co. Case (Interim Measures),* ICJ 1951, 89.
55. See, for example, *Chorzow Factory (Indemnity) Case*, PCIJ Series A No. 9 (1927).
56. See the *Nuclear Test Cases*, ICJ 1973 and 1974; *Tunisia v. Libyan Arab Jamahiriya* 1982, ICJ 18; *Malta v. Libya Arab Jamahiriya* (1985), ICJ 19. See also Article XVIII of the Agreement.
57. See Report of the First Meeting of the Preparatory Committee on the Establishment of the Caribbean Court of Justice, REP. 99/1/51 CCJ/PC, p.9.
58. See Report of the Second Meeting of the Preparatory Committee on the Establishment of the Caribbean Court of Justice, REP. 99/2/77 CCJ/PC, p.14.
59. See Report of the Third Meeting of the Preparatory Committee on the Establishment of the Caribbean Court of Justice, REP. 2000/3/12 CCJ/PC, p.10-11.
60. See Report of the Fourth Meeting of the Preparatory Committee on the Establishment of the Caribbean Court of Justice, REP. 2000/4/29 CCJ(PC), p.16.
61. See Report of the Fifth Meeting of the Preparatory Committee on the Establishment of the Caribbean Court of Justice, REP. 2000/5/54 CCJ/PC, p.10.

62. See Report of the Fifth Meeting of the Preparatory Committee on the Establishment of the Caribbean Court of Justice, REP. 2000/5/54 CCJ/PC, p.10.
63. See Report of the Seventh Meeting of the Preparatory Committee on the Establishment of the Caribbean Court of Justice, REP. 2001/7/6 CCJ/(PC), p.14.
64. See Report of the Seventh Meeting of the Preparatory Committee on the Establishment of the Caribbean Court of Justice, REP. 2001/7/6 CCJ/(PC), p.22.

CHAPTER TWO

The CCJ in Judicial Institution Building

UNIQUENESS OF THE CARIBBEAN COURT OF JUSTICE

By any rigorous, dispassionate standard of assessment applicable to regional or international judicial institutions today, it would be difficult to avoid the conclusion that the Caribbean Court of Justice is a unique international judicial institution in terms of its jurisdiction, the institutional arrangements devised for the appointment, removal and disciplining of its judges and the mechanism agreed for the financing of its operations. At the time of this writing, no other regional judicial institution in the world can lay a claim to being vested with an appellate jurisdiction in respect of municipal law matters and an original jurisdiction in respect of international law issues arising in relation to the interpretation and application of a treaty. The uniqueness of the Caribbean Court of Justice as a regional judicial institution would be further enhanced if, as is the case with the Supreme Court of Canada, it is vested with jurisdiction to determine appeals from the Member States of the Community with civil law systems, for example, Haiti and Suriname. Indeed, the Caribbean Court of Justice is the only regional judicial institution of its kind in the world whose judges will not be appointed, directly or indirectly, by the political directorate of the States participating in the regime. Cases in point are the International Court of Justice (ICJ), the European Court of Justice (ECJ), the Court of First Instance of the European Union (CFI), the Andean

Court of Justice (ACJ), the Central American Court of Justice (CACJ), the Court of Justice of the European Free Trade Area (CJEFTA) and the Court of Justice of the Common Market for Eastern and Southern Africa (COMESA) (CJC). Financially, too, the CCJ is likely to be only regional judicial institution in the world which will be financially independent of the executive and, by compelling inference, also administratively independent of the central executives of participating Member States.[1]

In a very real sense, the unique features of the CCJ are the product of peculiar historical conditions characterised by deep-seated suspicions of participating governments, suspicions born of unfortunate incidents involving the indiscreet employment of executive power,[2] and widespread regional skepticism about the willingness and readiness of regional governments to contribute to the budget of the Court on a reliable, sustainable basis in the light of past experience. Given the historical antecedents of the initiative to establish a regional court of last resort, especially those of the last 40 years, public acceptance of the establishment of a regional court of last resort has to be achieved by dint of hard work and credible, bankable assurances that commitments made by Governments in this regard would be respected and complied with. In the premises, the regional political directorate were persuaded to maintain a hands-off approach in the appointment of judges of the Court and to approve arrangements for funding of the Court well outside the political control and influence of regional decision-makers.

From the time that a firm, definitive decision was taken by the Conference of Heads of Government of the Caribbean Community to establish the Caribbean Court of Justice at their Eighteenth Meeting in Castries, Saint Lucia, the regional Attorneys General adopted an inclusive approach to the elaboration of the CCJ's constituent instrument and instructed the CARICOM Secretariat to circulate a draft Agreement to the presidents of Bar Associations in the Region for their consideration and reaction. The response was as masterly in its inactivity as it was resoundingly resonant in its protracted quiescence, and the

CARICOM Secretariat was constrained to elaborate the constituent instrument of the CCJ without the benefit of informed input from the regional Bar. To its credit, the Jamaican Bar Association did submit, somewhat belatedly, commendable proposals to amend the texts of the Draft Agreement Establishing the Caribbean Court of Justice and the Draft Enabling Bill. The majority of these proposals were accommodated in the text of these instruments which were considerably enhanced as a result. If all of the proposals of the Jamaican Bar Association were not taken on board, it was largely the result of the consensus approach adopted by the Attorneys General and Heads of Government in elaborating these instruments. Some of these proposals did not commend themselves to other Member States of the Caribbean Community.

In the ultimate analysis however, what might be said with conviction about the process adopted, is that the regional political directorate did make a good faith effort to establish a regional court of last resort that attempted to address the legitimate concerns of important stakeholders. History will determine the extent, if any, to which these efforts yielded positive outcomes. However, in the submission of Lord Slynn, the arrangements for selecting judges and financing the Caribbean Court of Justice do offer useful precedents for the establishment of regional judicial bodies.[3]

THE CARIBBEAN COURT OF JUSTICE AS AN INTEGRATION COURT

As an integration court, the Caribbean Court of Justice is also unique in having the provisions of its constitution relating to the exercise of its original jurisdiction replicated in the disputes settlement provisions of the constituent instrument of the integrating institution, the Caribbean Community, including the CARICOM Single Market and Economy (CSME). The effect of this drafting technique, in the present submission, is to make the Caribbean Court of Justice, in the exercise of its original jurisdiction, the institutional centrepiece of the CSME. Indeed, the absence of adequate arrangements for the definitive and authoritative settlement of disputes in the original Treaty of Chaguaramas (1973) is perceived as largely responsible for the lack of cohesion and structured development of the earlier economic integration arrangements. Provision was indeed made for arbitration,[4] but in the present submission this was not appropriate nor effective for the purpose. Determinations of arbitral tribunals are legally binding on the parties to the proceedings only and not on third parties. However, economic integration arrangements require determinations of disputes arising from the interpretation and application of the integration instrument to be legally binding on all participants in the regime in order to create uniformity and certainty in the applicable norms. As pointed out below, legal certainty in the economic environment is required for stability of expectations on the part of an investor, predictability of outcomes and, *a fortiori*, an attractive investment climate. The experience of the Caribbean Community and Common Market established by the original Treaty of Chaguaramas (1973) would appear to confirm that the absence of credible mechanisms for disputes settlement and sanctioning non-compliance with obligations, encourage deviant conduct by participants in the regime and, ultimately, the frustration and nullification of benefits expected to arise from operation of the integration arrangements. The drafters of the Revised Treaty of Chaguaramas appeared to have benefited from the experience of earlier efforts at regional economic integration, especially as these related to disputes settlement mechanisms, and made the compulsory judicial settlement of disputes concerning the interpretation and application of the Revised Treaty of Chaguaramas an integral feature of the regime.

Thus, by becoming parties to the Revised Treaty of Chaguaramas, Member States agreed to submit to the jurisdiction of the Caribbean Court of Justice. For example, Article 216 of the Revised Treaty provides that Member States recognise, *ipso facto*, and without special agreement, the compulsory jurisdiction of the Court. In the absence of this provision, parties to the Revised Treaty would have had to make other credible arrangements for the settlement of disputes arising in connection with the Treaty or by employing one or another mode of disputes settlement set out in Chapter Nine of the Treaty. One such option would be to become a party to the Agreement Establishing the Caribbean Court of Justice since the Court's jurisdiction in this context is set out in Article XII of the instrument. But as the situation now stands, Member States of the Community may submit to the jurisdiction of the Court without becoming a party to the Agreement Establishing the Caribbean Court of Justice by becoming a party to the Revised Treaty of Chaguaramas.

In fact, an examination of the relevant instruments would confirm that the Revised Treaty addresses the original jurisdiction of the court far more comprehensively than its constituent instrument. Thus Article 187 of the Revised Treaty provides as follows:

> (i) The provisions of this Chapter shall apply to the settlement of disputes concerning the interpretation and application of the Treaty including:
>
> (a) allegations that an actual or proposed measure of another Member State is, or would be, inconsistent with the objectives of the Community;
>
> (b) allegations of injury, serious prejudice suffered or are likely to be suffered, nullification or impairment of benefits expected from the establishment and operation of the CSME;
>
> (c) allegations that an organ or body of the Community has acted *ultra vires*; or
>
> (d) allegations that the purpose or object of the Treaty is being frustrated or prejudiced.

Article 188[5] then expressly provides that the disputes mentioned in Article 187 shall be settled by any one of the disputes settlement modes identified, including adjudication which was addressed in Articles 211 to 222, provisions which replicate the Articles of the Agreement establishing the CCJ relating to its original jurisdiction. The scheme of drafting of Chapter Nine of the Revised Treaty does appear to confirm that the drafters intended the adjudicatory provisions mentioned above to be a critical part of the Revised Treaty especially as it related to the CSME. In the premises, submission to the jurisdiction of the Caribbean Court of Justice in the exercise of its original jurisdiction, was perceived to be a compelling incident of participating in the CSME. This interpretation is consistent with the scheme of drafting of the Agreement Establishing the Caribbean Court of Justice which allows for reservations to be entered to the provisions relating to the appellate jurisdiction of the Court but not those relating to its original jurisdiction.[6]

In order to underscore the centrality of the Caribbean Court of Justice in the regime establishing the CSME, Article 211 of the Revised Treaty accords the Court exclusive jurisdiction for the settlement of disputes concerning the interpretation and application of the Revised Treaty.[7] The clear intention of this provision is to render all courts and tribunals within the jurisdiction of participating states incompetent to hear and determine disputes concerning the interpretation and application of the Revised Treaty. The implications of the exclusivity of the Court's jurisdiction in this context are addressed in Chapter IV. Suffice it to say that concurrent jurisdiction by courts or tribunals of the Caribbean Community in respect of matters relating to the interpretation and application of the Revised Treaty could lead to conflicting determinations and legal uncertainty in the operational environment with a probable negative impact on the regional investment climate. Similar concerns about legal certainty explain the thrust of Articles 214 and 221 of the Revised Treaty. Several of these provisions are peculiar to the Caribbean Court of Justice and operate to underscore its *sui generis* status as a regional economic integration judicial institution in international institutional law.

As an international integration judicial institution, the Caribbean Court of Justice is required to employ rules of international law in reaching its determinations.[8] However, the Court is not precluded from resorting to general or equitable principles to arrive at its determinations in the circumstances identified.[9] In this regard, the jurisdiction of the Caribbean Court of Justice is conspicuously different from that of the European Court of Justice which is empowered to apply Community Law, a body of norms peculiar to the European Union by virtue of its status as a supranational organisation and which is neither international law nor municipal law.

Supranationality speaks to voluntary derogations from sovereignty and to the competence of a collectivity to undertake sovereign acts, such as to make laws with direct effect for persons, natural and juridical, within the territorial jurisdiction of constituent state entities, without confirmation or promulgation by the state.[10] The status of supranationality is perceived to require in the ordinary course of events, the state in relation to which the competence is exercised voluntarily surrendering attributes of sovereignty or statehood to the relevant supranational entity. Of course, exceptionally, supranationality may be a function of coercion where, for example, a conquering state legitimately employing military coercion effects a transfer of sovereignty from the vanquished state. The classical examples of supranational jurisdiction, however, are to be found in treaties establishing the European Coal and Steel Community (ECSC) and the European Economic Community, now incorporated in the European Union since the Treaty of Maastricht.[11]

In the characterisation of the European Court of Justice,

> In contrast with ordinary international treaties, the EEC treaty has created its own legal system which . . . became an integral part of the legal systems of the Member States and which their courts are bound to apply.[12] By creating a Community of unlimited duration, having its own institutions, its own personality, its own legal capacity and capacity of representation on the international plane and, more particularly, real powers stemming from a limitation of sovereignty or a transfer of powers from the states to the Community, the Member States have limited their sovereign rights . . . and have thus created a body of law which binds both nationals and themselves. It follows from all these observations that the law stemming from the Treaty, an independent source of law, could not, because of its special nature, be overridden by domestic legal provisions . . .

> The transfer by the States from their domestic legal system to the Community's legal system of the rights and obligations arising under the Treaty, carries with it a permanent limitation of their sovereign rights against which a subsequent unilateral act incompatible with the concept of the Community cannot prevail.[13]

The peculiar status of the European Union as a supranational entity with power to make laws with direct effect for States and private entities without the intervention of their national assemblies is balanced by the right of private entities to enjoy *locus standi* in proceedings before the European Court of Justice where measures with direct effect impact negatively on the interests of these entities. However, nationals of the Caribbean Community do not have *locus standi* in proceedings before the Caribbean Court of Justice as a legal entitlement. Where nationals are accorded *locus standi* it is with the leave of the Court and at its discretion.[14]

Not unlike other international tribunals, the Caribbean Court of Justice is competent to review its judgments in circumstances identified in Article 219 of the Revised Treaty. It does not appear, however, that the European Court of Justice and the Andean Court of Justice have a similar competence. By dispensing justice as a court of reference,[15] the Caribbean Court of Justice would be in a position to enhance the economic and social cohesion of the Caribbean Community. Referring to the European Court of Justice in this context, Lord Denning submitted: 'When it comes to matters with a European element, the Treaty is like an incoming tide. It flows into the estuaries and up the rivers. It cannot be held back.'[16] In fact, the European Court of Justice is perceived in some quarters as the most potent force for economic and social cohesion in the European Union. There is reason to believe, moreover, that this reputation of the European Court of Justice is largely a function of judicial activism. At this point in time, it would be idle to speculate on the innovative propensities of the judges occupying the Bench of the Caribbean Court of Justice.

The peculiarity of the Caribbean Court of Justice as an integration court is informed by the status of the Caribbean

Community as an association of sovereign states unlike the European Union which is a supranational entity. Sovereignty, as an international law doctrine, speaks to the totality of exclusive rights, powers and privileges which international law recognises a state as entitled to exercise in relation to an ascertainable area of territory,[17] including its superjacent air space, and the persons, assets and resources therein, subject to compliance with the obligations correlative to the enjoyment of those powers, rights and privileges. As a constitutional international law doctrine, sovereignty does not involve the unfettered employment of competences by the state which is constrained by the applicable rules of international law, especially those set out in the United Nations Charter by which the legality of state acts is determined.[18] One such power of the state is the exclusive right of legislation in relation to persons and resources within its jurisdiction. The effect of this in an association of sovereign states like the Caribbean Community is the potential for legal uncertainty in the normative framework resulting from the interpretation and application of the integrating treaty with probable negative consequences on the regional macro-economic environment – hence the standardising and unifying jurisdiction of the Caribbean Court of Justice.

THE CARIBBEAN COURT OF JUSTICE AS A MUNICIPAL COURT

The Agreement Establishing the Caribbean Court of Justice offers little or no guidance about the doctrinal position the Court is likely to adopt on one or another issue. And it would be idle and inappropriate to speculate on the likely doctrinal disposition of the Court on any given issue or to indulge a value judgment on what it ought to be, especially since the Court has not been inaugurated and is yet to hold its first sitting. The foregoing notwithstanding, it does appear to be apposite to canvass some of the considerations which seem to be relevant in the present context. As a point of departure, a legal ethic to be controlling must be as dynamic as its environment of control. In other terms, law as an effective and relevant normative tool for social engineering must reflect the collective social ethos of the society it controls. Dissonance between the normative regime and the operational environment is a built-in prescription for tension between the law and human conduct. But the intractable issue falling to be determined is the extent, if any, to which normative prescriptions should direct human conduct or the requirement of normative prescriptions to adjust to developments in the socio-economic and technological environment. In both situations there must be an overriding concern about balancing public and private interests. In both situations it must be possible to discern the inclusive and egocentric imperatives informing human behaviour and to arrive at the balance by reference to an appreciation of the minimal requirements of social organisation. To do otherwise might involve rejection of those primordial values which distinguish *homo sapiens* from other forms of life.

An issue of seminal concern which is bound to agitate stakeholders of the Court, especially those of the legal fraternity, is the extent, if any, to which the Caribbean Court of Justice is required to follow previous decisions of the Judicial Committee of the Privy Council. In other words, to what extent would the Caribbean Court of Justice in its determinations be bound by the doctrinal disposition of its predecessor. Does the constituent instrument of the Court offer any guidance on this issue? At first blush, it would not be unreasonable to indulge the view that it does, to the extent that in addressing its original jurisdiction, competent decision-makers determined that the doctrine of *stare decisis* shall apply to determinations of the Court.[19] This requirement was informed by the conviction that legal certainty and uniformity in the applicable norms were necessary for stability of expectations and predictability of outcomes for relevant decisions of investors, in the absence of which the regional investment climate would be unattractive.

It may also be persuasively argued that it must have been the subject of an axiomatic assumption on the part of competent decision-makers that the Caribbean Court of Justice would follow the decisions of its predecessor, the Judicial Committee of the Privy Council – hence the resounding silence on the issue. The same arguments addressed in favour of applying the doctrine of *stare decisis* in the exercise of the Court's original jurisdiction may be advanced *a fortiori* in respect of the decisions of the Court in the exercise of its appellate jurisdiction. But even more persuasive are the provisions of Article III (2) which provide that 'decisions of the Court shall be final'. The implications of the language of commitment employed here are considered in chapter 3.

But even assuming that the Caribbean Court of Justice will be bound by previous decisions of the Judicial Committee of the Privy Council, there is sound reason for submitting that the doctrine of precedent must be regarded as a guide to lead rather than a chain to shackle. For precedent is not to be construed as a potent force for the petrification of law but a flexible instrument for the achievement of a dynamic social equilibrium, promoting measured social change without engendering disruptive social instability.[20]

In the present submission the alleged instability introduced into the administration of criminal justice in the Caribbean Community[21] by a line of decisions which seems to depart from precedent appears to be a function of the convergence of emergent norms, which, if they have not yet attained the status of *lex lata* certainly appear to be in the nature of *de lege ferenda*. On the one hand, there appears to be an emerging consensus, particularly in the area of international human rights law, that the ratification of a treaty by a State gives rise to a legitimate expectation on the part of persons entitled that the State will honour obligations assumed in the treaty, even where the State for one reason or another, omitted to enact the instrument into domestic law.[22] In this context consider the majority opinion in *Thomas and Hilaire v. Baptiste and Ors.* (1999) 54 WIR 387 when Lord Willet submitted:

> By ratifying a treaty which provides for individual access to an international body, the Government made that process for the time being part of the domestic criminal justice system and thereby . . . extended the scope of the due process clause in the Constitution.

This emerging consensus might be traced to the *lex lata* norm that a State may not plead its domestic law as a bar to the performance of an international obligation,[23] including a restrictive provision of its constitution. Postulated in other terms, a state is presumed to know its municipal law, including its constitution, and would only assume an international obligation if it knows it was in a position to give effect to it in its domestic law. Third parties are not presumed to be familiar with the domestic obligations of other parties to an international instrument. On the other hand, it could very well be that the highest judicial institutions in Britain are inclined not to accept the doctrine of transformation but to adopt the doctrine of incorporation articulated by Lord Denning in the *Trendtex* case.[24] If this is the case, then emerging rules of international humanitarian law would be automatically incorporated into the common law, which is, presumably, common to both Britain and Member States of the Caribbean Community, and could operate to enlarge the rights of individuals in respect of due process without the direct intervention of the legislature or an appropriate decision of the House of Lords or the Judicial Committee of the Privy Council.[25]

Given the foregoing, an evaluation of degrading and inhuman treatment, which is proscribed by the constitutions of Caribbean Member States, would appear to be a variable magnitude vulnerable to modification consistently with changing international social values and circumstances.[26] This submission appears to derive considerable justification from the articulated position of Robin Cooke who sat on the Privy Council and concurred in the doctrinal position of the majority in the *Neville Lewis* case. In this submission 'prolonged confinement in such circumstances could indeed make an ultimate execution unconstitutional; cumulatively the punishment may be ruled out as inhuman and degrading treatment. A sentence of five years extremely rigorous imprisonment to be followed by execution could not be accepted as civilised. The majority judgment is also important as recognising both a right to natural justice when the prerogative of mercy is being considered and the bearing of international law norms and treaty obligations on the requirements of natural justice. These rights, norms and obligations are relevant even when not expressly incorporated.'[27]

It also appears to be the subject of a reasonable inference that if the assumption regarding the doctrine of incorporation is correct, a flexible application of the *stare decisis* doctrine in the area of international humanitarian law would yield more modifications in the applicable norms than would normally be the case. But this would be due in no small measure to the rapid advances in international humanitarian law and its impact on municipal law, especially when the doctrine of incorporation is perceived to be determinative, and would not be expected to affect *aequo vigore*, other areas of international law and municipal law in the same way. In the premises, it is submitted that the instability which negatively impacts the normative regime of criminal law, and in particular, due process, would not necessarily impact developments in civil law in the same manner.

By way of indulging a measure of juridical heresy and intellectual candour, it is submitted that the line of decisions of the Judicial Committee of the Privy Council commencing with *Pratt and Morgan* must be seen as a wake-up call for the jurists of the Caribbean Community to address the philosophical, ethical and doctrinal foundations of an emerging humanitarian municipal jurisprudence. This emerging jurisprudence appears to be the outcome of the convergence of several norms, moral imperatives and doctrines, including the legal incidence of executive commitments at the international plane on the exercise of executive discretion at the domestic level - *Thomas and Hilaire v. Baptiste and Ors*;[28] the flexibility to be accorded the doctrine of *stare decisis* which is to be perceived more as a catalyst for a dynamic equilibrium in the normative environment than a potent force for the petrification of the law on traditional lines – *Trendtex Trading Corp. v. Central Bank of Nigeria*;[29] and the rule that the Courts will not follow a previous judgment in a case involving the liberty of the subject if the requirements of justice advise otherwise – *Reg v. Parole Board ex parte Wilson*, [1992] QB 740.

THE CARIBBEAN COURT OF JUSTICE IN AUTONOMOUS JUDICIAL DECISION-MAKING

The qualities of personal integrity and judicial independence required by the Bangalore Principles[30] and which are indispensable for autonomous judicial decision-making, would appear to be impossible of attainment in the absence of a credible, apolitical system for the selection, appointment and removal of the judges of the Caribbean Court of Justice. Further, the system of selection, appointment and removal of the judges would have to be underpinned by such institutional arrangements for the remuneration of these officials and the financing of the operations of the Court as would inspire public confidence that the political directorate is not in a position to employ the power of the purse to influence the determinations of the Caribbean Court of Justice. Consequently, it is proposed to evaluate the prospects of the CCJ for autonomous judicial decision-making by an examination of the arrangements contemplated for the appointment and removal of judges of the Court and for its financing on a sustainable, reliable basis.

Unlike other international judicial institutions existing today, the Judges of the Caribbean Court of Justice are to be appointed by an independent, apolitical Regional Judicial and Legal Services Commission from candidates in the Commonwealth and appropriate civil law jurisdictions, on the basis of open competition.[31] The qualifications stipulated for prospective candidates[32] are designed to facilitate access to the Bench of the Court by a cross-section of applicants including attorneys-at-law who would be qualified in international law, a discipline which was not accorded much attention in the syllabuses for the teaching of law by competent decision-makers who were more focused on matters relating to civil and criminal law in municipal jurisdictions. Consequently, the threshold for access to the Bench was agreed to be 15 years – five years on the bench of a court of unlimited jurisdiction in civil and criminal matters in the territory of a Contracting Party, assuming that practitioners were elevated to the bench after 10 years standing at the Bar and service in the lower judiciary, and 15 years standing at the Bar for teachers of law or professional practitioners. In addition, candidates for the Bench of the Court are required to be persons of high moral character, intellectual and analytical ability, sound judgment, integrity and understanding of people and society.[33] Compare in this context section 129 (4) of the Constitution of Ghana which reads: 'A person shall not be qualified for appointment as a Justice of the Supreme Court unless he is of high moral character and proven integrity and is of not less than fifteen years' standing as a lawyer'.

In identifying categories of persons to sit on the Commission, the regional Attorneys General were adamant that its composition must reflect a broad genre of stakeholders consistently with the required degree of professional competence and commanding the public confidence that this institution would not pay obeisance to the regional political directorate. And, although there appeared to be a bias against making the Commission a lawyers' body, nominees of the regional private Bar outnumbered other nominees on the Commission. The Commission which was inaugurated on August 21, 2003, will eventually consist of the President, as Chairperson; two persons nominated jointly by the Organisation of Commonwealth Caribbean Bar Associations (OCCBA) and the Organisation of Eastern Caribbean States (OECS) Bar Association; one chairman of the Judicial Services Commission of a Contracting Party selected in rotation in the English alphabetical order for a period of three years; the chairman of a Public Service Commission of a Contracting Party selected in rotation in the reverse English alphabetical order for a period of three years; two persons from civil society nominated jointly by the Secretary-General of the Caribbean Community and the Director-General of the OECS for a period of three years following consultations with regional non-governmental organisations; two distinguished jurists nominated jointly by the Dean of the Faculty of Law of the University of the West Indies, the Deans of the Faculty of Law of any of the Contracting Parties and the Chairman of the Council of Legal Education, and two persons nominated jointly by the Bar or Law Association of the Contracting Parties.[34]

Given the persistent opposition of the regional private Bar to the establishment of the Court and the fact that the majority of nominees emanated from this source, the regional Attorneys General determined to preempt any initiative by this class of stakeholders to frustrate the establishment of the Commission by declining to make nominations to the Commission – hence the belated inclusion of paragraph 2 of Article V in the text of the Agreement and which reads as follows:

> Where any person or body required to nominate a candidate for appointment to the Regional Judicial and Legal Services Commission in accordance with paragraph 1 fails to make such nomination within thirty (30) days of a written request in that behalf, the nomination shall be made jointly by the heads of judiciaries of the Contracting Parties.[35]

No provision is made in the Agreement Establishing the Caribbean Court of Justice for the dismissal of Members of the Commission for cause. However, the members of the Commission, in exercising their functions, are forbidden to seek or receive instructions from any body or persons external to the Commission.[36] Moreover, it does appear to be the subject of a reasonable assumption that the President may request a member of the Commission to resign for acts incompatible with the status and functions of a member. In the alternative, appointing bodies may be presumed to have the power of recall for activities incompatible with the status and functions of a member of the Commission. The independence of the Commission is reinforced by its enjoyment of functional privileges and immunities.[37] In the present submission, the institutional arrangements agreed for the appointment of members of the Commission appear to provide a credible expectation that in the performance of their functions the Commissioners would not be influenced by the regional political directorate.

Judges of the Bench of the Caribbean Court of Justice, other than the President, are to be appointed by the Regional Judicial and Legal Services Commission. Such appointments are to be made by a majority vote of all the members of the Commission.[38] Similarly, the removal of a judge from the Bench requires a majority vote of all members of the Commission. However, a judge may only be removed from office for inability to perform the functions of his office, whether arising from illness or any other cause, or for misbehaviour in accordance with the relevant provisions of Article IX of the Agreement.[39]

In order to enhance the security of tenure of judges, the Agreement expressly provides that the Commission may remove a judge from office only if the question of his removal has been referred by the Commission to a tribunal and the tribunal has advised the Commission that the judge ought to be removed from office for inability or misbehaviour. Further, the office of a judge shall not be abolished while there is a substantive holder thereof[40] and a judge may sit until he attains the age of 72 years.[41] No provision is made for the extension of the period of office of a judge for fear that the exercise of such a power may be manipulated in order to influence the judge in his judicial determinations. Similarly, there is also a proposal that judges of the Court in the exercise of its original jurisdiction should be precluded from handing down separate or dissenting judgments or opinions in order to insulate them from external influences. Anonymity in the delivery of judgments frustrates improper attempts to discover the doctrinal position of one or another judge on issues with a view to influencing them one way or another.[42]

Separate provisions have been elaborated for the appointment and removal of the President. The President of the Court is restricted to one term of seven years or until he attains the age of 72 years.[43] The President is appointed or removed from office by a qualified majority vote of three quarters of the Contracting Parties on the recommendation of the Commission.[44] The appointment of the President must be signified by letter under the hand of the Chairman for the time being of the Conference of the Heads of Government. The President may be removed from office by the Heads of Government on the recommendation of the Commission. Such a recommendation, however, must be based on the advice of a tribunal set up to investigate allegations of impropriety or inability to perform the functions of President.[45] The establishment of the tribunal must be accomplished by the Heads of Government acting on the initiative of at least three Heads of Government.[46] From the language of commitment employed in Article IV (6) it does not appear that a decision of the Heads of Government is required for the appointment or removal from office of the President. Article IV (6) provides that the President 'shall be appointed or removed by the qualified majority vote of three-quarters of the Contracting Parties on the recommendations of the Commission'. As such any representative of a Contracting Party may participate in the vote. It is doubtful, however, if this was the intention of the drafters, given the articulated role of the Heads of Government in the removal of the President from office.

The institutional arrangements agreed for the appointment and removal of the President should inspire confidence that this appointment will not be subject to determinative political influence or control. The Contracting Parties, in appointing the President, are required to act on the affirmative recommendation of the Commission and may not reject the Commission's nominee and substitute their own for appointment. Where the Contracting Parties (not the Heads of Government) cannot agree on the appointment, the Commission is entitled to make other nominations *ad nauseum* until a recommendation commends itself to a qualified majority of three-quarters of the Contracting Parties. As such, the appointment of the President is insulated from political control to a much greater degree than similar appointments of other international or regional integration, tribunals. For even though the Presidents of the European Court of Justice and the International Court of Justice are elected by their peers on the Bench, the persons electing and elected are appointed or elected directly by political representatives of States. The arrangement agreed for the appointment and removal of the President are a far cry from those contemplated in the Draft Inter-Governmental Agreement of 1992 and confirm the readiness of the regional political directorate to address seriously the legitimate concerns of stakeholders. Yet, in one submission,

> the Agreement Establishing the Caribbean Court of Justice does not shield the process of selection of judges from political interference to any greater degree. The Heads of Government have too large an opportunity to influence the appointment of the President and the Chairman of the Regional Judicial and Legal Services Commission and consequently the whole process of the judicial appointments.[47]

As pointed out above, the role of the political directorate in the appointment of the President is substantially qualified. Similarly, it is not shown how the President controls appointments to the Bench of the Court by the Commission nor has there been any demonstration of how the appointment, discipline and removal of the President from office remained 'steadfastly' under the control of the Heads of Government and how this compromised the whole process of selection of judges. These perceptions appear to lack merit.

The institutional arrangements devised for the financing of the Caribbean Court of Justice are likely to make this institution the envy of judicial institutions the world over in terms of the financial independence it is likely to enjoy. These arrangements are a function of the historical experience of the Commonwealth Caribbean Region where regional institutions were not known to be funded by participating governments on a reliable and sustainable basis. Indeed, this was among the most potent and persuasive arguments advanced by the detractors of the Court against its establishment, especially since it represented a legitimate concern of stakeholders. In order to establish their credibility in terms of honouring their financial commitment to the Court and desisting from employing the power of the purse to exercise leverage with judges of the Court, the regional Attorneys General proposed, and the Heads of Government accepted, the mechanism of the Trust Fund. In this connection, the President of the Caribbean Development Bank (CDB) with the authority of the Board of Governors undertook to raise US$100 million in international capital markets for on-lending to Member States of the Community. This amount was to be deposited by the Bank in the Trust Fund. Prior to approaching the international capital markets, the President of the CDB required the Member States of the Caribbean Community to conclude a Trust Fund Agreement satisfactory to the Bank and to conclude loan agreements with the Bank in respect of the repayment of their moieties of the US$100 million. The CARICOM Secretariat was also requested by the regional Attorneys General to elaborate an appropriate vesting deed to vest the capital and other assets of the Fund in the Trustees of the Fund. The Trustees of the Fund were identified by the CARICOM Secretariat drawn from reputable private sector bodies and the Fund was to be managed by a professional manager to be selected by the Caribbean Development Bank. These arrangements for financing the operations of the Court appeared to have silenced some of its most virulent and skeptical detractors. The Council of the Jamaican Bar Association, however, appears to entertain reservations about the adequacy and sustainability of these arrangements.[48]

The institutional arrangements agreed for the appointment of the members of the Regional Judicial and Legal Services Commission, for the appointment and removal of the President and judges of the Caribbean Court of Justice and for financing the operations of the Court should constitute plausible assurances that the regional political directorate is not engaged in any invidious attempt to control or subvert the judiciary thereby compromising the democratic principle which forms the basis of governance in the Caribbean Community. The institutional arrangements devised for remunerating, appointing and dismissing judges of the Bench of the Caribbean Court of Justice appear to be important innovations in the configuration of international judicial institutions. Indeed, in the view of informed commentators these arrangements are likely to provide extremely useful precedents for similar institutions in the international community.

The purpose of the Trust Fund as set out in Article III of the Agreement Establishing the Caribbean Court of Justice Trust Fund is 'to provide the resources necessary to finance the biennial capital and operating budget of the Court and the Commission in perpetuity'. The Fund is precluded from soliciting or accepting grants, gifts or any other material benefit from any source, except with the consent of all the Members.[49] The intention of this provision is to protect the integrity of the Fund and, *ipso facto*, of the Caribbean Court of Justice which may be compromised in the eyes of the public by accepting financial gifts or other material benefits from sources whose public image leaves much to be desired. In this connection it is important to note that the Board is required to 'review the adequacy of the resources of the Fund, not later than two years after the entry into force of this Agreement and thereafter at least once within every succeeding biennium'[50] and the Members are required to make additional contributions to the Fund where resources are found to be inadequate.[51] The Board of Trustees, drawn primarily from the private sector and civil society, has broad responsibility, *inter alia*, for directing the operations of the Fund, evaluating the performance of the Fund, establishing regulations of the Fund and guidelines for prudential investments of the Fund's resources and the appointment of the executive officer and investment manager of the Fund.[52]

Consistently with Article XXXVII of the Agreement Establishing the Caribbean Court of Justice which provides for withdrawal from the regime, Article XVIII of the Agreement Establishing the Caribbean Court of Justice Trust Fund also provides for withdrawal from the Fund subject to the withdrawing

Member settling all outstanding obligations to the Fund. The Agreement is silent on the entitlement of a withdrawing Member to be refunded capital from the Fund. Any such capital amount would have to be negotiated and agreed among the Contracting Parties, the withdrawing State, and the Board of Trustees of the Fund especially since the Vesting Deed of the Caribbean Court of Justice Trust Fund vests the assets of the Fund in the Trustees. The purpose of the Trust, not unlike the purpose of the Trust Fund, is to hold the assets of the Fund on 'trust to provide the resources necessary to finance the biennial capital and operating budget of the Court and the Commission in perpetuity'.[53]

In performing their duties under the Vesting Deed, the Trustees are expressly authorised to 'balance competing claims on the resources of the Fund, bearing in mind that when there is conflict between the provisions of the Agreement Establishing the Caribbean Court of Justice Trust Fund and the Vesting Deed of the CCJ Trust Fund, the provisions of the former prevails'.[54] The Trust Fund , insofar as it is subject to the vesting deed, may be terminated where two-thirds of the Trustees have so decided and the Settlor, consisting of the Member States Parties to the Agreement, have so concurred. The law applicable to the Trust Fund is the law of Trinidad and Tobago which could be modified by the Board of Trustees with the consent of the Settlor.[55] However, the foregoing submissions may have to be modified if the Vesting Deed is incorporated in the Regulations of the CCJ Trust Fund as recommended by the CDB.

NOTES

1. Consider in this context the controversy between the Chief Justice and Attorney General of Trinidad and Tobago which led to the setting up of a Commission of Enquiry under the Chairmanship of Lord Mackay of Clashfern on February 29, 2000.
2. See paper presented by Bernice Lake. 'The Caribbean Court of Justice: Public Confidence and the Role of the Media'. Paper delivered at

the Fifth Annual Caribbean Media Conference, St. John, Antigua and Barbuda, May 16, 2002.

3. Observations made at the meeting of the International Law Association in Bridgetown, Barbados, on March 28 and 29, 2003.
4. See Articles 11 and 12 of the Treaty of Chaguaramas establishing the Caribbean Community and Common Market, 1973, in Duke E.E. Pollard, *The CARICOM System: Basic Instruments*, (Kingston: The Caribbean Law Publishing Co., 2003) 184.
5 See the Revised Treaty of Chaguaramas establishing the Caribbean Community including the CARICOM Single Market and Economy.
6. See Article XXXIX of the Agreement.
7. Contrast in this context Article 29 (1) of the COMESA Treaty which gives the COMESA Court of Justice (CJC) concurrent jurisdiction with national courts and tribunals of participating states.
8. See Article 217 (1) of the Revised Treaty.
9. See Article 217 (2) and (3) of the Revised Treaty.
10. See J.T. Lang, *The Common Market and Common Law*, (Illinois: Chicago University Press, 1966), 10.
11. See, The Treaty on Political Union adapted by the Heads of State and Government of the Community on 10 December 1972.
12. See, for example, Articles 189-92 of the Rome Treaty which address the legal incidence of regulations, directives, decisions and recommendations for Member States and Private entities.
13. *Costa v. ENEL*, No. 6/64, 1964 CMLR 425
14. See Article 222 of the Revised Treaty. Contrast the right of private entities *to locus standi* in the Court of Justice of COMESA(CJC). Article 24 (2) of the COMESA Agreement.
15. See Article 214 of the Revised Treaty.
16. *H.P. Bulmer v. Bollinger S.A.* [1974] 2 All ER 1226; [1974] Ch 401.
17. See, for example, Ian Browlie, *Principles of Public International Law*, (Oxford: Clarendon Press, 1988) 291-2.
18. See *Starke's International Law*, 11th ed., (London: Butterworths, 1994), 91.
19. See Article 221 of the Revised Treaty.
20. See opinion of Stephenson, L.J. in *Trendtex Trading Corp. v. Central Bank of Nigeria* [1977] QB 359.
21. See Sir David Simmons, 'The Caribbean Court of Justice: An Historic Necessity'. Paper presented to the Commonwealth Meeting of the

Expert Group to Examine the Removal of the Appellate Jurisdiction of the JCPC, Marlborough House, London, June 10-13, 2003.

22. See *Lewis v. Attorney General of Jamaica* (2000). Also *Thomas and Hilaire v. Baptiste and Ors.* (1999) 54 WIR 275; [1999]3 WLR 249.

23. See *Starke's International Law*, 11th ed., (London: Butterworths, 1994), 78-79; also *United Nations Headquarters Agreement Case*, ICJ 1988, 12; and *Case of Free Zones of Upper Savoy and Gex* (1932), PCIJ Series A/B, no.46.

24. See *Trendtex Trading Corp. v. Central Bank of Nigeria* [1977] QB 359; also *Lewis v. Attorney-General of Jamaica*, (2000) 57 WIR 275.

25. See Lord Denning, *idem.*

26. Consider in this context Article 7 of the International Covenant on Civil and Political Rights which reads: 'No one shall be subjected to torture or to cruel, inhuman or degrading treatment or punishment. In particular, no one shall be subjected without his free consent to medical or scientific experimentation.'

27. Robin Cooke, 'Final Appeal Courts: Some Comparisons', *Journal of Commonwealth Lawyers Associations*, 2001, 49.

28. (1999) 54 WIR 387; [1999] 3 WLR 249.

29. [1977] QB 359.

30. See *Code of Conduct – the Bangalore Draft* prepared by the Working Group of the Consultative Council of European Judges, Strasbourg, April 30, 2002.

31. There is some consideration being given by some Commissioners to inviting potential candidates to apply where personal pique may constitute a disincentive for some eminently qualified persons to respond to a general advertisement.

32. See Article IV (10) of the Agreement.

33. See Article IV (11) of the Agreement. The requirement of fifteen years standing at the Bar was established in one of the earliest drafts of the Inter-Governmental Agreement appearing in 1992. It was extended to twenty years in the draft Agreement appearing in the Compendium of CCJ Instruments Rev. 7, prepared by the CARICOM Secretariat. The Agreement finally settled on 15 years.

34. See Article V of the Agreement.

35. This was one of the last amendments made by the regional Attorneys General and had to be effected by round robin prior to transmission of the Draft Agreement to Heads of Government for approval.

36. See Article V (12) of the Agreement.
37. See the Protocol on Privileges and Immunities of the CCJ and the RJLSC set out in Appendix III.
38. See Article IV (7) of the Agreement.
39. See Article IX (4) of the Agreement.
40. See Article IX (1) of the Agreement.
41. See Article IV (3) of the Agreement.
42. See the Report of the Expert Group established by the Meeting of Commonwealth Law Ministers to Examine the Removal of Appellate Jurisdiction from the Judicial Committee of the Privy Council by Member Countries, Commonwealth Secretariat, 2003. The European Court of Justice does not allow dissenting or separate opinions to be delivered by its judges.
43. See Article IX (2) of the Agreement. This was not the position adopted earlier by competent decision-makers. See the Draft Agreement set out in the Compendium of CCJ Documents Rev. 7, dated 8 June 1999 prepared by the CARICOM Secretariat; and the Draft Agreement of 1992.
44. See Article IX (6) of the Agreement.
45. See Article IX (5) (1) of the Agreement.
46. See Article IX (6) of the Agreement.
47. See Bernice Lake, 'The Caribbean Court of Justice: Public Confidence and the Role of the Media', Paper delivered at the Fifth Annual Caribbean Media Conference, St. John's, Antigua and Barbuda, on May 16, 2002.
48. But, see submissions made by a representative of the Council of the Jamaica Bar Association at the 6th Annual Meeting of the OCCBA held at the Savannah Hotel in Bridgetown, Barbados on September 7, 2003.
49. See Article IV (2) of the Agreement Establishing the CCJ Trust Fund.
50. See Article IV (5) of the Agreement Establishing the CCJ Trust Fund.
51. See Article IV (5) of the Agreement Establishing the CCJ Trust Fund.
52. See Article VII (1) of the Agreement Establishing the CCJ Trust Fund.
53. See Clause 5 of the Vesting Deed of the CCJ Trust Fund.
54. See Clause 3 (2) of the Vesting Deed of the CCJ Trust Fund.
55. See Clause 8 of the Vesting Deed of the CCJ Trust Fund.

CHAPTER THREE

Appellate Jurisdiction of the Caribbean Court of Justice

APPELLATE JURISDICTION OF THE COURT

The Caribbean Court of Justice is a unique model of a multinational court enjoying both an original jurisdiction as an international tribunal and an appellate jurisdiction in respect of municipal law issues arising in the jurisdictions of Member States of the Caribbean Community and heard on appeal from national appellate courts. Like many other Commonwealth countries, the Member States of the Caribbean Community have determined to terminate the jurisdiction of the Judicial Committee of the Privy Council as being inconsistent with their status as sovereign states and to replace that body with a regional court of last resort. Such a court, it is believed in official circles, would not only complete the circle of independence which was being drawn as early as 1962, but would also constitute the apotheosis of judicial institutional arrangements contemplated as long ago as 1970 when the Council of Legal Education was established to promote the development of an indigenous jurisprudence. In this context, a faculty of law has been established at the University of the West Indies campus at Cave Hill, Barbados, and the Council of Legal Education has law schools at Mona (Jamaica), St. Augustine (Trinidad and Tobago) and Nassau (The Bahamas). The establishment of another law school at the University of Guyana is under active consideration. Serious consideration is, therefore, being given to accommodate the growing regional demand for trained lawyers and to augment the export of regional professional services, an area in which the Region is perceived to enjoy a comparative advantage.

Since the Caribbean Court of Justice is a multinational court, its jurisdiction is set out in a treaty, the Agreement Establishing the Caribbean Court of Justice, which must be eventually enacted into law by the Parliaments of Member States subscribing to the common law system to give it the force of law in their respective jurisdictions. The situation is different in Suriname and Haiti which subscribe to the monist doctrine of international law. For the purpose of accommodating the common law jurisdictions, the CARICOM Secretariat has elaborated a model Draft Enabling Bill to implement the Agreement Establishing the Caribbean Court of Justice discussed below. The Agreement provides for the appellate jurisdiction of the Court as set out in Article XXV which reads as follows:

> 1. In the exercise of its appellate jurisdiction, the Court is a superior Court of Record with such jurisdiction and powers as are conferred on it by this Agreement or by the Constitution or any other law of a Contracting Party.
>
> 2. Appeals shall lie to the Court from decisions of the Court of Appeal of a Contracting Party as of right in the following cases:
>
> (a) final decisions in civil proceedings when the matter in dispute or appeal to the Court is of the value of not less than twenty-five thousand dollars Eastern Caribbean currency (EC$25,000) or where the appeal involves directly or indirectly a claim or a question respecting property or a right of the aforesaid value;
>
> (b) final decisions in proceedings for dissolution or nullity of marriage;
>
> (c) final decisions in any civil or other proceedings which involve a question as to the interpretation of the Constitution of the Contracting Party;
>
> (d) final decisions given in the exercise of the jurisdiction conferred upon a superior court of a Contracting Party relating to redress for contravention of the provisions of the Constitution of a Contracting Party for the protection of fundamental rights;

(e) final decisions given in the exercise of the jurisdiction conferred on a superior court of a Contracting Party relating to the determination of any question for which a right of access to the superior court of a Contracting Party is expressly provided for by its constitution;

(f) such other cases as may be prescribed by any law of the Contracting Party.

3. An appeal shall lie to the Court with the leave of the Court of Appeal of a Contracting Party from the decisions of the Court of Appeal in the following cases:

(a) final decisions in any civil proceedings where, in the opinion of the Court of Appeal, the question involved in the appeal is one that by reason of its great general or public importance or otherwise, ought to be submitted to the Court; and,

(b) such other cases as may be prescribed by any law of the Contracting Party.

4. Subject to paragraph 2, an appeal shall lie to the Court with the special leave of the Court from any decision of the Court of Appeal of a Contracting Party, in any civil or criminal matter.

5. Nothing in this Article shall apply to matters in relation to which the decision of the Court of Appeal of a Contracting Party is, at the time of the entry into force of the Agreement, pursuant to the Constitution or any other law of that Party, declared to be final.

6. The Court shall, in relation to any appeal to it in any case, have all the jurisdiction and powers possessed in relation to that case by the Court of Appeal of the contracting Party from which the appeal was brought.

Like the Judicial Committee of the Privy Council which it will replace, the Caribbean Court of Justice in the exercise of its appellate jurisdiction, will be the court of final appeal for each Member State of the Caribbean Community participating in the regime establishing the Court and which has not entered a reservation to Article XXV of the Agreement. Consequently, the Court may find itself in the paradoxical position of having to rule differently on similar facts depending on the legislation in place in the jurisdiction from which an appeal is brought. An interesting case in point concerns the prerogative of mercy which the Judicial Committee of the Privy Council has ruled is amenable to judicial review in its exercise,[1] thereby reversing earlier decisions of the Court on this issue.[2] Since the Government of Barbados has enacted legislation reversing the relevant decision of the Judicial Committee of the Privy Council, is the Caribbean Court of Justice expected to rule differently on the exercise of the prerogative of mercy in Jamaica than in Barbados, if the Jamaican Government omits to enact legislation ousting the judgment in the *Neville Lewis* case? A similar predicament may confront the Caribbean Court of Justice in other situations and clear practice directions would be required in this context or unified or harmonious national legislation on the employment of the ultimate sanction by Member States of the Caribbean Community parties to the Agreement Establishing the Caribbean Court of Justice.

COMPARISONS WITH OTHER COMMONWEALTH COURTS

It is proposed here to consider briefly the approach of some other Commonwealth Countries in delinking from the Judicial Committee of the Privy Council where the outcome was the establishment of a new court of last resort or retention of the existing Court of Appeal as the court of last resort. In the case of Ghana, a new supreme court was established to replace the Judicial Committee of the Privy Council. A similar approach was adopted by Singapore which abolished appeals to the Judicial Committee of the Privy Council by the Judicial Committee (Repeal) Act, 1994. New Zealand is also contemplating establishing a Supreme Court on delinking from the Judicial Committee of the Privy Council.

In the case of the Member States of the Caribbean Community, the issue was not merely one of delinking from the Judicial Committee of the Privy Council and establishing a court of last resort; it also involved establishing a multinational court of last resort for civil and criminal appeals coupled with an original jurisdiction, not as in the case of the Supreme Court of Ghana for specific municipal law issues, but for the settlement of disputes relating to an international instrument through the employment of applicable rules of international law. The Supreme Court of Canada was created in 1875 but it was not until 1949 that the Judicial Committee of the Privy Council ceased to be court of last resort for appeals from this Supreme Court and from provincial appellate courts. The Supreme Court of Canada is alleged to have discharged its remit conservatively and somewhat self-effacingly despite numerous opportunities after 1949 to challenge old sacred judicial cows inherited from the British Court system and to address issues by reference to the peculiar Canadian experience. The Supreme Court of Canada is the court of last resort for both common law and civil law jurisdictions of Canada and could provide an excellent precedent for the Caribbean Court of Justice in respect of its appellate jurisdiction for Suriname and Haiti. The Supreme Court of Canada aspires to unanimity in the delivery of judgments, but separate concurring and dissenting opinions are allowed. It is envisaged that the Caribbean Court of Justice in the exercise of its appellate jurisdiction will follow the Judicial Committee of the Privy Council in delivering its judgments, but a strong case is being advanced for the approach adopted by the European Court of Justice in respect of its original jurisdiction. The European Court of Justice does not allow separate or dissenting opinions *ex abundante cautela* to protect the independence of the Court.

In the case of Australia, the Parliament had legislative power to abolish appeals to the Judicial Committee of the Privy Council from all Australian courts, federal and state courts, in matters involving federal jurisdiction. This was done in 1903, 1968 and 1975. Finally, in 1986, Australia abolished all appeals to the Privy Council and the British Parliament surrendered the right to legislate for the Commonwealth of Australia. When appeals to the Judicial Committee of the Privy Council were abolished, the High Court of Australia automatically became the court of last resort. No new court was established, as is currently being contemplated in New Zealand and the Commonwealth Caribbean, to replace the jurisdiction of the Judicial Committee of the Privy Council.

Although the experience of delinking by the Commonwealth countries considered here might not have much relevance for groups of commonwealth countries desiring to establish a multinational court of last resort like the Caribbean Court of Justice, important lessons may be learned from their experiences relating to such issues as *stare decisis* and the original or exclusive jurisdiction of their final appellate courts. Consequently, it is proposed to set out below the relevant constitutional provisions relating to some of these judicial bodies.

Relevant constitutional provisions of Ghana in respect of of its Supreme Court read as follows:

> *Article 129*
>
> (1) The Supreme Court shall be the final court of appeal and shall have such appellate and other jurisdiction as may be conferred on it by this Constitution or by any other law.
>
> (2) The Supreme Court shall not be bound to follow the decisions of any other court.
>
> (3) The Supreme Court may, while treating its own previous decisions as normally binding, depart from a previous decision when it appears to it right to do so; and all other courts shall be bound to follow the decisions of the Supreme Court in questions of law.
>
> (4) For the purposes of hearing and determining a matter within its jurisdiction and the amendment, execution or enforcement of a judgment or order made on any matter, and for the purposes of any other authority, expressly or by necessary implication given to the Supreme Court by this Constitution or any other law, the Supreme Court shall have all the powers, authority and jurisdiction vested in any Court established by this Constitution or any other law.
>
> *Article 130*
>
> (1) Subject to the jurisdiction of the High Court in the enforcement of the Fundamental Human Rights and Freedoms as provided in Article 33 of this Constitution, the Supreme Court shall have exclusive original jurisdiction in –
>
> (a) all matters relating to the enforcement or interpretation of this Constitution; and

(b) all matters arising as to whether an enactment was made in excess of the powers conferred on Parliament or any other authority or person by law or under the Constitution.

(2) Where an issue that relates to a matter or question referred to in clause (1) of this article arises in any proceedings in a court other than the Supreme Court, that court shall stay the proceedings and refer the question of law involved to the Supreme Court for determination; and the court in which the question arose shall dispose of the case in accordance with the decision of the Supreme Court.

Article 131

(1) An appeal shall lie from a judgment of the Court of Appeal to the Supreme Court

(a) as of right in a civil or criminal cause or matter in respect of which an appeal has been brought to the Court of Appeal from a judgment of the High Court or a Regional Tribunal in the exercise of its original jurisdiction; or

(b) with the leave of the Court of Appeal in any cause or matter, where the case was commenced in a court lower than the High Court or a Regional Tribunal and where the Court of Appeal is satisfied that the case involves a substantial question of law or is in the public interest.

(2) Notwithstanding clause (1) of this article, the Supreme Court may entertain application for special leave to appeal to the Supreme Court in any cause or matter, civil or criminal and may grant leave accordingly.

(3) The Supreme Court shall have appellate jurisdiction, to the exclusion of the Court of Appeal, to determine matters relating to the conviction or otherwise of a person for high treason or treason by the High Court.

(4) An appeal from a decision of the Judicial Committee of the National house of Chiefs shall lie to the Supreme Court with the leave of that Judicial Committee or the Supreme Court.

Article 132

The Supreme Court shall have supervisory jurisdiction over all courts and over any adjudicating authority and may, in the exercise of that supervisory jurisdiction issue orders and directions for the purpose of ensuring or securing the enforcement of its supervisory power.

Article 133

(1) The Supreme Court may review any decision made or given by it on such grounds and subject to such conditions as may be prescribed by rules of court.

(2) The Supreme Court, when reviewing its decisions under this article, shall be constituted by not less than seven Justices of the Supreme Court.

The relevant provisions of the constitution of Nigeria relating to the Supreme Court read as follows:

(1) The Supreme Court shall have jurisdiction, to the exclusion of any other court of law in Nigeria, to hear and determine appeals from the Court of Appeal.

(2) An appeal shall lie from the decisions of the Court of Appeal to the Supreme Court as of right in the following cases -

(a) where the ground of appeal involves questions of law alone, decisions in any civil or criminal proceedings before the Court of Appeal;

(b) decisions in any civil or criminal proceedings on questions as to the interpretation or application of this Constitution;

(c) decisions in any civil or criminal proceedings on questions as to whether any of the provisions of Chapter IV of the Constitution has been, is being, or is likely to be contravened in relation to any person.

(d) decisions in any criminal proceedings in which any person has been sentenced to death by the Court of Appeal or in which the Court of Appeal has affirmed a sentence of death imposed by any other court.

(e) .....

(3) Subject to the provisions of sub-section (2) an appeal shall lie from the decisions of the Court of Appeal to the Supreme Court with the leave of the Court of Appeal or the Supreme Court.

The relevant provisions of the Constitution of Australia relating to the High Court of Australia read as follows:

Section 73 [Jurisdiction of the High Court]

The High Court shall have jurisdiction, with such exceptions and subject to such regulations as the Parliament prescribes, to hear and determine appeals from all judgments, decrees, orders, and sentences –

(i) Of any Justice or Justices exercising the original jurisdiction of the High Court;

(ii) Of any other federal court, or court exercising federal jurisdiction; or of the Supreme Court of any State, or of any other court of any State from which at the establishment

> of the Commonwealth an appeal lies to the Queen in Council;
>
> (iii) Of the Inter-State Commission, but as to questions of law only: and the judgment of the High Court in all such cases shall be final and conclusive.
>
> But no exception or regulation prescribed by the Parliament shall prevent the High Court from hearing and determining any appeal from the Supreme Court of a State in any matter in which at the establishment of the Commonwealth an appeal lies from such Supreme Court to the Queen in Council.
>
> Until the Parliament otherwise provides, the conditions of and restrictions on appeals to the Queen in Council from the Supreme Courts of the several States shall be applicable to appeals from them to the High Court.

Since the jurisdiction of the Judicial Committee of the Privy Council was set out in the constitutions of Member States of the Caribbean Community, with the exception of Guyana which delinked from the Privy Council in 1970 and Suriname and Haiti which are civil law jurisdictions and never inherited the Judicial Committee of the Privy Council as their court of final appeal, delinking from this body would require an amendment to the constitutions of the countries concerned. Constitutional provisions for replacing the jurisdiction of the Privy Council vary among the Member States of the Caribbean Community and range from the requirement of a simple majority vote of Parliament in Jamaica to a qualified majority vote in Parliament in addition to a referendum in Antigua and Barbuda, The Bahamas, Grenada, and St. Vincent and the Grenadines. Other Member States may require a two-thirds majority vote or a three-quarters majority vote of their Parliament.

To date only one Member State, Barbados, has enacted legislation to delink from the Judicial Committee of the Privy Council and that legislation is yet to be proclaimed into law. The Draft Enabling Bill prepared by the CARICOM Secretariat was drafted in such a way as to repeal the jurisdiction of the Judicial Committee of the Privy Council (section 4) and to confer an original jurisdiction on the Court in respect of disputes concerning the interpretation and application of the Revised

Treaty of Chaguaramas (section 5) as well as an appellate jurisdiction in respect of a range of matters set out in sections 8A, 8B, 8C, 9, 10 and 11 as follows:

Section 8

A. Appeals shall lie to the Court from decisions of the Court of Appeal of a Contracting Party as of right in the following cases:

(a) final decisions in civil proceedings where the matter in dispute on appeal to the Court is of the value of not less than twenty-five thousand dollars Eastern Caribbean currency (EC$25,000) or where the appeal involves directly or indirectly a claim or a question respecting property or a right of the aforesaid value;

(b) final decisions in proceedings for dissolution or nullity of marriage; final decisions in any civil or other proceedings which involve a question as to the interpretation of the Constitution of the Contracting Party;

(c) final decisions given in the exercise of the jurisdiction conferred upon a superior court of a Contracting Party relating to the determination of any question for which a right of access to the superior court of a Contracting Party is expressly provided by its Constitution;

(d) such other cases as may be prescribed by any law of the Contracting Party.

B. An appeal shall lie to the Court with the leave of the Court of Appeal of a Contracting Party from the decisions of the Court of Appeal in the following cases:

(a) final decisions in any civil proceedings where, in the opinion of the Court of Appeal, the question is one that by reason of its great general or public importance or otherwise, ought to be submitted to the Court; and

(b) such other cases as may be prescribed by any law of the Contracting Party.

C. An appeal shall lie to the Court with the leave of the Court of Appeal from the decisions of the Court of Appeal:

(a) in respect of final decisions in any civil proceeding where, in the opinion of the Court of Appeal, the question involved in the appeal is one that by reason of its great general or public importance or otherwise, ought to be submitted to the Court;

(b) in such other cases as may be prescribed by any law (of the Contracting Party).

> *Section 9*
>
> An appeal shall lie to the Court with the special leave of the Court from any decision of the Court of Appeal from any civil or criminal matter.
>
> *Section 10*
>
> Nothing in this Act shall confer jurisdiction on the Court to hear matters in relation to any decision of the Court of Appeal which at the time of entry into force of the Agreement was, pursuant to the Constitution or any other law, declared to be final.
>
> *Section 11*
>
> Applications to the Court of Appeal for leave to appeal shall be made by motion or petition within forty-five days from the date of the relevant judgment, and the applicant shall give all parties directly affected by the appeal, notice of the application for leave to appeal.

Within the last two decades the jurisdiction of the Judicial Committee of the Privy Council has contracted beyond all recognition with the delinking of most Commonwealth countries and the establishment of their own courts of last resort. At present, the jurisdiction of the Judicial Committee of the Privy Council comprehends a final appellate court for independent Commonwealth countries and non-independent entities as well as a court of original jurisdiction for various disputes.[3] With devolution, the Judicial Committee of the Privy Council is expected to play an important role as a court of last resort to Ireland, Scotland and Wales.

Notwithstanding that the relevant legislation of the countries examined here makes it quite clear that the highest appellate court in the land is the court of last resort, the language of commitment employed in every case differs. Thus section 233 (1) of the constitution of Nigeria provides: 'The Supreme Court shall have jurisdiction, to the exclusion of any other court of law in Nigeria, to hear and determine appeals from the Court of Appeal.' Article 129 (1) of the Constitution of Ghana, on the other hand, states: 'The Supreme Court shall be the final court of appeal and shall have such appellate and other jurisdiction as may be conferred on it by this constitution or by any other law.'

In the case of the Caribbean Community, Article III (2) of the Agreement Establishing the Caribbean Court of Justice says quite succinctly 'The decisions of the Court shall be final'. But this provision of the Agreement has to be read in conjunction with other provisions of the Agreement and Draft Article 4 of the Draft Enabling Bill. The language employed in the Agreement Establishing the Caribbean Court of Justice is ominously reminiscent of that attributed to Lord Halsbury in *London Street Tramways Co. Ltd. v. London County Council* [1898] AC 375. to wit, '. . . a decision of this House upon a question of law is conclusive'. This statement is alleged to have established the doctrine of *stare decisis* and must be seen to have important implications for the determinations of the Caribbean Court of Justice. Prior to the Practice Statement which issued from the House of Lords in 1966, the House was considered to be bound, without qualification, by its previous decisions. And, by adopting in Article III (2) of the Agreement language similar to that employed by Lord Halsbury, it may be persuasively argued that the intention of the drafters was to accord determinations of the Caribbean Court of Justice the same status as decisions of the House of Lords prior to 1966.

A similar error was avoided by the drafters of the Constitution of Ghana which in Article 129 (3) gave the Supreme Court the option of departing from its previous decisions 'when it appears right to do so' – language whose similarity to that employed in the House of Lords Practice Statement in 1966 underscores the difficulty likely to be created for the Caribbean Court of Justice by the language of commitment employed in Article III (2) of the Agreement. In the present submission, it is not clear whether the Caribbean Court of Justice may escape the judicial straightjacket by issuing a practice statement in the sense of the Practice Statement of the House of Lords in 1966. The main difficulty perceived here is that the doctrine of *stare decisis* articulated by Lord Halsbury in 1898 lacked a treaty or legislative basis and could have been revoked in 1966 in the manner described. An amendment of the Agreement Establishing the Caribbean Court of Justice would be required since Member States would be precluded from passing legislation in the sense of Article 129 (3) of the constitution of Ghana since such legislation would go contrary to treaty obligations. The language of commitment employed in Article III (2) of the Agreement has the same judicial effect as that employed in Article XXII of the same instrument.

Comparison of the constitutional provisions of the courts of last resort of Canada, Nigeria, Ghana, Australia with the relevant provisions of the Agreement Establishing the Caribbean Court of Justice does appear to confirm the existence of only two classes of appeals – appeals as of right and appeals with the leave of the court below. Only the Supreme Court of Nigeria and the Caribbean Court of Justice appear to have retained the third class of appeals current during the existence of the Judicial Committee of the Privy Council, to wit, appeals with special leave of the court of last resort. Further, only the Caribbean Court of Justice among the courts of last resort considered here, appears to have established a threshold for appeals in civil matters. It is not clear what negative implications establishment of such a threshold may have for access to justice. In the absence of legal aid available to appellants in civil matters to be considered by the court of last resort, litigants below the threshold might not find it financially feasible to appeal to the court of last resort as a matter of right.

The jurisdiction of the Supreme Court of Ghana also holds some important differences from that of the Caribbean Court of Justice. Prominent among these is the exclusive original jurisdiction of the court of last resort to hear and determine all matters relating to the enforcement and interpretation of the constitution, the validity of acts of Parliament, subject to the jurisdiction of the High Court in matters touching on the Fundamental Rights and Freedoms provided in the constitution; and exclusive appellate jurisdiction in relation to treason and high treason. In this connection it is important to note that the jurisdiction of the Caribbean Court of Justice is ousted in respect of 'matters in relation to which the decision of the Court of Appeal of a contracting Party is, at the time of the entry into force of the Agreement pursuant to the constitution or any other law of that Party, declared to be final'.[4]

Having decided to delink from the Judicial Committee of the Privy Council and set up the Supreme Court of Ghana as the court of last resort, competent decision-makers appeared to have determined to fashion Ghana's court of last resort in the image of the House of Lords. Thus, the provisions of the constitution addressing the Supreme Court of Ghana were crafted in language reminiscent of language employed in the Practice Statement issued by the House of Lords in 1966. Further, Article 129 (2) of the Constitution provided that the Supreme Court of Ghana was not bound to follow the decisions of any other court. One important implication of this provision is that previous decisions of the Judicial Committee of the Privy Council did not necessarily bind the Supreme Court of Ghana.

Finally, the Supreme Court of Ghana was given power to review its own decisions. This power of review is similar to the power of the Caribbean Court of Justice to revise its determinations in the exercise of its original jurisdiction.[4] The power of review enjoyed by the Supreme Court of Ghana appears to be consistent with the Constitution's interpretation of the doctrine of *stare decisis* to be applied by that Court. In the premises, the constitution of Ghana has clarified several issues which the Caribbean Court of Justice would have to clarify in the exercise of its appellate jurisdiction.

LAW RELATING TO THE APPELLATE JURISDICTION OF THE CARIBBEAN COURT OF JUSTICE

Unlike the provisions set out in Part II of the Agreement Establishing the Caribbean Court of Justice, the instrument is conspicuously silent on the manner of exercise of the appellate jurisdiction of the Court. Part II of the Agreement not only vests the Court with original jurisdiction in various classes of disputes regarding the interpretation and application of the Revised Treaty but also addresses the law to be applied,[6] advisory opinions of the Court,[7] the status of determinations of the Court,[8] *locus standi* of private entities in proceedings before the Court[9] and so forth. Despite its resonant silence in this context, however, it is submitted that the practice of other superior common law courts of last resort does offer some useful guidelines for the Court regarding the legal policy to be adopted in the exercise of its appellate jurisdiction. In this context reference may be made to the recommendation of the Advisory Group appointed by the Government of New Zealand in November 2001 to advise on the purpose, structure, composition and role of a final appeal court.[10] The Advisory Group recommended:

> that in keeping with the need for certainty and uniformity, the Supreme Court (to replace the Judicial Committee of the Privy Council) should normally follow decisions of the Judicial Committee delivered when it was New Zealand's final court of appeal. However, the Supreme Court should be able to depart from previous decisions of the Judicial Committee when it appears right to do so, particularly in light of features unique to New Zealand . . .

Consider in this context, too, the provisions of Article 129(3) of the constitution of Ghana which read as follows: 'The Supreme Court may, while treating its own previous decisions as normally binding, depart from a previous decision when it appears to it right to do so, and all other courts shall be bound to follow the decisions of the Supreme Court in questions of law.'

It is clear that the Caribbean Court of Justice would need to establish the basis of its legal policy given the silence of the Agreement on this issue. In this context two discrete issues of legal policy suggest themselves for resolution. Firstly, how would the Caribbean Court of Justice treat previous decisions of the Judicial Committee of the Privy Council when this judicial institution was the court of last resort for the Member States of the Caribbean Community. One approach is to adopt the position articulated by the Government of New Zealand in respect of its own Supreme Court. Another approach would be to treat all such previous decisions either as binding or not binding. The other issue to be resolved concerns how the Caribbean Court of Justice would treat its own previous decisions, assuming as this author does, that the provisions of Article III (2) of the Agreement establishes the *stare decisis* doctrine. This the Court can do by issuing a practice statement within the meaning of the Practice Statement issued by the House of Lords in 1966. In terms of the traditional practice of superior appellate courts of common law jurisdictions, the Caribbean Court of Justice must be perceived as competent to 'correct errors in the law made by a subordinate court' as well as to clarify and develop the law in light of the circumstances and peculiar needs of the Member States of the Caribbean Community.

In applying the doctrine of *stare decisis* the Caribbean Court of Justice may be guided by decisions of superior courts of Britain, including the Court of Appeal and the House of Lords. In this connection the decision of the Court of Appeal in *Young v. Bristol Aeroplane Company, Ltd.* [1944] KB 718 offers reliable guidance. The *ratio decidendi* of that case was succinctly adumbrated by Lord Greene, M.R. as follows:

> The court is entitled and bound to decide which of two conflicting decisions it will follow. The court is bound to refuse to follow a decision of its own which, though not expressly overruled, cannot in its opinion, stand with a decision of the House of Lords. The Court is not bound to follow a decision of its own if it is satisfied that the decision was given *per incuriam*.

The Caribbean Court of Justice will also be required to address the issue of selective application of the doctrine of *stare decisis* depending on the classification of the proceedings as civil or criminal. In this connection, Lord Diplock, in giving the decision of the court in *Regina v. Gould* [1968] 2 QB at pp.68-69 submitted:

> In its criminal jurisdiction, which it has inherited from the Court of Criminal Appeal, the Court of Appeal does not apply the doctrine of *stare decisis* with the same rigidity as in its civil jurisdiction. If we were to be of the opinion that the law had been earlier misapplied or misunderstood in an earlier decision of this court or its predecessor, the Court of Criminal Appeal, we should be entitled to depart from the view as to the law

> expressed in the earlier decision, notwithstanding that the case could not be brought within any of the exceptions laid down in *Young v. Bristol Aeroplane Company, Ltd.* (1944) 718 . . . . As a matter of principle we respectfully find it difficult to see why there should in general be any difference in the application of the principle of *stare decisis* between the Civil and Criminal Divisions of this court, save that we must remember that in the latter we may be dealing with the liberty of the subject and if a departure from authority is necessary in the interests of justice to an appellant, then this court should not shrink from so doing.

This interpretation of the application of the doctrine of *stare decisis* appears to be consistent with a line of cases addressing the liberty of the subject and would appear to justify the considered and careful attention of the judges of the Caribbean Court of Justice especially since the decisions of the Judicial Committee of the Privy Council in the line of cases commencing with *Pratt and Morgan* were expressed to be turning the doctrine of *stare decisis* on its head and introducing unacceptable levels of uncertainty and instability in the administration of criminal justice in the Caribbean Community. Thus in *Regina v. Spenser* [1985] QB 771, 778, May L.J. submitted:

> Counsel accepted that in general the Criminal Division of the Court of Appeal is bound to follow its own decisions in the same way as the Civil Division of the Court. He referred us to the well know decision in *Young v. Bristol Aeroplane Company, Ltd.* [1944] KB 718, and we accept that the principles laid down in that case apply, subject to the one point with which we deal hereafter, to any decision of the Court of Appeal, whether sitting in its civil or criminal jurisdiction. Although in may not be necessary to decide the point in the instant appeals, we appreciate that in *Rex v. Taylor* [1950] 2 KB 368, a Court of Criminal Appeal comprising seven members departed from a previous view assumed by the court and declined to follow an earlier authority. In our respectful opinion the *ratio* of that decision was that to which Widgery L.J. first referred in *Reg v. Newsome* [1970] 2 QB 711, 716, namely, that the court justified its action to a very large degree by the fact that in that case a departure from authority was necessary in the interests of the appellant. Lord Goddard, CJ, in giving his judgment of the court in *Rex v. Taylor* [1950] 2 KB, 368 took a robust view that if a man be in prison and in the judgment of the court wrongly

> in prison, it should not allow such matters as *stare decisis* to stand in the way . . .

Support for a more flexible application of the doctrine *of stare decisis* where the liberty of the subject is involved appears to come also from Lord Taylor in *Regina v. Parole Board, ex parte Wilson* [1992] QB 740 where the *ratio decidendi* of the case was that the court was not bound to follow an earlier decision where the liberty of the subject was involved and the interest of justice prescribed otherwise. The nature of the doctrine of *stare decisis* and its role in developing the law were also addressed in some other decisions of superior appellate courts of Britain. In this context it has been asseverated that the courts should only depart from precedent where they are satisfied that the principle laid down is wrong or that an earlier decision adopted a wrong approach: *Regina v. Secretary of State for the Home Department ex parte Khawoja* [1984] AC 74 p. 125 D-H per Lord Bridges of Harwick; *Regina v. Parole Board ex parte Wilson* [1992] QB 740 at p.754 per Taylor L.J., *Pratt and Morgan v. Attorney General of Jamaica* [1994] 2 AC 1, and *Regina v. Governor of Brockhill Prison ex parte Evans* [1997] QB 443 at p.462. Thus in *Pratt and Morgan* it was submitted that: 'The Board is not bound by its previous decisions and it does not follow them if there are cogent reasons for not doing so. It should not hesitate to overrule a decision in relation to human rights if it is of the opinion that the decision is wrong.'

On the basis of the foregoing decisions on the doctrine of precedent, it is submitted that the Caribbean Court of Justice is likely to find itself at the crossroads of judicial decision-making and would be free to follow any one of two conflicting paths of legal policy depending on whether it is satisfied that one or another decision of the Privy Council was wrong or whether or not it is prepared to adopt the doctrine of transformation or the doctrine of incorporation in relation to the reception of international law into the common law. After careful examination of relevant decisions of British superior courts and reflection on the arguments addressed, the perceived doctrinal position of the Judicial Committee of the Privy Council appears to be the syncretisation of several ideas in addressing the imposition of the ultimate sanction for socially deviant conduct on the part of convicted felons. These ideas comprehend such issues like the super-ordinate/subordinate relationship of international law and domestic law, the requirement of domestic law to accommodate commitments undertaken by the State at the international plane particularly as they relate to humanitarian law;[11] the competing claims of the doctrines of incorporation and transformation as the vehicle for the reception of international law into the common law;[12] the obligation of municipal law courts to adopt a flexible interpretation of the *stare decisis* doctrine where the liberty of the subject is involved, and the legitimacy of the cumulative impact of these ideas on the domestic normative regime. Consequently, an important, and probably rewarding, area of research for regional jurists appears to be the philosophical, juridical and ethical foundations of decisions of the Judicial Committee of the Privy Council on the employment of the ultimate sanction.

Given the charged political context in which the Caribbean Court of Justice is being created, an issue of seminal public concern thrusting itself to the forefront of the regional agenda is the approach to be adopted by the Court towards the doctrine of *stare decisis* in its appellate jurisdiction. This issue has already been resolved in relation to the original jurisdiction of the Court and it would be reasonable to assume that the same considerations arguing for the innovative introduction of this doctrine in the Court's original jurisdiction apply *aequo rigore* if not *a fortiori* to determinations of the Court in its appellate jurisdiction – certainty, uniformity, consistency and predictability in the normative environment. However, resolution of the issue regarding the manner of interpreting the doctrine of *stare decisis* in relation to determinations of the Court still leaves unresolved the issue of the binding nature of previous decisions of the Judicial Committee of the Privy Council and the manner of treating with it. On the occasion of Canada and Australia delinking from the jurisdiction of the Judicial Committee of the Privy Council, both the Supreme Court of Canada and the High Court of Australia ruled that previous and future decisions of the Judicial Committee were no longer binding but had persuasive force. In the case of Australia, the ruling of the High Court came a mere three years after the event in 1975[13] while in the case of the Supreme Court of Canada the ruling came 30 years after.[14] It appears that this was the practice employed by Commonwealth courts.[15]

Assuming that the Caribbean Court of Justice regards the practice of Commonwealth courts of last resort determinative, the Caribbean Court of Justice may wish to consider issuing a Practice Statement like that of the House of Lords in 1966 or the Supreme Court of Singapore indicating how the doctrine of *stare decisis* would be construed and applied. In one submission '(a)n ultimate appellate court which has abandoned the convenient crutch of binding precedent is much more likely to analyse with care all the issues involved in a case than is an ultimate appeal court which permits itself to take refuge in the delusion of the binding precedent'.[16]

In terms of offering guidance concerning the approach to be adopted by the Caribbean Court of Justice in relation to the doctrine of *stare decisis* reference may be made to the practice statement of the House of Lords which was issued in 1966 in which the House of Lords affirmed its competence to depart from precedent when it was right to do so.[17] However, this self-declaratory power of the House of Lords to depart from precedent has been expressed to be employed with caution and circumspection.[18] For example, the House does not depart from precedent merely because the decision was wrong. Something more has to be shown, like some material change in circumstances.[19] Where statutory construction is involved, the House would not normally depart from precedent but would await an amendment by legislative enactment.[20] Further, where the decision sought to be reconsidered has been acted upon, it should be set right by the legislature.[21] Decisions may be overruled when they are no longer appropriate in light of changed circumstances,[22] where they have laid down a commercially irrelevant and inconvenient test,[23] or where a serious error has distorted the law.[24] Decisions which are recent and are unlikely to have been acted upon are more readily overruled.[25]

On the basis of the foregoing, courts of last resort may adopt the following policy regarding the doctrine of *stare decisis*:

(a) To ensure continuity, certainty and coherence departures from the doctrine of *stare decisis* should be made with caution and circumspection;

(b) Departures from precedent are justified where previous decisions were wrong and there was some material change in the circumstances;

(c) Departures from precedent are justified where social or commercial conditions have changed substantially and adherence to precedent would create practical difficulties;

(d) Departures from precedent are not justified where statutory interpretation is involved; the aid of the legislature should be invoked.

It has been suggested that in making a determination whether or not to depart from a previous decision, the court should weigh the need for certainty and consistency in the law against the injustice caused by adherence to a mistaken decision. In this submission, the weighing process should address the following issues:

> (a) Does the decision rest upon a principle that has been carefully worked out in a succession of cases?
>
> (b) Is it a decision in which there was a difference of opinion among the decision judges?
>
> (c) Has the previous decision resulted in inconvenience?
>
> (d) Has the decision been acted upon subsequently in a way that militates against reconsideration?[26]

NOTES

1. *Lewis et al v. Attorney General of Jamaica* (2000) 57 WIR 275.
2. See the dissenting judgment of Lord Hoffman in *Lewis et al v. AG of Jamaica* (2000) 57 WIR 275; also *de Freitas v. Benny* [1976] AC 239; *Reckley v. Minister of Public Safety and Immigration* No. 2 [1996] AC 527.
3. The jurisdiction of the Judicial Committee of the Privy Council as at March 2000 is set out in chapter 5.
4. See Article III (5) of the Agreement Establishing the Caribbean Court of Justice.
5. See Article XX of the Agreement Establishing the Caribbean Court of Justice.
6. See Article XVII of the Agreement Establishing the Caribbean Court of Justice.
7. See Article XIII of the Agreement Establishing the Caribbean Court of Justice.
8. See Article XXII of the Agreement Establishing the Caribbean Court of Justice.
9. See Article XXIV of the Agreement Establishing the Caribbean Court of Justice.
10. See Margaret Wilson, 'Preparatory Steps to be Taken so as to Achieve a Smooth Transition in Removing the Jurisdiction of the Judicial Committee of the Privy Council'. Paper presented to the Commonwealth Meeting of the Experts Group to Examine the Removal of Appellate Jurisdiction from the Judicial Committee of the Privy Council, Marlborough House, London, June 10-13, 2003.
11. See, for example, *Higgs v. Minister of National Security* [2000] 2 WLR 1368, where the Judicial Committee of the Privy Council maintained 'the existence of a treaty may give rise to a legitimate expectation on the part of citizens that the Government in its acts affecting them will observe the terms of the treaty'.
12. Consider in this context the emerging consensus that natural justice in municipal systems must accommodate changes in international norms and obligations assumed in treaties: Robin Cooke, 'Final Appeal Courts: Some comparisons' in the *Journal of the Commonwealth Lawyers Association*, 2003, p.49.
13. See *Virgo v. The Queen* (1978) 52 ALJR 418 where the High Court held, unanimously, that judgments of the Privy council were no longer binding in spite of their date of delivery.

14. See Gordon Bale, *Cutting Off the Mooring Ropes of Binding Precedent*, Canadian Bar Association, Vol. XVIII No. 2, p.257.
15. Consider in this context the Supreme Court of Singapore, and the Supreme Court of Ghana.
16. See Bale, 'Cutting Off' at p.261.
17. Consider the statement of Lord Reid for the rationale of this practice statement in *Jones v. Secretary of State for Social Services* [1972] AC 944 at 966.
18. *The Doctrine of Binding Precedent: Cutting the Gordian Knot – Stare Decisis in Singapore before the Reforms of 1993-1994.* pp. 169-181.
19. See *Fitzlect Estates Ltd. v. Clorry* [1977] 3 All ER 996 (HL).
20. *Jones v. Secretary of State for Social Services* [1972] AC 944, 966.
21. *Knutter (Publishing, Printing and Promotions) Ltd. v. DPP* [1973] 2 All ER 898, 903.
22. *British Railway Board v. Herrington* [1972] 1 All ER 749 (HL).
23. *The Johanna Oldendorff* [1974] AC 479 (HL).
24. *R v. Shirpuer* [1986] 2 All ER 334, 345.
25. *Ibid.*
26. Walter Woon, *Reforms to the Hierarchy of the Courts and Their Legal Implications in Reforms to the Court System, Judicial and Legal Reforms in Singapore 1990-1998* in A Review of Legislative and Judicial Reform of Criminal Evidence, 1990-95.

CHAPTER FOUR

Original Jurisdiction of the Caribbean Court of Justice

DEVELOPMENT OF INTERNATIONAL ADJUDICATION

An appreciation of the attributes and functions of the Caribbean Court of Justice would be considerably enhanced if viewed against the historical background of international adjudicatory bodies. In this context, it is important to bear in mind the emergence of the nation state in the sixteenth century as a product of the Renaissance and Reformation. The legitimisation of the nation state as the unit of governance and the modern state system as the basis of international relations followed at the Treaty of Westphalia, 1648, which terminated a century of unprecedented blood-letting in Europe, benignly called the wars of religion, where religious dogmatism provided a convenient and callous rationalisation for conquest, territorial expansion and personal aggrandizement. The ensuing decades witnessed an appalling intensification of the attributes of personal sovereignty culminating in a century characterised by unqualified absolutism and enlightened despotism which, in turn, gave way to the era of popular sovereignty heralded by the French Revolutionary and Napoleonic Wars at the turn of the eighteenth century. Although international disputes continued to be settled by force, the Jay Treaty 1794 between Britain and the United States introduced a method of disputes-settlement through mixed commissions. The novelty of the procedure, however, precluded its taking root in the practice of states.

The nineteenth century, however, saw no abatement at the international level of the doctrine of untrammelled national sovereignty and international disputes continued to be settled, traditionally, on the basis of military might, or innovatively, on the basis of *ad hoc* third party adjudicatory bodies, for example, the Alabama Arbitration, 1872 until the creation of the Permanent Court of Arbitration whose establishment after the Hague Conferences of 1899 and 1907 was a significant turning point in international adjudication. Predictably, the Permanent Court of Arbitration was not a spectacular success. The preferred modes of disputes settlement continued to be good offices, mediation and negotiation which did not compromise national sovereignty. Conciliation, as a mode of dispute settlement, received a fillip from the Hague Conferences of 1899 and 1907. And, as wars became more calamitous, genocidal, catastrophic and costly to the national treasury, as exemplified by the two world wars of 1914 and 1939, serious consideration was given to the peaceful settlement of international disputes through the establishment of norms to be applied by permanent adjudicatory bodies. The most celebrated cases in point were the Permanent Court of International justice (PCIJ) 1921 and its worthy successor, the International Court of Justice (ICJ) 1946 which was accorded the status of an organ of the United Nations. The establishment of these organisations set a commendable precedent for the setting up of a plethora of international adjudicatory bodies in the twentieth century both at the regional level and the wider international plane. The more distinguished of these are the European Court of Justice, the Court of First Instance of the European Union, the European Court of Human Rights, the Inter-American Court of Human Rights, the Court of Justice of the European Free Trade Area, the Andean Court of Justice, the Central American Court of Justice, the Disputes Settlement Body of the World Trade Organization, the International Tribunal on the Law of the Sea, the International Centre for the Settlement of Investment Disputes, the Court of Justice of the Common Market for Eastern and Southern Africa (COMESA) and latterly, the Caribbean Court of Justice, whose gestation period spanned the entire twentieth century and which is due to come on stream during the first quarter of 2004.

Some of these adjudicatory bodies leaned heavily on the traditional doctrines of international law and located states at the centre of the international adjudicatory process. Thus, only states were ordinarily accorded *locus standi* in proceedings before these bodies,[1] and only agents of states parties before the Court could represent the interests of litigants. Consider in this context the practice of the International Court of Justice and contrast the applicable law of the Caribbean Court of Justice. Interestingly enough, this hallowed tradition was broken by a Member State of the Caribbean Community when Saint Lucia, a microstate by international standards, intervened in the Banana Dispute in the World Trade Organization as an interested party and the Appellate Body allowed Saint Lucia to be represented by private lawyers. In the submission of the Appellate Body:

> ... representation by counsel of a government's own choice may well be a matter of particular significance – especially for developing country Members – to enable them to participate fully in dispute settlement proceedings. Moreover, given the Appellate Body's mandate to review only issues of law or legal interpretation in panel reports, it is particularly important that governments be represented by qualified counsel in Appellate Body proceedings.[2]

Reliance by international adjudicatory bodies on traditional international law doctrines also informed the general exclusion of private entities, natural and juridical, from their proceedings which did not cater for objects of international law. This practice was eroded by the advent of international human rights adjudicatory bodies and inter-governmental bodies boasting attributes of supranationality to a greater or lesser extent. Cases in point are the European Court of Human Rights, the Inter-American Court of Human Rights, the European Court of Justice, and the European Court of First Instance, institutions of the European Union, the Court of Justice of the Cartagena Agreement and the Court of Justice of COMESA (CJC) which accorded *locus standi* to private entities aggrieved by acts of policy-making institutions with direct effects. Of importance, too, was the international legal principle that sovereign states could not be brought before these tribunals in the absence of their consent, as an attribute of their sovereign immunity. But even this venerable doctrine has been eroded by emerging rules of international law as evidenced in the *Pinochet* case.[3] There exists no universal compulsory jurisdiction for the settling of disputes among states in the international community. Despite this, the trend towards the compulsory settlement of international disputes has taken hold and several international adjudicatory bodies have been accorded jurisdiction to consider and determine disputes between States Parties which have submitted beforehand to their jurisdiction. This is the position in respect of most of the international adjudicatory bodies mentioned above. Despite the growing significance of international adjudicatory bodies, however, there is no settled policy about their functions. What, for example, is the relationship between these international adjudicatory bodies and national judicial bodies? Or, how do their determinations impact the policies of national executives which have submitted to their jurisdiction? Some guidance is given by recent decisions of the Judicial Committee of the Privy Council in *Thomas and Hilaire v. Baptiste and Ors.*[4] and *Lewis et al v. Attorney-General of Jamaica.*[5] And although international adjudicatory bodies are required more often than not, to apply rules of international law in reaching determinations, they are sometimes not precluded from applying general principles of law or deciding a case *ex aequo et bono* with the consent of the parties. Consider in this context Article 38 of the Statute of the International Court of Justice, and Article 217 of the Revised Treaty of Chaguaramas Establishing the Caribbean Community including the CARICOM Single Market and Economy.

ORIGINAL JURISDICTION OF THE CARIBBEAN COURT OF JUSTICE[6]

When the original jurisdiction of the Caribbean Court of Justice (CCJ) was first mooted for inclusion in the Agreement, the most ardent detractors of the Court disingenuously maintained that it was merely a ruse to distract attention from the real purpose of the Court – the promotion of hanging in the Caribbean Community, given the diametrically opposite doctrinal position of the Judicial Committee of the Privy Council to regional officialdom regarding employment of the ultimate sanction for murder. In fact, however, an original jurisdiction for a Caribbean Court of Appeal had been proposed as early as 1972 in the Report of the Representative Committee of the Organisation of Commonwealth Caribbean Bar Associations (OCCBA) on the Establishment of a Caribbean Court of Appeal in Substitution for the Judicial Committee of the Privy Council, June 1972.

Recommendation No. 16 of the Summary of Recommendations of the Report read as follows:

> 16. That the Court be vested with original jurisdiction in respect of matters referred to it by agreement between the Caribbean States, or by any two or more of them, arising out of such original treaties, as the CARIFTA Agreement or by the Council of the Area, or such matters as the interpretation of the Agreement . . . [7]

Two decades later, the West Indian Commission in its celebrated Report, 'Time for Action', also strongly recommended an original jurisdiction for the Caribbean Supreme Court to interpret and apply the Revised Treaty of Chaguaramas, and even the Charter of Civil Society.

Both sets of recommendations envisaged an original jurisdiction for the Court much wider than that accorded to it by the current Agreement Establishing the Caribbean Court of Justice.[8]

On careful analysis of the role envisaged by the West Indian Commission for the proposed CARICOM Supreme Court, it would not be difficult to conclude that the West Indian

Commission perceived the Court, in the exercise of its original jurisdiction, as the institutional centerpiece of the proposed CARICOM Single Market and Economy (CSME). The CSME is being designed to create a single economic space stretching from Belize in Central America in the north to Suriname in South America, in which the factors of production would be able to move to any part of the Caribbean Community where they can be most productively and efficiently employed. The rights envisaged for Community nationals in this expanded economic space include the right of establishment, the right to provide services and the right to move capital.[9] But in order to facilitate the transborder movement of these rights without unnecessary restrictions, there is need for an institution to authoritatively and definitively interpret and apply the Revised Treaty of Chaguaramas establishing the Caribbean Community including the Caricom Single Market and Economy, in the absence of which rights would tend to be illusory and the obligations correlative thereto, merely vacuous commitments on the part of the Governments concerned. And this is where the Caribbean Court of Justice, in the exercise of its original jurisdiction, is expected to play a critical role.

Unlike the European Union, which is a supranational entity to which participating Member States have voluntarily surrendered attributes of sovereignty[10] and, in particular, the exclusive competence to make laws with direct effect for nationals in the jurisdictions of Member States without the intervention of their legislatures, the Caribbean Community, for historical reasons, is, and is likely to remain for the foreseeable future, an association of sovereign States. This political status of the Caribbean Community finds cogent juridical expression in Article 28 (1) of the Revised Treaty, which requires the Conference, the supreme organ of the Caribbean Community, to take decisions by an affirmative vote of all its members, subject to the exceptions identified, and such decisions shall be legally binding. And, even though the unanimity rule has been relaxed in respect of decisions by other organs of the Community, where any Member State can establish that any issue under consideration in these organs is of critical importance to its national well being, decisions on such an issue must be taken by an affirmative vote of all the Member States.[11]

This status of the Caribbean Community as an association of sovereign states has important implications for Member States, their nationals and the role of the Caribbean Court of Justice in the CSME. In the first place, rights accorded by a treaty and obligations assumed under a treaty are, according to the applicable norms of traditional international law, enjoyed by or imposed, initially, on States Parties to the instrument in their capacity as subjects of international law. Where such rights are intended to be enjoyed by nationals of States Parties to the treaty, the relevant instrument has to be enacted into domestic law before nationals can enjoy such rights, unless the monist doctrine of international law applies in the particular case. When this happens, however, in relation to States Parties to the Revised Treaty, every court in every jurisdiction of the Member States participating in the regime would be competent to pronounce on the Treaty thereby raising the forbidding prospect of a cacophony of interpretations of the same instrument. In short, a disequilibrating prescription for legal uncertainty with probable negative consequences for macro-economic stability in the regional investment climate.

CARICOM, as we all know, is largely a capital-importing region; it does not generate the capital required for significant investment purposes but depends on foreign direct investment for large-scale infrastructural and developmental projects. The foreign investor, however, requires a stable, predictable investment climate in which to commit his investment. Postulated in other terms, the prudent investor requires certainty in the investment climate, certainty that will foster stability of expectations and enable him to predict outcomes with a fair degree of success. Outcome predictability for the investor is, more often than not, a function of legal certainty in the normative environment. And this is where the CCJ is required to play a critical role by importing certainty, stability, uniformity and predictability in the regional investment environment.

As a first step in the establishment of the desired investment climate in the region, all Member States of the Caribbean Community are required to submit to the jurisdiction of the Caribbean Court of Justice in the exercise of its original jurisdiction.[12] Thus, by Article 216 of the Revised Treaty the Member States agreed to recognise as compulsory, *ipso facto*, and without special agreement the original jurisdiction of the Court established by Article 211 of the Revised Treaty. Article 211 provides that the Court shall have compulsory and exclusive jurisdiction to hear and determine disputes concerning the interpretation and application of the Treaty. The exclusivity of the Court's jurisdiction is addressed in the context of Article 214 of the Revised Treaty, which speaks of referrals to the Court. In order to appreciate the significance of Articles 211 and 216, it is important to bear in mind that in traditional international law, States, as an attribute of sovereignty, cannot be brought before international tribunals in the absence of their consent. States must consent or submit to the jurisdiction of the tribunal voluntarily or the tribunal will not exercise jurisdiction. Similar provisions exist in the statutes of international tribunals. Consider in this context the statutes of the International Court of Justice[13] and the International Criminal Court. When the Court's jurisdiction in a particular matter is disputed, the Court is competent to determine the issue.[14]

Article 217 (1) of the Revised Treaty provides that the law to be applied by the Caribbean Court of Justice in exercising its jurisdiction under Article 211 shall be international law. International tribunals are not presumed to know the municipal law of States appearing in proceedings before them; this has to be proved, like foreign law, by experts who know the national law of states parties before them. International law, however, governs the activities of all states in the international community, large and small, be they socialist, communist, democratic or authoritarian in political disposition or whether they belong to the civil law or common law systems. Consequently, both Haiti and Suriname, subscribing as they do to the civil law system, would have no difficulty, like their common law brothers, to sign on to the jurisdiction of the Court in the exercise of its original jurisdiction. However, Article 217 (2) expressly provides that the Court shall not bring in a finding of *non liquet* on the ground of silence or obscurity of the law, while Article 217 (3) empowers the Court to determine an issue before it *ex aequo et bono*, if the parties to the dispute so agree. The implications of these last-mentioned provisions are addressed below in the context of the alleged supranational attributes of the Caribbean Court of Justice.

The provisions of paragraph 1 of Article 217 could, however, give rise to nice juridical issues. For example, one intractable issue falling to be determined is the status of an alleged rule of international law to be applied by the Court. Is the alleged rule a norm *de lege ferenda* or *lex lata* and, if so, which tribunal is competent to make the determination definitively? In the submission of Lord Denning, the rules of international law are subject to change.[15] When, therefore, can it be determined that a new rule of international law has emerged and where is the determination to be made? Can such a determination be made by a municipal court or only by a competent, generally recognised international tribunal like the International Court of Justice? Is a determination by the Caribbean Court of Justice in the exercise of its original jurisdiction on the status of an alleged rule of international law appealable to the Caribbean Court of Justice in the exercise of its appellate jurisdiction? In this context, it is important to bear in mind that the exclusivity of the Court in the exercise of its original jurisdiction extends only to the interpretation and application of the Revised Treaty and does not comprehend rulings on the juridical status of norms of international law to be applied in the settlement of disputes. The uncertainty attending this issue has been addressed by international lawyers.[16]

However, the appellate jurisdiction of the CCJ as set out in Article XXV of the Agreement Establishing the Caribbean Court of Justice does not contemplate appeals from international courts but only from municipal courts below in the jurisdiction of Member States participating in the regime. Similarly, the Court in the exercise of its original jurisdiction, does not contemplate appeals to any higher court from its determinations. In the premises, it is submitted that the Court, as an appellate judicial body, could reach a determination diametrically apposed to one reached by the Court as an international tribunal on the status of an alleged rule of international law. In point of fact, nothing in the practice of courts appears to preclude the Court in the exercise of any of its jurisdictions from determining the existence of a rule of international law since both municipal and international courts, in the absence of a contrary intention, appear to have jurisdiction on the issue.

Thus, in *The Paquette Habana*[17] the Supreme Court of the United States was required to rule on the existence of a customary rule and in the *Lotus* case[18] the Permanent Court of International Justice was similarly required to rule on the existence of a customary rule. The methodology employed by both courts was the same, namely, an exhaustive examination of state legislation and state practice, treaties, decisions of competent tribunals and the writings of outstanding publicists on the relevant issues. In the first case, the Supreme Court of the United States found for the existence of a custom and in the second case, the international court decided against the existence of a customary rule. Conflicting outcomes are apparently facilitated by the absence of any rules regarding the standard of proof to be applied and one or another tribunal may be more rigorous in establishing the facts of the case. Conflicting determinations on the existence or non-existence of a customary rule of international law by the two jurisdictions of the Caribbean Court of Justice may easily be avoided by the employment of the normal practice of judicial comity by either jurisdiction of the Court.

It will be recalled that the status of the Caribbean Community as an association of sovereign states was expressed to have important implications for the uniform application of Community law in the CARICOM Single Market and Economy. Consequently, in order to avoid a situation of conflicting interpretations of the Revised Treaty by the courts and tribunals of the Member States, Article 211 accorded the Court compulsory and exclusive jurisdiction to hear and determine disputes in relation to interpreting and applying this instrument. It follows, therefore, *stricto juris*, that national courts do not enjoy concurrent jurisdiction with the CCJ in matters concerning the interpretation and application of the Revised Treaty. Furthermore, Article 214 of the Revised Treaty peremptorily provides that where a national court or tribunal is seised of an issue whose resolution involves the interpretation or application of the Revised Treaty and the court or tribunal is satisfied that a decision on the question is necessary for it to deliver judgment, the court or tribunal concerned shall refer the question to the Caribbean Court of Justice (CCJ) for its determination before delivering judgment. The ineluctable inference, of course, is that in delivering judgment the court or tribunal will act on the determination of the Caribbean Court of Justice in respect of the issue referred thereto.

Article 214 of the Revised Treaty is similar to Article 177 of the Rome Treaty[19] but is different in an extremely important particular. For, whereas Article 177 (2) of the Rome Treaty gives the national court or tribunal a discretion of referral to the European Court of Justice where such a court or tribunal is not a court of last resort, Article 214 of the Revised Treaty allows for no such discretion. It is only where, in the case of the European Union's constituent instrument, that the court or tribunal concerned is an institution of last resort that the requirement of referral is established.[20] As such, there is room in the European Union for many conflicting opinions on the interpretation and application of its constituent instrument prior to a final determination by a court of last resort. The situation is somewhat different in the Caribbean Community where the referral requirement is automatic, assuming a finding for a ruling by the Caribbean Court of Justice by the judges of a municipal court.

However, there appears to be some room for conflicting judgments of national courts or tribunals on the interpretation and application of the Revised Treaty. On careful scrutiny it is easy to establish that national courts within the European Union have a discretion to interpret and apply the Rome Treaty *propio motu*. For it is only where the court or tribunal considers that a decision on the question is necessary to deliver judgment that the referral requirement comes into play. Lord Denning, in addressing the application of Article 177 of the Treaty of Rome established some very useful guidelines.[21] He submitted that in determining whether a decision on the question of referral is necessary, the court or tribunal must conclude that it would be impossible to deliver judgment without such a decision. Further, where the European Court of Justice has decided the same point, the court or tribunal may act on the decision of the European Court of Justice without referral. Thirdly, where the court or tribunal considers that the question in issue leaves little room for doubt, then the task is to apply the Treaty of Rome and not to seek an interpretation of it. But all these determinations of the court or tribunal, in the present submission, are highly subjective and leave room for conflicting outcomes.

Similar considerations apply *aequo vigore* in the interpretation of Article 214 of the Revised Treaty and place on all national judges of municipal courts or tribunals of Member States of the Caribbean Community the unenviable task of understanding and appreciating the applicable rules of international law in reaching a determination in the context of this provision. Where however, a court or tribunal in the Caribbean Community considers that a decision on a question relating to the interpretation or application of the Revised Treaty is involved, Article 214 obliges the Court or tribunal concerned to refer the matter to the CCJ which has exclusive jurisdiction. The advantage of the approach adopted by CARICOM decision-makers is that it leaves less discretion to the judge than the provisions of Article 177 (2) of the Rome Treaty. The downside of this approach however, is that it could lead to an inundation of the Caribbean Court of Justice (CCJ) with referrals from courts and tribunals of the Member States parties to the Agreement Establishing the CCJ. For the referral procedure is one way of avoiding expensive litigation before the Caribbean Court of Justice.

Article 221 of the Revised Treaty stipulates that judgments of the Court shall constitute legally binding precedents for parties in proceedings before the Court unless such judgments have been revised in accordance with Article 219. This provision constitutes, in the present submission, an important innovation in traditional international law which applies the principle of *jurisprudence constant*, that speaks to the tendency of international tribunals to follow previous decisions on an issue, but establishes no requirement to do so. By requiring the CCJ to apply the doctrine of *stare decisis* in arriving at judgments, however, competent decision-makers of CARICOM were concerned to ensure certainty in the applicable norms, stability of expectations on the part of economic actors in the Community, and predictability of outcomes for investment decisions by investors. It is contemplated that the doctrine of *stare decisis* would be applied flexibly. In effect, competent decision-makers sought to ensure that the Court would promote dynamic stability in the applicable law and not espouse the petrification of relevant norms. Consider in this context the dictum of Stephenson, L.J. in the case of *Trendtex Trading Corporation v. Central Bank of Nigeria* [1977] QB 529 at 568 who quoted Sir Samuel Evans in *The Odessa* (1915) 52, 61-2:

> In the domain of international law, in particular, there is room for the extension of old doctrines or the development of new principles, where there is, or is even likely to be, a general acceptance of such by civilized nations. Precedents handed down from earlier days should be treated as guides to lead, and not as shackles to bind. But the guides must not be lightly deserted or cast aside.

This submission eloquently encapsulates the doctrine of *stare decisis* employed in Article 221 of the Revised Treaty of Chaguaramas. In the final analysis, however, the CCJ will have to determine the scope of application of the doctrine of *stare decisis* and the extent to which it constrains judicial activism or innovativeness in establishing and declaring applicable norms. Common law courts in Britain do not construe the doctrine of *stare decisis* as precluding them from distinguishing the instant case from previous decisions thereby contributing to the avoidance of retrogressive petrification of the applicable law. And the Judicial Committee of the Privy Council does not apply the doctrine of *stare decisis* in an unqualified manner.[22] Thus, it was held that the court is not bound to apply an earlier decision perceived to be based on a wrong principle, or one handed down *per incuriam* an Act of Parliament,[23] or where subsequent developments had so altered public policy considerations that the correctness of the earlier decision was now in doubt.[24]

The provisions of Article 221 of the Revised Treaty, however, might have farreaching implications for the reception of international law in the common law of the Caribbean Community. Addressing the issue regarding the place of international law in English common law, Lord Denning, M.R. submitted that there were two schools of thought on the matter. One school supported the doctrine of incorporation which held that international law formed part of English common law and that rules of international law were incorporated automatically into English law. The other school of thought supported the doctrine of transformation which held that international law was no part of English law except in so far as the rules of international law have been adopted and made part of the law of the land by judges, or by an Act of Parliament or by long established custom.

Under the doctrine of transformation, English common law is governed by precedent and cannot develop *pari passu* with international law but has to be changed by the House of Lords or Act of Parliament. After citing persuasive examples of modifications to English common law in accordance with changing norms of international law, Lord Denning continued:

> Seeing that the rules of international law have changed – and do change – and that the courts have given effect to the changes without any Act of Parliament, it follows to my mind inexorably that the rules of international law as existing from time to time do form part of our English law. It follows, too, that a decision of this court – as to what was the ruling of international law 50 or 60 years ago – is not binding on this court today. International law knows no rule of *stare decisis*. If this court today is satisfied that the rule of international law on a subject has changed from what it was 50 or 60 years ago, it can give effect to that change – and apply the change in our English law – without waiting for the House of Lords to do it.[25]

This dictum of Lord Denning appears to be the culmination of a process of reasoning dating as far back to Blackstone who submitted that the law of nations, as it was called at the time, was a part of the law of England. It appears that Lord Mansfield and other judges of the eighteenth century supported Blackstone on this point and several cases were determined on the basis of this principle:[26]

> During the nineteenth century it was reaffirmed in a succession of decisions by distinguished common law and equity judges; in *Dolder v. Huntingfield* (1805) by Lord Eldon, in *Wolff v. Orholm* (1817) by Lord Ellenborough, in *Novello v. Toogood* (1823) by Abbott CJ, in *De Wutz v. Hendricks* (1824) by Best CJ, and in *Emperor of Austria v. Day and Kossuth* (1861) by Stuart V-C.

The doctrine of incorporation also found favour with Lord Atkin in *Chung Chi Cheung v. Rex* [1939] AC 160 who submitted that international law was incorporated into the common law of England to the extent that it was not inconsistent with statute law or final decisions of the courts.[27]

One important implication of the provisions of Article 221 of the Revised Treaty is that by compelling inference, the drafters appear to have legitimised the doctrine of transformation in the common law of the Caribbean Community. Further, Article III (2) of the Agreement Establishing the Caribbean Court of Justice, which provides that the decisions of the Court shall be final, replicates the sense of the language of Lord Halsbury in *London Street Tramways Co. Ltd. v. London County Council.*[28] It follows from this that the Caribbean Court of Justice in the exercise of its appellate jurisdiction is required apply the doctrine of *stare decisis*. It follows, too, that where the Caribbean Court of Justice in the exercise of its original jurisdiction has ruled on one or another issue of international law, the Court in the exercise of its appellate jurisdiction will have to apply the decision of the former unless such decision is ousted by a subsequent decision of the Court in the exercise of its original jurisdiction or by statute pursuant to a relevant determination of the Conference of Heads of Government. However, the competence of the Court under Article 219 of the Revised Treaty to revisit its judgments may also prevent the petrification of the law along undesirable lines. In the alternative, the Court may consider issuing a practice statement in the sense of the one issued by the House of Lords in 1966 indicating a flexible interpretation of the *stare decisis* doctrine.

Article 222 of the Revised Treaty addresses the issue of *locus standi* of private entities in proceedings before the CCJ. In traditional international law only states and collectivities of States, as subjects of international law, are accorded *locus standi* in proceedings before international tribunals. Exceptionally, as is the case of the European Union or the Andean Community where provisions of the regime's constituent instrument are considered as having direct effect, that is, having the force of law for private entities without the intervention of their national legislatures, such entities are accorded *locus standi* in relevant proceedings before the European Court of Justice and the Andean Court of Justice.[29] Article 222 of the Revised Treaty, however, does not confer on private entities the right of *locus standi* in proceedings before the CCJ. It merely gives the Court the discretion to allow private entities to appear as parties in proceedings before it where, in the opinion of the Court the interest of justice requires it. Since, in traditional international law, only the states of nationality of persons aggrieved are entitled to espouse a claim of an object of international law in proceedings before an international tribunal, competent decision makers of the Caribbean Community had to cater for the situation where an aggrieved private entity may have a claim against its state of nationality which might decline to espouse the claim of its national – hence the formulation of Article 222 of the Revised Treaty.

Article 218 of the Revised Treaty also empowers the Court to prescribe interim measures in order to preserve the rights of parties to a dispute pending delivery of judgment. In this connection it is interesting to note that Article 41 of the Statute of the International Court of Justice only allows the ICJ to *indicate* interim measures. Consequently, there was some doubt whether an indication of interim measures had to be complied with.[30] And so the competent decision makers of CARICOM attempted to put the issue beyond all doubt by empowering the CCJ to *prescribe* interim measures. It is submitted, however, that the obligation to comply could have been more compelling had language been employed similar to that set out in Article 290 (6) of the United Nations Convention on the Law of the Sea which requires parties to 'comply promptly with any provisional measures prescribed'.

As the situation currently obtains in the Caribbean Community, litigation in municipal courts of Member States, which have not delinked from the Judicial Committee of the Privy Council, could, *inter alia*, involve issues touching on the interpretation and application of the Revised Treaty which is being provisionally applied by most Member States. Omission by Member States to oust the jurisdiction of the Judicial Committee of the Privy Council could lead to a ludicrous situation where that institution could have a determinative role in respect of issues concerning the interpretation and application of the Treaty and on which the Caribbean Court of Justice has ruled. Indeed, this is the position as it exists today and which, in the present submission, is juridically feasible but politically unacceptable. In an era of liberalisation and globalisation, where the lines between jurisdictional boundaries are blurred and rules of competition governing the behaviour of enterprises are susceptible to tendentious interpretations consistent with self-serving perceptions of the national interest, autonomous judicial decision-making in the Region is likely to be the only plausible guarantee that companies operating in the CARICOM Single Market and Economy play by the applicable rules determined by CARICOM decision-makers. Consider in this context the ruling of the Judicial Committee of the Privy Council in *Cable and Wireless (Dominica) Ltd. v. Marpin Telecoms and Broadcasting Co. Ltd.* [2001] 1 WLR 1123.

In the situation described above, however, the Judicial Committee of the Privy Council could rely on judicial comity to decline jurisdiction. For example, British courts rely on comity in recognising the legislative, executive and judicial principles of a *forum non conveniens* whereby the court declines jurisdiction where a foreign court is perceived to be more appropriate for the relevant proceedings.[31] However, it appears that the courts will not apply judicial comity to prevent the United Kingdom, as an attribute of sovereignty, from protecting its revenue laws from abuses.[32] In the premises, it does not appear that omission to delink from the Judicial Committee of the Privy Council in its appellate jurisdiction may be fatal for the efficient functioning of the Caribbean Court of Justice in the exercise of its original jurisdiction.

The Court, in the exercise of its original jurisdiction, is the only body competent to deliver advisory opinions on the interpretation and application of the Treaty. Such advisory opinions are delivered on the request of the Member States parties to a dispute or by the Community. Consequently, one way of avoiding the costs of litigation before the Court is for the member States parties to a dispute to request an advisory opinion on the issue by the Court.[33] It does appear that the request for an advisory opinion must come from the Member States, parties to a dispute, or from the Community either at the instance of a competent organ or the Secretary-General. As such, Member

States may not request advisory opinions on hypothetical issues; in every case where such a request is made there must exist a dispute about the interpretation or application of the Treaty. Similarly, Member States or private entities may avoid the costs of litigation before the CCJ by resort to the referral procedure set out in Article 214 of the Treaty. It is conjectured that much of the time of the Court will be taken up with the preparation and delivery of advisory opinions and with referrals from municipal courts and tribunals.

THE CARIBBEAN COURT OF JUSTICE IN REGIONAL ECONOMIC DEVELOPMENT[34]

> . . . justice sectors in the Caribbean have been seen historically as users of resources, rather than as contributors to economic and social development.[35]

Having examined the original jurisdiction of the Caribbean Court of Justice, it is now proposed to determine how the Court will contribute to the structured development of the CARICOM Single Market and Economy.

The signing of the Agreement Establishing the Caribbean Court of Justice by Heads of Government of the Caribbean Community in Barbados, on February 14, 2002 must be seen as a momentous event constituting one of the most defining determinations in the institutional and historical development of the regional economic integration movement. By this act, the political directorate of the Caribbean Community did not only assert their right to exercise autonomy of decision-making in judicial matters by severing the last colonial link with Britain, but emphatically demonstrated their political will to honour their commitments to regional economic integration set out in the Revised Treaty of Chaguaramas establishing the Caribbean Community including the CARICOM Single Market and Economy. For, on the basis of a dispassionate analysis of the institutional arrangements contemplated for the effective operation of the CARICOM Single Market and Economy, the Caribbean Court of Justice, in the exercise of its original jurisdiction, must be considered as constituting the institutional centrepiece of the regional integration movement. Among its other attributes, the Caribbean Court of Justice will be the only judicial institution of its kind, being on the one hand, a municipal court and on the other, an international tribunal employing rules of international law to settle disputes. At the same time the Court would be a unique international judicial body in terms of the institutional arrangements agreed for the appointment of its judges and the funding of its operations.[36]

An understanding of the role of the Caribbean Court of Justice in regional economic development would be greatly facilitated by adopting as the point of departure an examination of the role of the justice sector, in particular, and that of the law, generally, in the national economic development process. For present purposes, law will be defined as the corpus of societal norms which is established, interpreted, applied and enforced by the central authorities of the State in order to regulate the conduct of persons, both natural and juridical, in their normal interface with one another. The central authorities which are normally involved in the process described are the legislative assemblies, offices of the solicitors-general, offices of the attorneys-general, ministers of justice, the courts, directors of public prosecutions, commissioners of prisons and police, probation officers, legal aid clinics, associations of public and private law practitioners approved by governments, and other relevant legal and administrative institutions. Collectively, this assemblage of organisations and institutions is known as the justice sector.

A generally acceptable compendium of factors perceived to influence structured national, social and economic development will probably include an impressive body of determinants of a psychological, geopolitical, economic, environmental, legal and institutional nature of a varying mix, depending on the peculiar circumstances of the political entities examined. Of the factors identified above, conventional economic wisdom would probably ascribe a very low rating to the legal determinant. This disposition may be explained by reference to generally uninformed and misconceived perceptions enjoying wide currency in various professions, including the legal fraternity, about the role of law and the justice sector in the national development process. Similar perceptions of a more deep-seated nature are entertained by the political directorate of various jurisdictions in the Caribbean Community where resources committed to enhancement of the justice sector are not perceived as translating into positive political outcomes at election time. Within recent times, however, the role of law and the justice sector in national economic development has been accorded favourable recognition by multilateral financial institutions which are insisting on improvements in the justice sector as a catalyst for attracting and sustaining investments for the economic development of disadvantaged States.[37] It has been observed in this context that high direct and indirect costs of violence can deter both domestic and foreign investment and stimulate the migration of scarce skills. Similarly, improvements in both the criminal and civil justice systems not only enhance social stability but also impact positively on the domestic investment environment and economic development.

Contrary to anecdotal information, however, the law and legal institutions play a critical, determinative, though oftentimes, unheralded role in national economic development. This is particularly the case in the Caribbean Community where the sole proprietor and family establishments continue to dominate and even impede economic activity. The vast majority of companies in the Caribbean Community are private companies and most of them comprise family businesses. Indeed, even some wholly owned Government companies and subsidiaries of large transnational corporations are registered as private companies entitled not to file accounts with the Registrar of Companies.[38] Financial economists like Hayek recognise, on the one hand, the importance of legal institutions for the efficient functioning of financial markets and, on the other hand, the contribution of financial markets to national economic development. In this context, it is worthy of note that the basic unit of any currency, legal tender, is a creature of law and underpins monetary and financial transactions of States in their international economic, monetary and financial transactions.[39] The critical importance of the financial sector in national economic development and the contribution of legal norms in establishing the architecture of the sector may be inferred from the submissions of the United States delegation in the FTAA negotiations which read, *inter alia*, as follows:

> In the view of the United States, a review of FTAA rules affecting the financial sector and the development of specialised provisions for that sector as appropriate should be pursued in a distinct FTAA forum. The sensitivity of financial markets and institutions and the complexity of financial regulations warrant establishing one forum to ensure the development of clear coherent rules for this section . . . [40]

In support of the perception of the positive role of law in national economic development it has been submitted that:

> (c)onsistent enforcement of understandable laws helps provide a stable environment where the long-term consequences of economic decisions can be reasonably predicted and assessed. An effective and efficient judiciary has the added benefit of making the legal system affordable and accessible for relatively small-sized enterprises and less privileged citizens, therebv achieving poverty and equity objectives as well as an increase in overall economic activity.[41]

In fact, the most critical actors in national economic activity are creatures of the law – juridical entities, like the corporation, the limited liability company and the firm. These legal creations are, in large measure, responsible for much of the economic activity in the so-called developed societies and the global reach of economic agglomerations. In this connection, it is submitted that the innovative, defining and expansionist role of the joint-stock/limited liability company in industrial and economic development in Britain and Europe during the nineteenth century must be accorded historical recognition, especially after the landmark decision of the House of Lords in *Salomon & Salomon* [1897] AC 22 which definitively and conclusively established the company as a legal entity separate and apart from its members.

Prior to this legal fiction, industrial development was likely to be stymied by entrepreneurial exposure to risk, unmitigated bankruptcy and even imprisonment. Indeed, current international economic activity is controlled and determined by mega-corporations resulting from transborder mergers of transnational corporations whose global reach is at best disconcerting and whose individual resources, natural, human, technological and financial, more often than not, dwarf the national resources of most developing nations.[42]

The role of the State as the primary determinant of national economic policy and as an important actor in international economic activity has been considerably undermined by the emergence of globalisation and liberalisation as national economic imperatives. At the same time, transnational corporate power has been inordinately augmented by trade liberalisation and globalisation as evidenced in the juridical configuration and operation of the World Trade Organization. Fortunately, though perhaps, belatedly, recognition of the importance of these legal entities by regional experts has come from no less a source than the Governor of the Eastern Caribbean Central Bank who, in attempting to establish a vision for the Caribbean Community in the new millennium, perceptively submitted, *inter alia*:

> The vehicle for the production of both goods and services is the firm (read company). In this region we have tended to put the major emphasis on creating the conditions for production instead on the actual unit of production. The dominant firm in the region has been the multinational corporation which has traditionally controlled the export sectors in both agriculture and mining.
>
> The predominant domestic enterprises have been in the distribution, wholesale and retail sectors. The very size and structure of our economies dictate that for us to achieve sustainable growth, our activities must be export-oriented and flexible enough to adapt to a dynamic and competitive environment.
>
> The Caribbean private sector and governments must meet the challenge of developing and supporting the kind of firm structures which are appropriate to our circumstances and which give us the capacity to insert ourselves into the global

> commodity chains which now have come to represent the locus of international production, distribution and consumption.
>
> One would want to suggest that the import/export firm so prevalent in East Asia could be an appropriate vehicle for mobilising enterprise and production across the region and forming the link between the international economy and the region, and between small firms and the export economy.
>
> The strategy will have to concentrate on the institutional and incentive arrangements we put in place to capture international business. The legal and financial infrastructure are critical to the success of this enterprise; in these two areas, cutting edge legislation and financial products have to be important factors . . .[43]

Such cutting edge legislation must address issues in the areas of companies, banking, financial institutions, incentives, intellectual property, commerce, bankruptcy, securities environment, international trade, competition, subsidies, dumping, economic integration, to mention a few. Although conventional economists consider themselves the movers and shakers of national development, the law is in fact the basic and essential catalyst of social and economic development. In the modern State, itself a creature of law, nearly all acceptable social and economic activities are conducted within parameters established by law. In this context, it is submitted that the state is society politically organised on the basis of enforceable legal rules. However, because the role of law in national economic and social development is not readily appreciated by competent decision-makers or, if it is, it is not accorded due prominence in the national political agenda, resources normally allocated to the establishment and maintenance of legal infrastructure are exiguous compared to resources allocated to other sectors like health and education, which continue to command relatively high political and electoral profiles.

Significantly, too, the role of law in the achievement and maintenance of macro-economic stability and, *ipso facto*, in national economic development is not readily understood by conventional economic gurus and critical decision-makers. An interesting example in this context is to be found in the area of currency values. Although it is reasonable to assume that economists worthy of the designation discern the importance of stable currency values in contributing to business efficiency and a healthy macro-economic environment in the modern State, it is not always the subject of a reasonable assumption, however, that economists recognise that the required stability and predictability in the national economic environment are necessarily a function of legal certainty and the ability of the law to adapt to the dynamics of the economic environment.[44] And this is where the legal fraternity has been conspicuously remiss in not informing itself of the role of law in national economic development and in publicising this role to important stakeholders.

Such a lack of appreciation is further compromised by the omission of some economists to distinguish between depreciation of a national currency – erosion of its purchasing power – and devaluation, which is a conscious governmental act established by law to lower the par value of the currency. Similarly, the law plays a determinative role in the establishment of interest rates, the independence of central banks, prudential management of financial institutions and markets, the control of money supply, access by governments to central banks' financial resources, permissibility and extent of budgetary deficits, the borrowing powers of national administrations and so on *ad nauseum*. All of the factors identified may contribute in varying degrees to macro-economic stability and, by the same token, the stability of investor expectations, in the absence of which the investment climate is unlikely to be inviting. In short, unless the prudent investor finds himself in a position to predict outcomes with reasonable accuracy and certainty, he is normally disinclined to commit his investment. And in this context, outcome predictability is, more often than not, a function of legal certainty.

Furthermore, the organisation of monetary systems, both internationally and nationally, including the establishment of par values, exchange rates and even legal tender, is a function of legislative enactments. Indeed, money is less an economic than a legal concept and may be defined as a chattel, issued under the authority of law, denominated with reference to a specific unit of account and endowed with the status of legal tender for the complete satisfaction of a debt or other monetary obligation. And it needs no arguing that monetary systems are indispensable for the organisation and successful operation of modern economies.[45]

At the international level, it is impossible to ignore the role of the law in determining developments in trade, finance, technology transfers, transportation, shipping, exploitation of the resources of ocean space and outer space, telecommunications, technological innovation and such like. Indeed, the extensive system of multilateralism established during and after the Second World War dictates, in large measure, State interaction in the international community at present. This system was the outcome of various multilateral conferences designed to legislate conduct in the post-war years in virtually every spatial dimension, with a view to restoring and promoting international trade. Beginning with the Bretton Woods Agreements in 1943, these multilateral instruments comprehended the Chicago Convention (1944), the aborted Havana Charter (1948), the General Agreement on Tariffs and Trade (1947), the Geneva Conventions on the Law of the Sea (1958 and 1960), the International Convention for the Protection of Industrial Property (1958), the General Assembly Declaration of Legal Principles Governing Activities of States in the Exploration and Use of Outer Space (1963), the United Nations Convention on the Law of the Sea (1962) and culminated in the Marrakesh Agreement (1994) establishing the World Trade Organization.[46] These multilateral regimes impact decisively on national decision-making and sometimes critically determine the direction and scope of national economic development.

ROLE OF THE JUSTICE SECTOR IN NATIONAL ECONOMIC DEVELOPMENT

Although law and the justice sector enjoy a symbiotic relationship, they are, nevertheless, discrete sociological phenomena. Law, as a centrally determined normative body of prescriptions, speaks to the regulation of human intercourse; the justice sector addresses the institutional and organisational arrangements which give tangible expression to the establishment, interpretation, application and enforcement of legal norms. And, if, as demonstrated in the previous section, the role of law in national economic development is perceived as critical, the justice sector must be seen to play an equally seminal role in the process.

Efficiently functioning institutions of the justice sector, by complementing and facilitating various legislative initiatives which, collectively, define conventional morality and the prevailing social ethos of a people, operate to institutionalise good governance, which is being posited by the international donor community as a conditionality of financial assistance in the form of grants, concessional loans and even preferential trading arrangements. Consider in this context the EU/ACP Cotonou Agreement and the unfolding FTAA Agreement. Institutions of the justice sector, particularly, judicial institutions, by enhancing the delivery of services both in terms of swiftly and decisively punishing socially deviant behaviour, ensuring that contractual obligations are performed and protecting and enforcing property rights through the expeditious, fair and transparent settlement of disputes, contribute to a healthy business and investment climate. In short, an efficient and effective justice sector instills confidence in the general populace and engenders conditions of stability conducive to predicting the consequences of critical decision-making, particularly in the area of investments.

More importantly, many functions of institutions operating in the justice sector contribute in large measure to a reduction in the transaction costs of conducting business with probable beneficial impact on the national investment climate. Addressing the issue of the investment climate, Owen Arthur, Prime Minister of Barbados observed:

> The environment must therefore be created within which the Region's enterprises can be adequately capitalised and acquire the critical mass to compete at home and to compete

> internationally. Widespread encumbrances and the high cost of doing business in the Region must be systematically reduced.[47]

Much of this cost is due to inefficiencies in the operation of the justice sector. In this context, mention must be made of affordable access to justice and expeditious, efficacious disputes settlement procedures, especially in the area of commercial disputes. Similarly, by effectively protecting property rights from various forms of fraud and brigandry, the justice system relieves property owners of expenditure on protective services thereby reducing the costs of business transactions. Furthermore, stability in the social and macro-economic environment issuing from an efficient justice sector lowers the incidence of investment risks and the price of capital to borrowers and entrepreneurs. In this context, too, it must be observed that social stability in the national environment coupled with plausible assurances of protection for life and limb of individuals, impacts favourably on the tourism industry which is the largest generator of foreign exchange in the economies of most Member States of the Caribbean Community. Lower transaction costs impact positively on production costs resulting in an enhanced competitive position for businesses.

On the basis of the foregoing, it appears to be the subject of a reasonable inference that much underdevelopment in countries of the Caribbean Community can be traced to inadequate legal infrastructure and inefficiencies in the functioning of national justice sectors and underscores the need for reforms in the justice sector.

> By raising the cost of conducting business, a poorly performing justice sector makes a nation's goods and services less competitive on international markets. At the extreme, inoperative justice sectors cannot prevent or control violence, thus diminishing existing physical capital and deterring new investment.[48]

Reforms in the justice sector, however, must go hand in hand with reforms dictated by developments associated with globalisation and liberalisation. In one submission:

> (g)lobalisation and technological advancements have the potential to free most developing countries from the restrictions

> imposed by a small domestic market, low savings and limited access to world technology and credit . . . . The creation and development of mechanisms to support more market-oriented economic policies - such as regulatory agencies in support of private sector led growth and anti-trust, anti-dumping and fair trading commissions - are urgently needed in most developing countries. Globalisation has also intensified the link between justice sector services and development, and it has raised the costs associated with an ineffective and inefficient justice sector.[49]

ROLE OF THE CARIBBEAN COURT OF JUSTICE IN REGIONAL ECONOMIC DEVELOPMENT

A credible evaluation of the role of the Caribbean Court of Justice in regional economic development must bear in mind two important factors. Firstly, the proposed Caribbean Court is intended to be a unique institution in international institutional relations. For not only is the Court designed to replace the Judicial Committee of the Privy Council (JCPC) as the highest appellate municipal court for the Member States of the Caribbean Community but it is also structured to be an international tribunal employing rules of international law in interpreting and applying the Revised Treaty of Chaguaramas Establishing the Caribbean Community including the CARICOM Single Market and Economy. In the exercise of its appellate jurisdiction, the Court will be the tribunal of last resort for participating Member States of the Community. As an international tribunal, however, the Court will exercise an original but exclusive jurisdiction in respect of the interpretation and application of the Revised Treaty. In the exercise of both jurisdictions, the Court is expected to play a critical role in ensuring legal certainty in the Community and CSME, in the absence of which there is unlikely to be the stability of expectations which investors require as a basis for predicting outcomes in respect of economic decisions, especially those relating to investments in one or another economic activity.

One or two policymakers in the Community at an earlier stage of the process, had wondered whether retention of the JCPC in respect of civil suits might not inspire greater investor confidence with probable positive impact on the regional investment climate. In the present submission, three observations may be tendered for consideration in this context. Firstly, the JCPC rarely overturns decisions of regional courts on civil matters, thereby attesting to the generally high quality of regional judicial pronouncements. Secondly, foreign investors proposing to commit substantial investments in developing regions normally provide for disputes settlement procedures in the relevant investment instrument. Such procedures usually provide for the settlement of disputes by the International Centre for the Settlement of Investment Disputes (ICSID), an instrumentality of the World Bank (IBRD). Thirdly, the Agreement Establishing the Caribbean Court of Justice expressly provided for the promotion and establishment of alternative disputes settlement modes and this should provide a vehicle for the expeditious and satisfactory resolution of a wide range of commercial disputes.

Of no less importance is the fact that despite its misleading nomenclature, the Caribbean Community remains, and was always intended to be, an association of sovereign States. Indeed, the principle of sovereign equality of States finds cogent legal expression in the unanimity rule prescribed for determinations on substantive issues in the highest decision-making organ of the Community – The Conference of Heads of Government.[50] The legal status of the Caribbean Community has important consequences for the functioning of its organs and the benefits intended to inure to nationals of Member States. And in all of this, it is worthwhile to remember that the express intention of competent decision-makers is the creation of a single economic space in the Community.

However, given that the Community consists of several sovereign jurisdictions, establishment of a single economic space would require the superimposition of collective economic decisions on discrete national administrations, which, in the ultimate analysis, retain autonomous decision-making powers in areas of national economic development. Furthermore, the relevant integrating instruments setting out the rights and obligations of nationals of Member States have to be enacted into law by the national assemblies concerned before such rights and obligations can be enforced in national jurisdictions. One important consequence of this is that, in the absence of constraining legislation to this effect, national courts would be competent to interpret and apply the relevant enabling legislation.

The rights inuring to nationals of Member States consist, in the first instance, of the right of establishment, the right to provide services and the right to move capital within the Community.[51] The right of establishment has been expressed to include the right to engage in any non-wage-earning activities of a commercial, industrial, agricultural, professional or artisanal nature, as well as the right to create and manage economic enterprises within the contemplation of the revised Treaty. In this connection, it is important to note that non-wage-earning activities means activities of an economic nature undertaken by self-employed persons or independent contractors. In order to facilitate the right of establishment, Member States will be required to eliminate all legislative prescriptions and administrative practices which impede the exercise of the right of establishment. Such constraining prescriptions and practices relate to the employment of managerial, technical and supervisory personnel in economic enterprises, the establishment by qualifying companies of agencies, branches or subsidiaries and conditions for entry of relevant personnel, their spouses and dependants.

One intractable outstanding issue relates to the question of other rights contingent on the right of establishment as defined and agreed. These so-called contingent rights relate to the terms of access by beneficiaries to social infrastructure of host States. Are the children of persons exercising the right of establishment entitled as of right to be accorded places in schools of their choice, assuming the satisfaction of non-discriminatory conditions? And if so, are such students entitled to be admitted on the same conditions as nationals in accordance with relevant provisions of the Revised Treaty proscribing discrimination on the grounds of nationality?

Similar considerations apply to access to health services and other social services. All such issues are to be addressed in a separate Protocol to be elaborated for the purpose.[52]

Similar problems may be expected to arise in relation to the provision of services by professionals and approved categories of skilled workers. In this connection, however, Member States are expected to put in place 'appropriate mechanisms to establish common standards to determine equivalency or to accord accreditation to diplomas, certificates and other evidence of qualification secured by nationals of other Member States'.[53] Both with respect to establishment and provision of services, Member States are prohibited from introducing new restrictions.

In all the situations contemplated for the removal of restrictions, competent organs of the Community are required to establish agreed programmes for the removal of such restrictions. Such programmes have been established and agreed by Conference and are in the process of being implemented. At the end of the time frames established for the removal of restrictions on the right of establishment, the provision of services and the movement of capital, it is envisaged that the most important factors of production would be free to move to any area of the Community where they can be most productively and efficiently employed. It is envisaged that all restrictions will be removed by the end of 2005.[54] The axiomatic assumption in all this is that skills will only be inclined to move with opportunities for beneficial employment and that persons entitled would not willingly become a charge on the exchequer of the host country. And in any event, Member States reserve the right to employ safeguard mechanisms in support of their balance of payments positions.[55] Moreover, disadvantaged countries, regions and sectors are allowed special derogations and concessions as appropriate to facilitate their participation in the CSME.

In terms of capital, Member States undertook to remove discriminatory restrictions on banking, insurance and other financial services. Similarly, Member States undertook not to introduce new restrictions on the movement of capital and payments connected therewith and on current payments and transfers.[56] In this context, the Council for Finance and Planning (COFAP) was tasked with establishing, in collaboration with the Committee of Central Bank Governors, a programme for the removal of the restrictions mentioned above. Member States also undertook to co-ordinate their foreign exchange policies in respect of the movement of capital between them and third States. However, given the position currently existing in the Community in the area of foreign exchange policies, with Barbados, Belize, The Bahamas and the OECS States maintaining fixed exchange rates and the rest floating currencies, it is difficult to be euphoric about the commitment to co-ordinated foreign exchange policies in the absence of an obligation to redirect national policies. In the long term it is proposed to move to a single currency for the Community based on voluntary compliance with agreed convergence criteria. Given, however, the temptation to break ranks especially where political and electoral imperatives prescribe such a course of action, it is submitted that nothing less than a legal obligation, backed by credible sanctions, to comply with the agreed convergence criteria, will facilitate the achievement of the stated objectives.

The rights identified above are some of the more important rights nationals of the Community will expect to enjoy in order to be persuaded that regional economic integration is indeed working. And for this to happen, there must exist somewhere in the Community credible mechanisms for authoritative and definitive identification and protection of such rights. And this is where the Caribbean Court of Justice must be seen to play an important role. As mentioned above, the municipal courts of all Member States, in the absence of legislative constraints, will be competent to interpret and apply the Revised Treaty as enacted into local law. This would be no less than a prescription for legal uncertainty issuing from a variety of judicial pronouncements which are not required to be consistent with one another. Legal uncertainty in this context is likely to engender instability by frustrating the predictability of economic decisions, particularly investment decisions, and their consequences. Such an environment is likely to impact negatively on macro-economic stability and the investment climate in general. This will not augur well for the Caribbean Community comprising in large measure capital-importing countries.

Viewed from this perspective, it would be possible to grasp the critical role of the Caribbean Court of Justice in the development of the CARICOM Single Market and Economy. As mentioned above, the status of the Community as an association of sovereign States, coupled with the requirement for every Member State to enact the Revised Treaty into local law, subjects this instrument to as many interpretations as there are national jurisdictions, thereby constituting a built-in prescription for legal uncertainty. In order to avoid this eventuality, the political directorate of the Community determined to invest the Caribbean Court of Justice with compulsory and exclusive jurisdiction in respect of issues relating to the interpretation and application of the Revised Treaty.[57] Consequently, where a municipal court in any national jurisdiction of a Member State party to the Agreement Establishing the Caribbean Court of Justice is seised of an issue concerning the interpretation and application of the Revised Treaty, it will be required to stay proceedings on such an issue pending a determination thereon by the Caribbean Court of Justice if the court or tribunal is satisfied that a determination of the CCJ is necessary to deliver judgment.[58] In fact, Article 177 of the Rome Treaty prescribes a similar requirement for municipal courts of Member States of the European Community from which there is no appeal.[59] In this way, uniformity of applicable norms is ensured with positive effects on legal certainty and the stability of the investment climate.

As concerns the referral procedure however, it is important to appreciate the absence of automaticity in the process set out in Article 177 of the Rome Treaty and Article XIV of the Agreement Establishing the Caribbean Court of Justice. In both situations there is a large element of discretion residing in the national courts as to which ruling of the European Court of Justice

(ECJ) and the Caribbean Court of Justice, as the case may be, is necessary for the delivery of judgment. There is no requirement for referral unless the national courts or tribunals so determine. But once a referral is made to the CCJ and the CCJ rules on the issue, this ruling establishes a legally binding determination for future similar cases given the requirement for the Court to follow previous decisions on the subject. The situation, however, is different in the case of the ECJ which is not bound by precedent. And national courts may keep referring the same issue to the ECJ if there is any plausible expectation that a change in relevant circumstances or even in the composition of the Court may prompt a revision of an earlier ruling by the European Court of Justice.[60]

A comparison of Article 177 of the Rome Treaty and Article 214 of the Revised Treaty reveals some interesting differences. Whereas Article 177 (2) gives a court or tribunal, which is not a municipal court of last resort, a double discretion to refer an issue to the European Court of Justice, Article 214 of the Revised Treaty restricts the discretion to situations where the court or tribunal considers that a referral to the CCJ is 'necessary to enable it to deliver judgment'. In the case of judicial institutions of the European Union, there is a further discretion to refer or not to refer even where it is considered that a decision on a question is necessary to enable judgment to be delivered. In effect, ordinary municipal courts and tribunals are competent to rule on issues concerning the interpretation and application of the Treaty of Rome, and unless those determinations are appealed to a court of last resort where referrals to the ECJ are a requirement, there may be various conflicting opinions on any given issue relating to the Treaty of Rome subsisting simultaneously. Such a situation, however, is unlikely to arise with the same degree of intensity in the Caribbean Community where the incidence of referrals, however, could inundate the Caribbean Court of Justice.

In addressing the application of Article 177 of the Rome Treaty, Lord Denning established some useful guidelines. Firstly, in determining whether a decision on a question is necessary, the court or tribunal must conclude that it would be impossible to deliver judgment without such a decision. Secondly, where the same point has been decided by the European Court of Justice, the court or tribunal may act on the decision of the European Court of Justice without a referral. But, since the European Court is not governed by the rule of *stare decisis* a court or tribunal may still refer a question on which the court has ruled in the expectation that a material change of circumstance might induce the European Court of Justice to rule differently on the same question. Where, however, the court or tribunal is persuaded that the question in issue leaves little room for doubt, then the task is to apply the Treaty of Rome and not to seek an interpretation of it. Finally, before making a determination on the necessity to secure a decision on the question, the court or tribunal must establish the facts of the case. Undoubtedly, similar considerations are likely to guide the courts of the Caribbean Community in construing and applying Article 214 of the Revised Treaty.

It is also important to bear in mind that the law to be applied by the Court in the exercise of its original jurisdiction is international law which is common to both civil law and common law jurisdictions.[61] This requirement, however, does not preclude the Court from reaching determinations *ex aequo et bono* where the parties to a dispute before the Court so agree.[62] Consequently, both Suriname and Haiti will have no problems in submitting to the jurisdiction of the Court in the exercise of its original jurisdiction. The fact that the jurisdiction of the Court in respect of those submitting thereto is both compulsory and exclusive contributes to uniformity in the applicable rules. This is enhanced by the binding nature of the Court's decisions for third parties. Thus Article 221 of the revised Treaty provides that decisions of the Caribbean Court of Justice constitute *stare decisis*.[63]

Consistently with traditional international law, only subjects of international law are normally accorded *locus standi* in proceedings before the Caribbean Court of Justice. In the premises, private entities or individuals aggrieved by a denial of rights to be accorded under the revised Treaty are required to have their claims espoused by their States of nationality in proceedings before the Court.[64] However, this requirement could result in a denial of access to justice when one party to a dispute is a Member State which declines to espouse the claim of its national. To pre-empt this eventuality, Article 222 of the revised Treaty provides for private entities to be accorded *locus standi* in proceedings before the Court with leave of the Court where the requirements of justice so prescribe.

Based on the foregoing, the role of the CCJ in ensuring the efficient operation of the CSME cannot be denied. In the absence of this institution to pronounce authoritatively and definitively on the rights and obligations of Member States of the Community and their nationals, rights may tend to become illusory and obligations vacuous commitments. An integration regime comprising an association of sovereign States requires an institution like the Caribbean Court of Justice to assist the justice sector in the delivery of services expected of the sector in any progressive, stable national economic environment. Indeed, despite its status as a supranational collectivity, the European Union still requires the European Court of Justice to inject legal certainty and provide social and economic cohesion in the operational environment. In the Caribbean Community, the Caribbean Court of Justice is expected to contribute no less.

NOTES

1. Consider, for example, Article 34 (1) of the Statute of the ICJ.
2. See P. Sands, R.Mackenzie and Y. Shany, *Manual on International Courts and Tribunals*, (London: Butterworths, 1999) p.xxix.
3. *Regina v. Bowstreet Metropolitan Stipendiary Magistrate and others, ex parte Pinochet Ugarte (No.1)* HL [2000] AC 19.
4. (1999) 54 WIR 387; [1999] 3 WLR 249.
5. (2000) 57 WIR 275.
6. Duke, E.E. Pollard, 'Original Jurisdiction of the Caribbean Court of Justice'. Paper presented at the 30th Course on International law

sponsored by the Inter-American Juridical Committee of the Organisation of American States, Rio de Janeiro, August 18-20, 2003.

7. See Appendix V of the Report at p. 66.

8. See *Time for Action, the Report of the West Indian Commission*, Black Rock, Barbados, 1992 at p.500.

9. See, for example, Articles 33, 37 and 40 of the Revised Treaty of Chaguaramas establishing the Caribbean Community including the CARICOM Single Market and Economy signed in Nassau, The Bahamas, on 5 July 2001.

10. See, for example, Dr. K. Borchardt, *The ABC of Community Law*, European Community. 1999.

11. Article 28 (1) of the Revised Treaty reads as follows:

> Save as otherwise provide in this Treaty and subject to paragraph 2 of this Article and the relevant provisions of Article 27, the Conference shall take decisions by an affirmative vote of all its members and such decisions shall be binding.

See articles 29 (3) and (4) of the Revised Treaty which reads as follows:

> Where issues have been determined to be of critical importance to the national well-being of a Member State, in accordance with paragraph 4 of this Article, such decisions shall be reached by an affirmative vote of all Member States

and

> Decisions that an issue is of critical importance to the national well-being of a Member State shall be reached by a two-thirds majority of the Member States.

12. See Article 215 of the Revised Treaty by which States Parties to the instrument undertake to comply with the judgments of the Court.

13. See, for example, Article 36 (2) of the Statutes of the International Court of Justice.

14. See Article 216 (2) of the Revised Treaty.

15. See *Trendtex Trading Corporation v. Central Bank of Nigeria* [1977] QB at p.35.

16. See *Starke's International Law*, 11th ed., (London: Butterworths, 1994, p.19. Here, the author describes the difficulty of determining when a rule of international law has emerged and gained general recognition by states of the international community.

17. See (1900) 175 US 677.

18. See (1927) PCIJ Series A, No.10.

19. Compare Article 234 of the Treaty of Maastricht 1992.
20. See Article 177 (3) of the Rome Treaty and Article 234 (3) of the Treaty of Maastricht.
21. See *H.P. Bulmer v. Bollinger S.A.* [1974] 2 All ER 1226.
22. See *Lewis et al v. Attorney General of Jamaica* (2000) 57 WIR 275.
23. See *Attorney General for Ontario v. Canada Temperance Federation* [1946] AC 193; *Nkarubule v. The King* [1950] AC 379; *Young v. Bristol Aeorplane Co. Ltd.* [1944] K-B 718 and *Rex v. Taylor* [1950] 2 KB 368. *Young v. Bristol Aeroplane Co. Ltd.* definitely established the essential principles of the doctrine of *stare decisis.*
24. *Reg v. Parole Board, ex parte Wilson* [1992] QB 740 where the court held that where the liberty of the subject is involved, it was not bound to follow an earlier decision if the interest of justice required otherwise.
25. See *Trendtex Trading Corporation v. Central Bank of Nigeria* [1977] QB 529 at pp.553-4.
26. See *Starke's International Law*, 11th ed. (London: Butterworths, 1994), 68.
27. *Ibid.*, 69.
28. *London Street Tramways Co. Ltd. v. London County Council* [1898] AC 375.
29. See Duke E.E. Pollard, 'The Caribbean Court of Justice: Challenge and Response', in *CARICOM Perspective*, Vol.1, 1999, p.32.
30. See Jerome B. Elkind, 'Interim Protection: A Functional Approach', *Cornell International Law Journal* (1981) 153-65.
31. See *Spiliada Maritime Corporation v. Cansulex Ltd.* [1987] AC 460.
32. See *Collco Dealing Ltd. v. IRC* [1962] AC 1.
33. See Article 212 of the Revised Treaty establishing the Caribbean Community.
34. Originally published in a slightly different form in *Governance in the Age of Globalisation*, Kenneth O. Hall and Denis Benn eds. (Kingston: Ian Randle Publishers, 2003), 555-567.
35. See *Challenges of Capacity Development: Towards Sustainable Reforms of Caribbean Justice Sectors – Volume I: Policy Document.* IDB/CGCED, May 2000 at p.4.
36. The Caribbean Court of Justice will be the only international tribunal of its class whose judges are not appointed directly or indirectly by political representatives of governments and which will be financially

independent of governments' subventions, its operational expenses being defrayed from the process of a trust fund established for the purpose.

37. See R.E. Messick, *Judicial Reform and Economic Development: A Survey of the Issues*, The World Bank Research Observer, Vol. 14, No. 1, Feb. 1995, 117.

38. *Report of the Working Party on the Harmonisation of Company Law in the Caribbean Community*, p.11. This state of affairs, in the present submission, is unacceptable and should be remedied by legislative enactments.

39. For the nature and impact of legal institutions on monetary policy and financial transactions, see generally, F.A. Mann, *The Legal Aspect of Money*, (Oxford: Clarendon Press, 1964).

40. See the non-paper circulated by the US Delegation during the FTAA negotiations on services.

41. See *Challenges of Capacity Development: Towards Sustainable Reforms of Caribbean Justice Sectors - Volume II: A diagnostic Assessment* - IDB/CGCED, May 2000 at p.1.

42. See Duke E. Pollard, *Law and Policy of Producers' Association*, (Oxford: Clarendon Press, 1982), 15-32.

43. Dwight Venner, 'The Challenges of Economic Policy and Circumstances in the 21st Century' in *The Caribbean Community: Beyond Survival*, Kenneth O. Hall, ed., (Kingston: Ian Randle Publishers, 2000) 695.

44. See generally, David Johnston et al, *Cyber Law*, (Toronto: Stoddart Publishing Co. Ltd., 1997).

45. For a comprehensive analysis of these issues, see F.A. Mann, *The Legal Aspect of Money*. 2nd edition. (Oxford: Clarendon Press, 1964), Chapters I and II.

46. For the impact of this system of multilateralism on the economies of developing countries, see Pollard, 'Law and Policy', 18.

47. 'The Future of the Caribbean Community and Common Market' in *The Caribbean Community – Beyond Survival*. Kenneth O. Hall, ed., (Kingston: Ian Randle Publishers, 2000) 622.

48. *Challenges of Capacity Development: Towards Sustainable Reforms of Caribbean Justice Sectors, Volume II: A diagnostic Assessment*, IDB/CGCRD, May 2000 2.

49. *Challenges of Capacity Development: Towards Sustainable Reforms of Caribbean Justice Sectors, Volume II: A diagnostic Assessment*, IDB/CGCRD, May 2000 at p.2.

50. See Article 28 (1) of the Revised Treaty of Chaguaramas.
51. See, for example, Articles 32, 38 and 40 of the Revised Treaty of Chaguaramas signed in Nassau, The Bahamas on July 5, 2001.
52. See Article 239 of the Revised Treaty of Chaguaramas.
53. See Article 35(2) of the Revised Treaty.
54. The CARICOM Legislative Drafting Facility which is headed by the author of this book is currently engaged in drafting amendments to various enactments in order to remove restrictions.
55. See Articles 39 and 40 of the Revised Treaty.
56. See Article 43 (2), 47 and 48 of the Revised Treaty.
57. See Article 211 of the Revised Treaty.
58. See Article 214 of the Revised Treaty which reads as follows:

    > Where a national court or tribunal of a Member State is seised of an issue whose resolution involves a question concerning the interpretation or application of this Treaty, the court or tribunal concerned shall, if it considers that a decision on the question is necessary to enable it to deliver judgment, refer the question to the Court for determination before delivering judgment.

59. Article 177 of the Treaty of Rome reads as follows:

    > 1. The Court of Justice shall have jurisdiction to give preliminary rulings concerning: (a) interpretation of this Treaty; (b) the validity and interpretation of acts of the institutions of the Community; (c) the interpretation of the statutes of bodies established by an act of the Council, where those statutes so provide. 2. Where such a question is raised before any court or tribunal of a Member State, that court or tribunal may, if it considered that a decision on the question is necessary to enable it to give judgment, request the Court of Justice to give a ruling thereon. 3. Where any such question is raised in a case pending before the Court or tribunal of a Member State, against whose decisions there is no judicial remedy under national law, that court or tribunal shall bring the matter before the Court of Justice.

60. See the judgment of Lord Denning in *H.P. Bulmer Ltd. v. J. Bollinger SA* [1974] 2 All ER 1226 at 1235.
61. See Article 217 of the Revised Treaty.
62. See paragraph 3 of Article 212 of the Revised Treaty.
63. Contrast the determinations of the European Court of Justice which 'is not absolutely bound by its previous decisions' per Lord Denning in *H.P. Bulmer Ltd. v. J Bollinger SA* [1974] 2 All ER 1226.
64. See Pollard, 'Law and Policy'.

CHAPTER FIVE

Delinking from the Judicial Committee of the Privy Council

THE JUDICIAL COMMITTEE OF THE PRIVY COUNCIL'S JURISDICTION

The genesis of the jurisdiction of the Judicial Committee of the Privy Council is traceable to the inordinate degree of arrogance associated with the disposition of royal power in the middle ages. Then, the crown was presumed to be an inexhaustible store of justice which legitimised the establishment of royal courts to dispense justice according to the common law of the land. Since the presumption about the inexhaustible supply of justice inhering in the crown appeared to be irrebuttable, a residium of justice was always deemed to be available to the crown, for deployment, as an attribute of royal prerogative, among its privy councillors to address matters of peculiar concern to the crown. Consider in this context royal courts like the infamous Court of Star Chamber which oftentimes ignored the procedural requirements of due process in addressing 'matters of riot or tending to riot, robbery, libel, slander, perjury and offences against royal proclamations'. In effect, matters tending to breaches of the king's peace or prejudicial to royal authority! These so-called prerogative courts came to be identified with instruments of royal oppression and the arbitrary employment of sovereign power, particularly under the Stuart kings, and fell into desuetude around 1689.

But the crown was always perceived to be competent to establish courts from its inexhaustible resources of justice and privy councillors were identified to deal with petitions to the crown, as the ultimate source of justice, as well as appeals from courts in the colonies comprising the British Empire. The latter were addressed by a small committee of privy councillors. Inevitably, this committee of privy councilors, which later came to be known as the Judicial Committee of the Privy Council, was perceived as an indispensable attribute of empire and the judicial symbol of colonialism. By the Judicial Committee Act, 1833, the Committee was formally accorded the status of a special judicial tribunal and determined its composition, procedures and jurisdiction which continues today with appropriate modifications. For a considerable period of its history the determinations of the Judicial Committee of the Privy Council did not admit of dissenting opinions and took the form of advice to the sovereign. The doctrine of *stare decisis* did not apply to its determinations since the royal disposition was subject to change with the vicissitudes of empire.

The jurisdiction of the Judicial Committee of the Privy Council as at March 2000 is as follows:[1]

1. Commonwealth Jurisdiction

Appeals to Her Majesty in Council

An appeal lies from the undermentioned countries and territories in the following circumstances:

(a) By leave of the local Court of Appeal – 'as of right' from final judgments in civil disputes where the value of the dispute is more than a stated amount. Some courts also have discretion to grant leave in interlocutory matters or matters of great public importance or constitutional matters.

(b) By special leave of Her Majesty in Council - usually in criminal cases but sometimes in a civil case where the appellant has failed to comply with the rules regarding leave by the local Court of Appeal, e.g. as to time for applying or lodging security for costs test:

Antigua and Barbuda
Bahamas
Barbados
Belize
Grenada
Jamaica
New Zealand
St. Christopher and Nevis
Saint Lucia
Saint Vincent and the Grenadines
Tuvalu

(c) The Sovereign Base Area of Akrotiri (in Cyprus)

(d) The United Kingdom Overseas Territories, which include -

Anguilla
Bermuda
British Antarctic Territory
British Indian Ocean Territory
British Virgin Islands
Cayman Islands
Falkland Islands
Gibraltar
Montserrat
St. Helena and dependencies
Turks and Caicos Islands

(e) Appeal to local head of state

Brunei

An appeal lies from the Court of Appeal of Brunei to the Sultan and Yang di-Pertuan - in civil cases only. By agreement between Her Majesty and the Sultan these appeals are heard by the Judicial Committee who report their opinion to him instead of to Her Majesty.

(f) Appeals to the Judicial Committee

(i) The Republic of Trinidad and Tobago

(ii) The Commonwealth of Dominica

(iii) Kiribati

(iv) Mauritius

These are independent republics within the Commonwealth and the appeal lies direct to the Judicial Committee. Its Orders are enforceable as orders of the Court of Appeal of the territory concerned. There are provisions for Trinidad and Tobago, Dominica and Mauritius governing the grant of leave by local courts on similar lines to the appeals to Her Majesty in Council (see 1 above) and the Board may grant special leave to appeal. For Kiribati the appeal lies only in constitutional cases affecting a Banaban.

2. Domestic Jurisdictions

(a) The Board hears appeals to Her Majesty in Council:

- (i) From the Courts of Appeal of Jersey and Guernsey and from the Royal Court when sitting in an appellate capacity.
- (ii) From the Isle of Man.
- (iii) From the disciplinary committees (and in the case of some professions also from other committees) of the regulatory bodies of the following professions: medical practitioners, dentists, opticians, veterinary surgeons, osteopaths, chiropractors and professions supplementary to medicine.
- (iv) Against Schemes of the Church Commissioners under the Pastoral Measure 1983.

(b) The Judicial Committee has jurisdiction to hear and determine questions relating to the competences and functions of the legislative and executive authorities established in Scotland and Northern Ireland by the Scotland Act 1998 and the Northern Ireland Act 1998, respectively, and questions as to the competence and functions of the Assembly established by the Government of Wales Act 1998. Cases can reach the Judicial Committee through four routes -

(i) direct references of a Bill of the Scottish Parliament or Northern Ireland Assembly, to be heard in the Judicial Committee as a court of first instance;

(ii) appeals to the Judicial Committee from certain superior courts;

(iii) references from

(a) appellate courts, including the House of Lords, and

(b) any court, made on the application of the appropriate Law Officer;

(iv) references by Law Officers to the Judicial Committee of issues that are not the subject of current legislation or litigation.

When exercising this jurisdiction the Board may consist only of members of the Judicial Committee who hold or have held high judicial office in the United Kingdom.

(c) The Board also has the following rarely used jurisdictions:

(i) Appeals from the Arches Court of Canterbury and the Chancery Court of York in non-doctrinal faculty causes.

(ii) Appeals from Prize Courts.

(iii) Disputes under the House of Commons Disqualification Act.

(iv) Appeals from the Court of Admiralty of the Cinque Ports.

(d) Her Majesty has the power to refer any matter to the Board for "consideration and report" under s.4 of the Judicial Committee Act 1833.

REGIONAL PERSPECTIVES ON DELINKING

Constitutional procedures for delinking from the Judicial Committee of the Privy Council by Member States of the Commonwealth vary according to the requirements of one or another constitution of the State proposing to sever judicial ties with this venerable institution.[2] Indeed, where the severing of judicial links with the Judicial Committee of the Privy Council assumed the dimension of a traumatic rupture by stakeholders in Commonwealth Countries, political demands were made for constitutional procedures which relevant constitutions did not require as appears to be the case in Jamaica. Commonwealth countries severing links with the Judicial Committee of the Privy Council tended to adopt one of two approaches. The first approach was to establish the highest existing domestic court as the final appellate court as were the cases of Canada in 1949 and Australia in 1977. The second approach was to establish a final appellate court like India did in 1950 and Hong Kong did in 1997 and New Zealand currently proposes to do. Where, for example, it was proposed to sever links with the Judicial Committee and to replace this institution with another judicial body as was the case in New Zealand and the Caribbean Community, the relevant enactment required not only delinking provisions but vesting provisions. Where, as was the case of Australia, it was not proposed to maintain the three-tiered system of judicial institutions, only delinking provisions were required since appeals terminated at the domestic appellate level.[3]

An examination of the delinking and vesting constitutional provisions perceived to be required in the countries of the Caribbean Community will serve to confirm the complexity and protracted nature of the process which is required to respond to peculiar, political and psychological conditions. Before addressing some of the provisions of relevant national enactments in this context, however, it is proposed to describe briefly the thrust of the various instruments involved in the process in the Caribbean Community.

In this context, the most important instrument is the constituent instrument of the Caribbean Court of Justice. The Agreement Establishing the Caribbean Court of Justice attempted to achieve several objectives. The primary objective was to establish a municipal court of last resort in substitution for the Judicial Committee of the Privy Council. The other important objective was to create a judicial institution with compulsory and exclusive jurisdiction to hear and determine disputes concerning the interpretation and application of the Revised Treaty of Chaguaramas establishing the Caribbean Community including the CARICOM Single Market and Economy. Consequently, the Caribbean Court of Justice, in the exercise of its original jurisdiction, must be perceived as the institutional centrepiece of the CSME. Of equal importance was the Enabling Act to enact into domestic law in Member States the Agreement Establishing the Caribbean Court of Justice. This Act was also intended to abolish the jurisdiction of the Judicial Committee of the Privy Council and to replace it with the jurisdictions of the Caribbean Court of Justice, both appellate and original. Other important supporting institutions are the Regional Competition Commission and the CARICOM Regional Organisation for Standards and Quality (CROSQ). Some institutions contemplated in this context are expected to address accreditation and intellectual property rights issues. Closely allied to the Agreement Establishing the Caribbean Court of Justice are the Agreement Relating to the Seat of the Caribbean Court of Justice and the Protocol on Privileges and Immunities of the Caribbean Court of Justice and the Regional Judicial and Legal Service Commission. Both of these instruments address the immunities of the Court and Commission as well as the functional immunities and privileges of officials of these institutions and persons required to appear in proceedings before the Court.

Due to legitimate reservations of stakeholders of the Caribbean Court of Justice about the diffidence of the regional political directorate in honouring financial obligations to regional institutions, competent decision-makers were constrained to put in place credible arrangements for financing the Caribbean Court of Justice on a reliable and sustainable basis – hence the Agreement Establishing the Caribbean Court of Justice Trust Fund. This instrument was designed to establish institutional arrangements perceived not only to place the financing of the Court on a sound, sustainable basis, but also beyond the control or political influence of the regional political directorate. In the premises, delinking from the Judicial Committee of the Privy Council by Member States of CARICOM appears to require much more professional and legislative effort than similar initiatives in other parts of the Commonwealth.

Barbados is the only Member State of the Community among those proposing to abolish the jurisdiction of the Judicial Committee of the Privy Council and to make the Caribbean Court of Justice the final appellate court, which has enacted legislation in this behalf. This Act is entitled the Constitution (Amendment) Act 2003 and is to come into operation on a date to be appointed by proclamation. The Act amends sections 24, 27 and 79 of the Constitution of Barbados by substituting the Caribbean Court of Justice for Her Majesty in Council wherever the latter term appears and inserts sections 79B, 79C, 79D, 79E, 79F, 79G, 79H, 79I. The Act also amends sections 80, 84, 87 and 88 of the Constitution of Barbados. Cumulatively, these amendments repeal the jurisdiction of the Judicial Committee of the Privy Council in Barbados, establish a Judicature consisting of the Caribbean Court of Justice, the Supreme Court of Judicature and the Magistrates Court empowered to exercise jurisdiction under the Constitution of Barbados or any other law (Section 79C). The Caribbean Court of Justice is vested with exclusive and compulsory jurisdiction in relation to specified categories of disputes concerning the interpretation and application of the Revised Treaty of Chaguaramas and the CCJ is made the final court of appeal from decisions of the Court of Appeal (Section 79D). The amendments also provide for the constitution of the Caribbean Court of Justice (Section 79E) and for the appointment of the judges thereof (Section 79F); regulate the tenure of the President and other judges of the Caribbean Court of Justice (Section 79G) their removal from office (Section 79H) and retirement (Section 79I).

Although the Act enacts various important provisions of the Agreement Establishing the Caribbean Court of Justice, it does not give the Agreement the force of law in Barbados thereby leaving several obligations assumed under the Agreement unimplemented. Presumably, the Government of Barbados intends to enact additional legislation to address those omissions.

The Draft Enabling Bill prepared by the CARICOM Secretariat and approved by the regional Attorneys General as a model for adoption by the Member States of the Caribbean Community, in addition to vesting the Caribbean Court of Justice with an original jurisdiction in the domestic jurisdiction of Member States, merely substituted the appellate jurisdiction of the Caribbean Court of Justice for that of the Judicial Committee of the Privy Council. In so doing the regional Attorneys General must be seen not to have adopted the recommendation of the West Indian Commission concerning the original jurisdiction of the Court in respect of the Charter of Civil Society whose interpretation and application were recommended to come within the jurisdiction of the Caribbean Court of Justice.[5] In any event, competent decision-makers, contrary to the confident expectation of the West Indian Commission, adopted the Charter of Civil Society as a recommendation of norms and principles as guides for good governance but declined to accord this instrument the status of a treaty. The Draft Enabling Bill also proposed to give the Agreement the force of law in the Member States of the Caribbean Community and provided for the enforcement of decisions of the Caribbean Court of Justice.

CONSTITUTIONAL PROCEDURES FOR DELINKING

The relevant sections of the Constitution of Antigua and Barbuda read as follows:

Section 47 (1):

> Parliament may alter any of the provisions of this Constitution or of the Supreme Court Order in the manner specified in the following provisions of this section.

47 (2):

> A bill to alter this constitution or the Supreme Court Order shall not be regarded as being passed by the House unless on its final reading in the House the bill is supported by the votes of not less than two-thirds of all the members of the House.

Section 47(3):

> An amendment made by the Senate to such a bill as is referred to in subsection (2) of this section that has been passed by the House shall not be regarded as being agreed to by the House for the purpose of section 55 of this Constitution unless such agreement is signified by resolution supported by the votes of not less than two-thirds of all the members of the House.

Section 55 deals with restrictions on the powers of the Senate as to bills other than money bills. It allows bills, which have been passed by the House but rejected by the Senate twice, to be submitted to the Governor-General for assent provided the procedure specified in section 55(2)(b) is followed. Section 55(2)(b) provides:

> A bill such as is referred to in subsection (5) of section 47 of this Constitution shall not be submitted to the Governor-General for his assent unless the provisions of that sub-section have been complied with and the power conferred on the House by this sub-section to resolve that a bill shall not be presented to the Governor-General for assent shall not be exercised in respect of such a bill.

Section 47(4) provides:

> For the purposes of section 55(4) of this Constitution, an amendment of a bill to alter this Constitution or the Supreme Court Order shall not be suggested to the Senate by the House unless a resolution so to suggest the amendment has been supported by the votes of not less than two-thirds of all the members of the House.

Section 55(4) deals with the procedure where a bill which has been sent to the Senate in the preceding session is then going before House and amendments are proposed by the House but not inserted in the bill. These amendments may be considered by the Senate and, if accepted, are treated as amendments made by the Senate and agreed to by the House. Section 47(5) reads:

> A bill to alter this section, *Schedule 1 to this Constitution or any of the provisions of this Constitution specified in Part I of that schedule or any of the provisions of the Supreme Court Order specified in Part II of that schedule shall not be submitted to the Governor-General for his assent unless*:
>
> a. there has been an interval of not less than ninety days between the introduction of the bill in the House and the

> beginning of the proceedings in the House on the second reading of the bill in that House;
>
> b. after it has been passed by both Houses of Parliament or, in the case of a bill to which section 55 of this Constitution applies, after its rejection by the Senate for the second time; and
>
> c. the bill has been approved on a referendum, held in accordance with such provisions as may be made in that behalf by Parliament, by not less than two- thirds of all the votes validly cast.

Chapter IX (sections 119-122) which deals with Judicial Provisions is not listed in Schedule I so the provisions of section 47(5) are not applicable. Section 46(8)(a) provides:

> A bill to alter this Constitution or the Supreme Court Order shall not be submitted to the Governor-General for his assent unless it is accompanied by a certificate under the hand of the Speaker (or, if the Speaker is for any reason unable to exercise the functions of his office, the Deputy Speaker) that the provisions of sub-sections (2), (3) or (4), as the case may be, of this section have been complied with and, where a referendum has been held, a certificate of the Supervisor of Elections stating the results of the referendum.

Section 46(8)(b) provides:

> The certificate of the Speaker or, as the case may be the Deputy Speaker, under this sub-section shall be conclusive that the provisions of sub-sections (2), (3) or (4) of this section have been complied with shall not be enquired into by any court of law.

The procedure for amending the Antiguan Constitution in order to delink from the Judicial Committee of the Privy Council is:

(a) a delay of 90 days between the introduction of the bill in the House and the commencement of proceedings in the House on the second reading of the bill;

(b) a bill passed by two-thirds of the House of Representatives. Either passage by the Senate; or

(c) where the senate has declined to pass the bill in two successive sessions, it is nevertheless passed by the House under section 55(2) of the Constitution;

(d) approval of the bill in a referendum held in accordance with such provisions as may be made in that behalf by Parliament by not less than two-thirds of all the votes validly cast;

(e) presentation of the bill to the Governor-General for his assent along with a certificate of the Speaker or Deputy Speaker of the House that the relevant provisions of sub-sections (2), (3) or (4) of section 47 have been complied with.

The Commonwealth of Dominica has a unicameral legislature. The relevant sections of the Constitution read as follows:

> 42(1) provides: Parliament may alter any of the provisions of this Constitution or of the Supreme Court Order in the manner specified in the following provisions of this section; section 42(2) reads: A bill to alter this section, Schedule 1 to this Constitution or any of the provisions of this Constitution specified in Part I of that Schedule or any of the provisions of the Supreme Court Order specified in Part II of that Schedule shall not be regarded as being passed by the House of Assembly unless on its final reading in the House the bill is supported by the votes of not less than three-quarters of all the elected members of the House; and a bill to alter any of the provisions of this Constitution or, as the case may be, of the Supreme Court Order not so specified shall not be regarded as being passed by the House unless on its final reading in that House the bill is supported by the votes of not less than two-thirds of all the elected members of the House.

Chapter VIII of the Constitution which deals with judicial provisions including appeals to the Privy Council is one of the sections listed in Part I of Schedule I to the Constitution. It is listed in sub-section (vi) and requires the special procedures set out above for amendment. Section 30(1) (a) and (b) of the Constitution provides that the House shall consist of a number of elected representatives and nine senators who may be elected or appointed in accordance with section 34.

Section 34 sets out the procedure for appointment of the senators and provides that Parliament may prescribe that senators may be elected. At the time of writing, information was not available as to whether Parliament had made any provision for the election of senators. As section 42 (2) refers to the votes of elected members, whether or not the senators are elected will be relevant in determining the number of votes needed to pass the bill. Section 42 (3) provides:

> A bill to alter any of the provisions of this Constitution or the Supreme Court Order shall not be submitted to the President for his assent-
>
> a. unless there has been an interval of no less than ninety days between the introduction of the bill in the House of Assembly and the beginning of the proceedings in the House on the second reading of the bill; and
>
> b. if the bill provides for the alteration of this section, Schedule 1 to this Constitution or any other provisions of this Constitution or the Supreme Court Order specified in that Schedule, unless after it has been passed by the House the bill has been approved on a referendum, held in accordance with such provision as may be made in that behalf by Parliament, by a majority of the votes validly cast on that referendum.

Section 42(4) provides:

> The provisions of paragraph (b) of subsection (3) of this section shall not apply in relation to any bill to alter-
>
> a. section 106 of this Constitution in order to give effect to any agreement between Dominica and the United Kingdom concerning appeals from any court having jurisdiction in Dominica to the Judicial Committee;
>
> b. any of the provisions of the Supreme Court Order in order to give effect to any international agreement to which Dominica is a party relating to the Supreme Court or any other court (or any office or authority having functions in respect of any such court) constituted in common for Dominica and for other countries also parties to the agreement.

The procedure for amending the Constitution in Dominica in order to delink from the Judicial Committee of the Privy Council is as follows:

(a) a relevant agreement between the Commonwealth of Dominica and the United Kingdom;

(b) a delay of 90 days between the introduction of the bill in the House and the commencement of proceedings in the House on the second reading of the bill;

(c) a bill passed on its final reading with the support of at least three-quarters of the elected Members of the House;

(d) on presentation to the President for his assent the bill is accompanied by a certificate of the Speaker or Deputy Speaker that the provisions of sub-sections (2) and (3) of section 42 have been complied with. Section 42 (7) deals with the requirement of a Speaker's certificate.

There is no requirement for a referendum in accordance with section 42(4)(a) if one accepts an interpretation of this section that includes an agreement between Dominica and the United Kingdom to terminate the Privy Council's appellate jurisdiction. Because the requirements of a certificate from the Speaker or the Deputy Speaker are identical in the OECS constitutions, the text will not be reproduced, but the relevant sections will be noted.

The events of Grenada's recent past, in particular the status of the different legal regimes which operated in the country, may still have some implications for the position of the Privy Council and any replacement of that body. The academic discussions of Caribbean jurists, such as Francis Alexis and Simeon McIntosh and Dr. Kenny Anthony have identified the issues involved. The identification of the Constitution's provisions below is without prejudice to this issue and does not identify any other laws, for example, the People's laws which may be applicable. The applicable sections are as follows: Section 39(1) provides:

> Parliament may alter any of the provisions of this Constitution or of the Courts Order or section 3 of the West Indies Associated States (Appeals to Privy Council) Order 1967(a) in the manner specified in the following provisions of this section.

Section 39(2) provides:

> A bill to alter this Constitution or the Courts Order or section 3 of the West Indies Associated States (Appeals to Privy Council) Order 1967 shall not be regarded as being passed by the House of Representatives unless on its final reading in that House the bill is supported by the votes of not less than two-thirds of all the members of the House.

Section 39(3) provides:

> An amendment made by the Senate to such a bill that has been passed by the House of Representatives shall not be regarded as being agreed to by the House of Representatives for the purpose of section 48 of this Constitution unless such agreement is signified by resolution supported by the votes of not less than two-thirds of all the members of the House of Representatives.

Section 39(4) provides:

> For the purposes of section 48(4) of this Constitution, an amendment of a bill to alter this Constitution or the Courts Order or section 3 of the West Indies Associated States (Appeals to Privy Council) Order 1967 shall not be suggested to the Senate by the House of Representatives unless a resolution so to suggest the amendment has been supported by the votes of not less than two-thirds of all the members of the House of Representatives.

Section 48 deals with the power of the House to pass a bill other than a money bill which has been approved by the House but rejected by the Senate in two successive sessions. While sub-section (4) deals with the case where the House proposes amendments to a bill without inserting them and sends them to the Senate for consideration and the power of the Senate to adopt these amendments as if they emanated from there. Section 39(5) provides:

> A bill to alter this section, Schedule 1 to this Constitution or any of the provisions of this Constitution specified in Part I of that Schedule or any of the provisions of the Courts Order specified in Part II of that Schedule or section 3 of the West Indies Associated States (Appeals to Privy Council) Order 1967 shall not be submitted to the Governor for his assent unless-
>
> a. there has been an interval of not less than ninety days between the introduction of the bill in the House of Representatives and the beginning of the proceedings in the House on the second reading of the bill in that House ;
>
> b. after it has been passed by both Houses of Parliament or, in the case of a bill to which section 48 of this Constitution applies, after its rejection by the Senate for the second time; and
>
> c. the bill has been approved on a referendum, held in accordance with such provision as may be made in that behalf by Parliament, by not less than two-thirds of all the votes validly cast on that referendum.

It is the reference to the West Indies Associated States (Appeals to the Privy Council) Order 1967 that will trigger the provisions of sub-section (5) of section 39 rather than the reference to Schedule I of the Constitution. Because although Chapter VIII which deals with Judicial Provisions is found in Part I subsection vi of Schedule I, section 104 which addresses appeals as of right to the Privy Council is specifically excluded from this Schedule I. The position is different from that in the other OECS constitutions. Again, it is not stated by which majority must the Senate adopt the bill. The procedure for amending the Constitution in Grenada in order to delink from the Judicial Committee of the Privy Council, subject to the provisos which appear at the beginning of this section is:

(a) A delay of at least ninety days between the introduction of the bill and the beginning of proceedings in the House on the second reading of the bill.

(b) The passing of the bill by both Houses of Parliament with the requirement that at least two-thirds of the members of the House vote in support; or approval by the House, according to section 48, where the bill has been rejected twice by the Senate.

(c) The bill has been approved in a referendum by two-thirds of all the votes validly cast.

(d) On submission to the Governor-General for his assent, the bill is accompanied by a certificate of the Speaker or Deputy Speaker as provided in section 39(8) stating that the provisions of sub-section (2), (3) or (4) of section 39 have been complied with; as well as a certificate from the Supervisor of Elections stating the results of the referendum'.

St. Kitts and Nevis has a unicameral legislature for the two islands. The applicable sections are: Section 38(2) which provides:

> A bill to alter any of the provisions of this Constitution or of the Supreme Court Order shall not be regarded as being passed by the National Assembly unless, on its final reading, the bill is supported by the votes of not less than two-thirds of all the representatives.

Representatives here refer to the elected members only of the Assembly. Section 38 (3) provides:

> A bill to alter this section, Schedule I to this Constitution or any of the provisions of this Constitution specified in Part I of that schedule or any of the provisions of the Supreme Court Order specified in Part II of that schedule shall not be submitted to the Governor-General for his assent unless-

> (a) there has been an interval of not less than ninety days between the introduction of the bill in the National Assembly and the beginning of the proceedings in the Assembly on the second reading of the bill; and
>
> (b) after it has been passed by the Assembly the bill has been approved on a referendum by not less than two-thirds of all the votes validity cast on that referendum in the island of Saint Christopher and two-thirds of all the votes validly cast on that referendum in the island of Nevis.

Section 38(4) provides:

> The provisions of paragraph (b) of subsection (3) shall not apply in relation to any bill to alter-
>
> (a) section 99 in order to give effect to any agreement between Saint Christopher and Nevis and the United Kingdom concerning appeals from any court having jurisdiction in Saint Christopher and Nevis to Her Majesty in Council;
>
> (b) any of the provisions of the Supreme Court Order in order to give effect to any international agreement of which Saint Christopher and Nevis is a party relating to the Supreme Court or any other court of law (or any officer or authority having functions in respect of any such court) constituted in common for Saint Christopher and Nevis and for other countries also parties to the agreement.

Therefore, the procedure for amending the Constitution in St. Christopher and Nevis to delink from the Judicial Committee of the Privy Council will be –

(a) A relevant agreement between St. Kitts and Nevis and the British Government.

(b) A delay of at least 90 days between the introduction of the bill in the National Assembly and the beginning of proceedings in the Assembly on the second reading of the bill.

(c) The passing of a bill supported on its final reading by at least two-thirds of the elected members of the Assembly.

(d) When the bill is presented to the Governor-General for his assent, there is also a certificate from the Speaker or Deputy Speaker as required by section 38(10) stating that sub-sections (2) and (3)(a) of Section 38 have been complied with.

Nevis has a separate Assembly which is created by section 104 of the Constitution. However, for amendment to the Constitution, it is the National Assembly which has the authority.

For Saint Lucia, the relevant constitutional provisions are: Section 41(1) which reads 'Parliament may alter any of the provisions of this Constitution or of the Supreme Court Order in the manner specified in the following provisions of this section.' Section 41(2) provides:

> A bill to alter this section, Schedule 1 to this Constitution or any of the provisions of this Constitution specified in Part 1 of that Schedule or any of the provisions of the Supreme Court Order specified in Part II of that Schedule shall not be regarded as being passed by the House unless on its final reading in the House the bill is supported by the votes of not less than three-quarters of all the members of the House.

Section 41(3) provides

> A bill to alter any of the provisions of this Constitution, as the case may be, of the Supreme Court Order other than those referred to in subsection (2) of this section shall not be regarded as being passed by the House unless on its final reading in the House the bill is supported by the votes of not less than two-thirds of all the members of the House.

Chapter VIII of the Constitution (Judicial Provisions) is listed in sub-section (vi) in Part I of Schedule I to the Constitution. This means that a vote of at least three-quarters of the House is needed to amend this section of the Constitution. Section 41(4) provides:

> An amendment made by the Senate to a bill to which subsection (2) of this section applies shall not be regarded as being agreed to by the House for the purposes of section 50 of this Constitution unless such agreement is signified by resolution supported by the votes of not less than three-quarters of all the members of the House.

Section 41(5) reads:

> Any amendment made by the Senate to a bill to which subsection (3) of this section applies shall not be regarded as being agreed to by the House for the purposes of section 50 of this Constitution unless such agreement is signified by resolution supported by the votes of not less than two-thirds of all the members of the House.

Section 41(6) provides:

> A bill to alter any of the provisions of this Constitution or the Supreme Court Order shall not be submitted to the Governor-General for his assent –

(a) unless there has been an interval of not less than ninety days between the introduction of the bill in the House and the beginning of the proceedings in the House on the second reading of the bill; and

(b) if the bill provides for the alteration of this section, Schedule 1 to this Constitution or any of the provisions of this Constitution or the Supreme Court Order specified in that Schedule, unless after it has been passed by the Senate and the House or, in the case of a bill to which section 50 of this Constitution applies after its rejection by the Senate for the second time, the bill has been approved on a referendum, held in accordance with such provision as may be made in that behalf by Parliament, by a majority of the votes validly cast on that referendum.

Section 47(7) provides:

The provisions of paragraph (b) of subsection (6) of this section shall not apply in relation to any bill to alter –

(a) section 108 of this Constitution in order to give effect to any agreement between Saint Lucia and the United Kingdom concerning appeals from any court having jurisdiction in Saint Lucia to Her Majesty in Council;

(b) any of the provisions of the Supreme Court Order in order to give effect to any international agreement to which Saint Lucia is a party relating to the Supreme Court or any other court (or any officer or authority having functions in respect of any such court) constituted in common for Saint Lucia and for other countries also parties to the agreement.

Section 50 deals with the procedure where the Senate rejects twice in succession any bill other than a money bill which has been passed by the House.

The procedure for amending the Saint Lucian Constitution in order to delink from the Judicial Council of the Privy Council is as follows:

(a) a relevant agreement between the Government of Saint Lucia and the United Kingdom;

(b) a delay of at least 90 days between the introduction of the bill in the House and the beginning of proceedings in the House on the second reading of the bill;

(c) the approval of the bill by at least three-quarters of the members of the House and by an unspecified majority in the

Senate; or where the Senate has declined in two successive sessions to pass the bill, approval by the House according to section 50;

(d) when the bill is presented to the Governor-General for his assent, as provided in section 41(1) and there is also a certificate by the Speaker or Deputy Speaker that the provisions of subsections (2), (3), (4) or (5) of section 41 have been complied with.

St. Vincent and the Grenadines also has a unicameral legislature. The relevant provisions are: Section 38(1)

> Parliament may alter any of the provisions of this Constitution or of the Supreme Court Order in the manner specified in the following provisions of this section.

Section 38 (2) provides:

> A bill to alter any of the provisions of this Constitution or of the Supreme Court Order shall not be regarded as being passed by the House unless on its final reading the bill is supported by the votes of not less than two-thirds of all the Representatives.

Section 38 (3) reads:

> A bill to alter this section, the Schedule to this Constitution or any of the Provisions of this Constitution specified in Part 1 of that Schedule or any of the provisions of the Courts Order specified in Part 2 of that Schedule shall not be submitted to the Governor-General for his assent unless-
>
> (a) there has been an interval of not less than ninety days between the introduction of the bill in the House and the beginning of the proceedings in the House on the second reading of the bill; and
>
> (b) after it has been passed by the House the bill has been approved on a referendum by not less than two-thirds of all the votes validly cast on that referendum.

Representatives refer to the elected members of the House, the votes of the six appointed Senators are not essential to the amendment process.

Section 38(7) provides:

> The conduct of any referendum for the purposes of this section shall be the responsibility of the Supervisor of Elections and the provisions of subsections (4), (5) and (6) of section 34 of this

> Constitution shall apply in relation to the exercise by the Supervisor of Elections or by any other officer of his functions with respect to a referendum as they apply in relation to the exercise of his functions with respect to elections of Representatives.

38(8)(a) reads:

> A bill to alter any of the provisions of this Constitution or of the Supreme Court Order shall not be submitted to the Governor-General for his assent unless it is accompanied by a certificate under the hand of the Speaker that the provisions of subsection (2) of this section have been complied with and, where a referendum has been held in pursuance of subsection (3)(b) of this section, by a certificate under the hand of the Supervisor of Elections stating the results of the referendum.

The procedure for amending Saint Vincent and the Grenadines' Constitution in order to delink from the Judicial Committee of the Privy Council will be:

(a) the approval of the bill by a two-thirds majority of the elected members;

(b) on presentation to the Governor-General for his assent, the bill must be accompanied by the Speaker's or Deputy Speaker's certificate specifying that in Saint Vincent and the Grenadines' case, sub-section (2) of section 38 has been complied with.

All of the OECS States' Constitutions have delaying provisions and require a Speaker's certificate of compliance in order to amend their constitutions. Thereafter, there are differences, two countries – possibly Grenada and St. Vincent and the Grenadines – must hold a referendum in order to go forward with the proposed amendment. The four other countries have provisions which oust the requirement for a referendum when the amendment relates to the jurisdiction of the Privy Council. Each State requires a qualified majority vote of either two-thirds or three quarters of elected representatives to pass this bill. Where there are two separate chambers in the Parliament, the majority required by the Senate to pass the bill has not been specified. As noted earlier in this case, it may be argued that the required vote in the Senate is that of an absolute majority, which is the smallest of special majority votes which may be required to amend constitutions in the Region. Also, wherever the Senate exists as a separate chamber, the House of Representatives is empowered to override the Senate's refusal to pass such a bill if the rejection occurs in two successive sessions of the Senate.

OTHER COMMON LAW COUNTRIES

The relevant provisions of the Bahamas Constitution are: Article 52 (2)

> Subject to the provisions of Articles 60, 61 and 62 of this Constitution, the power of Parliament to make laws shall be exercised by Bills passed by both Houses, either without amendment or with such amendments only as are agreed to by both Houses, and assented to by the Governor General in accordance with Article 63 of this Constitution.

Article 54(1) reads:

> Subject to the provisions of this Article, Parliament may, by an Act of Parliament passed by both Houses, alter any of the provisions of this Constitution or (in so far as it forms part of the law of the Bahamas) any of the provisions of The Bahamas Independence Act, 1973.

Article 105 deals with the jurisdiction of the Privy Council and in subsection 3 provides that

> Parliament may by law provide for the functions of this chapter to be exercised by the Judicial Committee of Her Majesty's Privy Council to be exercised by any other court established for that purpose in substitution for the Judicial Committee.

Article 54 (3) provides:

> In so far as it alters –
>
> (a) this Article;
>
> (b) Articles 2, 3, 4, 5, 6, 7, 8, 9, 10, 11, 12, 13, 14, 15, 16, 17, 18, 19, 20, 21, 22, 23, 24, 25, 26, 27, 28, 29, 30, 31, 38, 39, 40, 45, 46, 51, 52, 60, 61, 62, 65, 66, 67, 68, 69, 70, 71, 72, 93, 94, 95, 96, 97, 98, 99, 100, 101, 102, 103, 104, or 105 of this Constitution; or
>
> (c) Articles 106, 127 or 137 of this Constitution in their application to any of the provisions specified in sub-paragraphs (a) or (b) of this paragraph; or

> (d) any of the provision of the Bahamas Independence Act 1973, a Bill for an Act of Parliament under this Article shall not be passed by Parliament unless: -
>
> (i) at the final voting thereon in each House it is supported by the votes of nor less than three-quarters of all the members of each House, and
>
> (ii) the Bill, after its passage through both Houses has been submitted to the electors qualified to vote for the elections of members of the House of Assembly and, on a vote taken in such manner as Parliament may prescribe the majority of the electors voting have approved the Bill.

Article 54(5) reads : 'No Act of Parliament shall be construed as altering this Constitution unless it is stated in the Act that it is an Act for that purpose.' Article 63(3) provides:

> Any Bill to which Article 54(2) or (3) of this Constitution applies shall be presented to the Governor-General endorsed with certificates of the requisite majorities in accordance with whichever of those paragraphs applies to the Bill, and with a certificate of the Parliamentary Registrar that it has been approved by the majority of the electors voting on the Bill.

Therefore, the procedure for amending the Constitution in the Bahamas in order to delink from the Judicial Committee of the Privy Council is:

(a) the approval of the bill by a vote of at least three-quarters of the members of each House;

(b) a recital in the bill that it is intended to amend the Constitution;

(c) on presentation to the Governor-General for his assent, the bill is endorsed with certificates of the Speaker and the President of the Senate that it has been passed by the required three-quarters majority;

(d) certificate by the Parliamentary Registrar that the majority of voters approve the bill.

The applicable provisions of the Barbados Constitution are:

Section 49(2)

> Subject to the provision of subsection (3), a Bill for an Act of Parliament under this section that alters any of the following provisions, that is to say -

> a. this section and section 1;
>
> b. Chapter II;
>
> c. Chapter III;
>
> d. section 28, 32, 35 to 39, 41, 42, 48, 60(2), 61, 62, 63 and 76 to 79 (other than subsection (7) of section 79);
>
> e. Chapter VII (other than section 83);
>
> f. Chapter VIII;
>
> g. Chapter IX;
>
> h. any provision of Chapter X in its application to any of the provisions specified in paragraphs (a) to (g),
>
> shall not be passed in either House unless at the final voting thereon in the House it is supported by the votes of not less than two-thirds of all the members of the House.

Section 49(3) reads:

> Sub-section (2) shall not apply to a Bill in so far as it alters any of the provisions specified in that subsection for the purpose of giving effect to arrangements for the federation or union of Barbados with any other part of the Commonwealth or for the establishment of some other form of constitutional association between Barbados and any other part of the Commonwealth.

Section 49 (4) reads:

> A Bill for an Act of Parliament under this section to which subsection (2) does not apply shall not be passed in either House unless at the final voting thereon in the House it is supported by the votes of a majority of all the members of the House.

Section 49 (6) provides:

> No Act of Parliament shall be construed as altering this Constitution unless it is stated in the Act that it is an Act for that purpose.

58(1) reads: 'A Bill shall not become law until the Governor General has assented thereto in Her Majesty's name and on Her Majesty's behalf and has signed it in token of such assent.'

The procedure for amending the Constitution of Barbados is:

(a) The approval of the bill on the final vote by at least two-thirds of the members of the House and the Senate;

(b) A recital in the bill that it is intended to amend the Constitution.

(c) Presentation of the bill to the Governor-General for his assent.

It would appear that the procedure for amending the Constitution in Barbados is one of the simplest in the Region. The requirement for two-thirds of the vote in each House represents the deepest level of entrenchment in the Barbados constitution.

The relevant provisions of the Belize Constitution are: Section 69 (1) which reads:

> The National Assembly may alter any of the provisions of this Constitution in the manner specified in the following provisions of this section.

Section 69(2) provides:

> Until after the first general election held after Independence Day a Bill to alter any of the provisions of this Constitution shall not be regarded as being passed by the National Assembly unless on its final reading in each House the Bill is supported by the unanimous vote of all member of that House.

Section 69(3)

> A Bill to alter this section, Schedule 2 to this Constitution or any of the provisions of this Constitution specified in that Schedule shall not be regarded as being passed by the House of Representatives unless on its final reading in the House the Bill is supported by the votes of not less than three-quarters of all the members of the House.

Judicial provisions, including section 104 which provide for appeals to the Privy Council are found in Part VII of the Constitution, which is listed as sub-section (3) of Schedule 2. It is curious that sub-section (2) of section 69 clearly indicates that before the first elections held after Independence, a specific vote was required in the Senate in order to amend the Constitution. After this time, according to section 69(3), there is no indication that a vote in the Senate is required to validly amend the Constitution. Sub-section (3) only refers to a vote of the members of the House of Representatives. The Belizean Constitution is similar to those in OECS countries with a bicameral legislature, both in time and its provisions. In those countries, a Senate vote is required even if a Senate veto can be overridden by the House. This issue may require further consideration.

Section 69(5) provides:

> A Bill to alter any of the provisions of this Constitution referred to in subsection (3) of this section shall not be submitted to the Governor General for his assent unless there has been an interval of not less than ninety days between the introduction of the Bill in the House of Representatives and the beginning of the proceedings in the House on the second reading of the Bill.

Section 69(6) provides:

> A bill to alter any of the provisions of this Constitution shall not be submitted to the Governor General for his assent unless it is accompanied by a certificate of the Speaker signed by him that the provisions of subsection (2), (3) or (4) of this section, as the case may be, have been complied with.

The procedure for the amendment of the Constitution of Belize is:

(a) a delay of 90 days between the introduction of the bill in the House and the beginning of proceedings in the House on the second reading of the bill;

(b) a vote in support of the bill by three-quarters of all the members of the House on the final reading of the bill;

(c) on submission to the Governor-General for his assent, the bill is accompanied by a certificate by the Speaker or Deputy Speaker that sub-section (3) of section 69 has been complied with.

As Guyana is the only country which does not have a two-tiered appeal system, the amendment to the Constitution will add to, rather than alter the existing appellate structure. Also, Guyana is another country with a unicameral legislature. The relevant provisions of the Guyana Constitution are: Article 66: 'Subject to the special procedure set out in Article 164, Parliament may alter this Constitution'. Article 164(1):

> Subject to the provisions of paragraphs (2) and (3), a Bill for an Act or Parliament to alter this Constitution shall not be passed by the National Assembly unless it is supported at the final voting in the Assembly by the votes of a majority of all the elected members of the Assembly.

Article 164(2):

> A Bill to alter any of the following provisions of this Constitution, that is to say - Articles . . . 120 to 163 inclusive,

> but excepting Article 132) . . . shall not be submitted to the President for his assent unless the Bill, not less than two and not more than six months after its passage through the National Assembly, has, in such manner as Parliament may prescribe, been submitted to vote of the electors qualified to vote in an election and has been approved by a majority of the electors who vote on the Bill:
>
> Provided that if the Bill does not alter any of the provisions mentioned in subparagraph (a) and is supported at the final voting in the Assembly by the votes of not less than two-thirds of all the elected members of the Assembly it shall not be necessary to submit the Bill to the vote of the electors.

The applicable provision is section 133 which deals with appeals from the High Court. The procedure for amending the Guyanese Constitution is:

(a) approval of the bill by the votes of at least two-thirds of all the elected members of the Assembly;

(b) submission of the bill to the President for his assent.

The provision of the Jamaica Constitution which deals with appeals to the Privy Council is section 110. The relevant provisions for the amendment of the Jamaican Constitution are Section 49(1) and (4).

Section 49(1):

> Subject to the provisions of this section Parliament may by Act of Parliament passed by both Houses alter any of the provisions of this Constitution or (in so far as it forms part of the law of Jamaica) any of the provisions of the Jamaica Independence Act, 1962.

Section 49(4):

> A Bill for an Act of Parliament under this section shall not be deemed to be passed in either House unless at the final vote thereon it is supported-
>
> a. in the case of a Bill which alters any of the provisions specified in subsection (2) or subsection (3) of this section by the votes of not less than two-thirds of all the members of that House, or
>
> b. in any other case by the votes of a majority of all the members of that House.

Section 61(3) provides:

> In every Bill presented to the Governor-General for assent under section 49 of this Constitution, the words of enactment shall be as follows: "Be it enacted by The Queen's Most Excellent Majesty, by and with the advice and consent of the Senate and the House of Representatives of Jamaica (or of the House of Representatives of Jamaica, as the case may be) in accordance with the provisions of section 49 of the Constitution of Jamaica, and by the authority of the same, as follows . . ."

The procedure for amending the Jamaican Constitution is:

(a) the bill is approved by a majority of votes in each House;

(b) the bill is submitted to the Governor-General for his assent endorsed with the words of enactment required by section 61(3).

Section 49(2) sets out the provisions of the constitution which are heavily entrenched. These do not include section 110 which deals with the jurisdiction of the Privy Council. It appears that the procedure for amending the Jamaican Constitution in this case will be the simplest one identified.

The relevant provisions in the Trinidad and Tobago Constitution are Section 54(1) and 54(3).

Section 54(1)

> Subject to the provisions of this section, Parliament may alter any of the provisions of this Constitution or (in so far as it forms part of the laws of Trinidad and Tobago) any of the provisions of the Trinidad and Tobago Independence Act, 1962.

Section 54(3):

> In so far as it alters-
>
> a. this section;
>
> b. sections 22, 23, 24, 26, 28 to 34, 38 to 40, 46, 49(1), 51, 55, 61, 63, 64, 68, 69, 71, 72, 87 to 91, 93, 96(4) and (5), 97, 109, 115, 138, 139 or the Second and Third Schedules;
>
> c. section 3 in its application to any of the provisions specified in paragraph (a) or (b); or
>
> d. any of the provisions of the Trinidad and Tobago Independence Act, 1962.

A Bill for an Act under this section shall not be passed by Parliament unless it is supported at the final vote thereon-

i. in the House of Representatives by the votes of not less than three-fourths of all the members of the House; and

ii. in the Senate by the votes of not less than two-thirds of all the members of the Senate.

Section 54 (5) provides:

> No Act other than an Act making provision for any particular case or class of case, inconsistent with provisions of this Constitution, not being those referred to in subsections (2) and (3), shall be construed as altering any of the provisions of this Constitution, or (in so far as it forms part of the law of Trinidad and Tobago) any of the provisions of the Trinidad and Tobago Independence Act, 1962, unless it is stated in the Act that it is an Act for that purpose.

Section 109 deals with appeals to the Privy Council.

The procedure for amending the Constitution of Trinidad and Tobago is:

(a) the approval of a bill by a vote of at least three-quarters of all the members of the House and at least two-thirds of the members of the Senate;

(b) the recital in the bill of the intention to amend the Constitution;

(c) submission of the bill to the President for his assent.

THE CIVIL LAW COUNTRIES

The differences in the civil law systems will raise specific issues if and when these countries opt to become members of the Court in the exercise of its appellate jurisdiction. At this time, there is insufficient information on this subject. The constitutional provisions are, therefore, cited with the understanding that a further evaluation will have to be undertaken regarding the issues raised by the membership of these countries.

Chapters IV and V of the Haitian Constitution deal with the judiciary and the court system set out in Articles 173 to 190. Article 173 provides:

> The Judicial Power shall be vested in the Supreme Court (Cour de Cassation), the Courts of Appeal, Courts of First Instance, Courts of Peace and special courts, whose number,

> composition, organization, operation and jurisdiction are set by law.

In addition, there is an entity known as the High Court of Justice, described in Article 185 which reads:

> The Senate may constitute itself as a High Court of Justice. The proceedings of this Court are presided over by the President of the Senate, assisted by the President and Vice President of the Supreme Court as Vice President and Secretary, respectively, except where the Justices of the Supreme Court and officers of the Public Prosecutor's Office assigned to that court are involved in the accusation, in which case, the Senators, one of whom shall be designated by the accused, and the Senators so appointed shall not be entitled to vote.

The amendment procedure is found in Articles 282 to 284 which read as follows: Article 282:

> On the recommendation, with reason given to support it, of one of the two (2) Houses or of the Executive Branch, the Legislature may declare that the Constitution should be amended.

Article 282(1) provides:

> This declaration must be supported by two-thirds (2/3) of each of the two (2) Houses. It may be made only in the course of the last Regular Session of the Legislative period and shall be published immediately throughout the territory.

Article 283 provides:

> At the first session of the following legislative period, the Houses shall meet in a National Assembly and decide on the proposed amendment.

Article 284(1) reads:

> No decision of the National Assembly may be taken without a majority of two-thirds (2/3) of the votes cast.

Article 284(2) reads:

> The amendment passed may enter into effect only after installation of the next elected President. In no case may the President under the Government that approved the amendment benefit from any advantages deriving therefrom.

Article 284(4):

> General elections to amend the Constitution by referendum are strictly forbidden.

The procedure for amending the Haitian Constitution appears to be:

(a) The legislature may declare on the recommendation of one of the two Houses or the Executive that the Constitution should be amended.

(b) The declaration must be supported by two-thirds of the members of each House and can only be made during the last regular session of the legislature. If supported, the declaration must be immediately published throughout the country.

(c) The proposed amendment will be examined in the first session of the new sitting of the legislature, during which the two Houses shall combine to form a National Assembly. The National Assembly must have two-thirds of the members of each House present to sit and deliberate on the amendment. Similarly, any decision on the amendment must be taken by a vote of two-thirds of the votes cast.

(d) The procedure which is equivalent to the Governor-General assenting to a bill is not clear. Perhaps the President signs the bill. However, the amendment only becomes effective when a newly elected President is installed. This suggests that there may be a delay of two years or more before an amendment may become effective.

Sections 138 to 146 of the Suriname Constitution deal with the court structure. There may have been some difficulty in the translation of these provisions.

Section 139 provides: 'The supreme body of the Judicial Power entrusted with the administration of justice is called the Court of Justice of Suriname. The Court shall supervise the regular course and settlement of all lawsuits.' Article 144 (The Constitutional Court) reads as follows:

> 1. An organ that is entrusted with judging the constitutionality of legal rules and measures shall be created by law.
>
> 2. The composition, tasks and jurisdiction of this organ shall be regulated by law.

As this court is established by an ordinary law, presumably its existence could be terminated by the repeal of this law.

The amending procedure is found in Article 72 which provides: 'Without prejudice to what is reserved elsewhere in the Constitution for regulation by law, the following subjects shall certainly be determined by law:

(a) Treaties, subject to what is determined in article 104;

(b) The amending of the Constitution;

(c) ...' (this section ends at sub-section (g)).

Therefore, the procedure for amending the Constitution of Suriname is set out in an ordinary law of Parliament. This legislation was not available at the time of writing so the specific provisions cannot be identified.

NOTES

1. Reprinted with permission from the Commonwealth Secretariat.
2. These procedures vary from a simple majority in Parliament in Jamaica to a qualified two-thirds majority in Parliament accompanied by a two-thirds majority vote in a national referendum.
3. See *Australia's Experience in Abolishing Privy Council Appeals*: Paper prepared for the Commonwealth Expert Group Meeting on Replacement of Appeals to the Privy Council, London, June 10-13, 2003 by the Commonwealth of Australia, p.3.
4. This appeared to be the position in Jamaica where delinking from the Judicial Committee of the Privy Council required a simple majority vote in the Parliament but diehard supporters of this institution were demanding a national referendum to determine the issue. Similar sentiments were expressed in other Member States of the Caribbean Community, like Dominica and St. Kitts and Nevis.
5. See *Time for Action Report of the West Indian Commission*, Black Rock, Barbados, 1992 p.500.

CHAPTER SIX

The Caribbean Court of Justice in International Law

THE CARIBBEAN COURT OF JUSTICE IN INTERNATIONAL LAW

Evaluation of the Caribbean Court of Justice as an institution in international law has to address both the juridical personality of the Court as well as the dual status of this institution, which, on the one hand, is a municipal tribunal, and, on the other, an international tribunal required to apply rules of international law for the resolution of disputes touching on the interpretation and application of an international instrument, namely, the Treaty establishing the Caribbean Community including the CARICOM Single Market and Economy.[1] For present purposes, international law will be construed to mean the corpus of norms generally recognised as regulating interstate intercourse as well as the conduct of collectivities of states or inter-governmental institutions in their mutual interactions. This body of norms also regulates their interface with other subjects of international law, such as private entities and individuals who have been accorded a measure of recognition in terms of espousing international claims. Whether or not the determinations of the Caribbean Court of Justice will be seen as generating or complementing general rules of international law or creating a body of regional norms applicable to the Member States of the Caribbean Community in their normal interface, like the Calvo doctrine, only the future will tell. But, as mentioned in Chapter Four the norms applicable to the Member States of the Caribbean Community are unlikely to have the *sui generis* status of 'Community law' issuing from the institutions of the European Union as a supranational entity and creating a normative regime recognised by the European Court of Justice and the courts of the Member States of the European Union as being superior to their own national law.[2]

The international instruments which speak to the juridical personality of the Court and Commission are the Agreement Establishing the Caribbean Court of Justice, the Protocol to the Agreement Establishing the Caribbean Court of Justice Relating to the Juridical Personality and Legal Capacity of the Court, the Agreement Establishing the Seat of the Caribbean Court of Justice and the Offices of the Regional Judicial and Legal Services Commission, and the Protocol on Privileges and Immunities of the Caribbean Court of Justice and the Regional Judicial and Legal Services Commission. Related instruments are the Agreement Establishing the Caribbean Court of Justice Trust Fund and the Vesting Deed of the Caribbean Court of Justice Trust Fund. On the advice of the Caribbean Development Bank, consideration is being given to incorporating the provisions of the Vesting Deed in the regulations of the Trust Fund in order to assimilate the applicable law.[3] These instruments impact variously on the Court and Commission, but at the end of the day the objective was to create a Court which was seen to be free from political control. All of these instruments to a greater or lesser degree contribute to the independence of the Court and the Commission. In this connection, it is useful to remember that independence of judicial institutions speaks to institutional arrangements and composition of these bodies, as distinct from integrity which speak to personal character attributes.

As an international tribunal, applying rules of international law in interpreting and applying the Revised Treaty, the Caribbean Court of Justice will be required to employ norms applicable to third states in such areas as subsidies and anti-dumping and rules of competition, all of which are addressed in relevant provisions of the Revised Treaty. All of these rules are based on international instruments currently forming part of the World Trade Organization regime or rules of law generally accepted in the international community. Of course, the constituent instrument of the Caribbean Community also contains rules peculiar to relations of the parties to the regime and not generally applicable to third states. It is also likely that norms developed and applied in the European Union relating to the rights of establishment, to provide services and to move capital in trans-border transactions will have considerable influence on determinations of the Caribbean Court of Justice which, like the European Court of Justice and European Court of First Instance, cannot be insensitive to the existence of two systems of law in the operational environment – the common law system and the civil law system, even though international norms apply equally to both systems. Where situations arise for which no generally applicable rules of international law are known to exist, the Treaty requires the Court to provide a solution, presumably by reference to general principles of law applied by states,[4] subscribing to both the civil law and common law traditions.

However, with the rapid convergence of values of both an economic and humanitarian genre, it does appear to be the subject of a reasonable assumption that the tension in norms applicable to jurisdictions of differing cultural orientation will be relieved and that juridical dissonance between the jurisdictions of North and South will diminish. But such dissonance may never disappear due to inherent divergencies in religious, ethical and moral imperatives and the disposition of human kind to hold firm to traditional values. Consequently, the Caribbean Court of Justice in the exercise of its original jurisdiction would be expected to weigh the regional interest against third party interests in determining the applicability of international norms to regional intercourse. And this is to be expected since many of the norms sought to be applied in interstate conduct emanate from older sovereignties, reflect the values and experiences of those sovereignties and which may not be appropriate for the needs of newly emerging states. A case in point relates to the rules of competition which were forged in an environment qualitatively and quantitatively different from those of emerging states and which may remain alien to occupants of newly emerging states for considerable periods of time, if not, forever. And, legal principles tend to assume a different dimension when applied to different societies. In the premises, fundamental adjustments or revision of such norms, would be necessary to make them amenable to less economically advanced societies.

Norms of conduct are necessarily the product of practical experiences peculiar to societies and might not be easily replicated in different societies. It follows, *a fortiori*, that rules of competition emanating largely from societies of the North and fashioned in an era of unbridled competition might not be readily assimilable in less developed societies of the South. Indeed, in some South American countries introduction of the rules of competition was met with hostility and even violence, especially in remote areas where traditional values prevailed. In this context, too, consideration may have to be given to employing the norm *rebus sic stantibus* to the TRIPS Agreement and other instruments of the World Trade Organization (WTO) regime, given the domestic and unforeseen consequences of the HIV/AIDS pandemic in Africa, the Caribbean, and other regions of the globe.

THE JURIDICAL STATUS OF THE COURT AND COMMISSION

Due to an unfortunate oversight, competent decision-makers of the Caribbean Community did not accord legal personality and legal capacity to the Caribbean Court of Appeal in the earliest drafts of the Inter-Governmental Agreement. This omission also crept into the Agreement Establishing the Caribbean Court of Justice and had to be rectified by way of a Protocol.[5] In this connection, it is important to note the distinction between the legal personality and legal capacity of intergovernmental organisations. In the present submission, 'legal personality' speaks to the capacity of an organisation at the international level, that is, as a subject of international law, for example, to espouse a claim, while 'legal capacity' ordinarily speaks to the competence of the organisation at the municipal level. In the premises, to assume that these discrete juridical phenomena are assimilable to each other because of their similarity is to betray egregious misappreciation of the applicable norms. In the submission of Harris, in which the author concurs:

> It is clear that the word "person" is used to refer to one who is a legal actor, but that it is of no assistance in ascertaining who or what is competent to act. Only the rules of law can determine this, and they may select different entities and endow them with different legal functions, so that it is a mistake to suppose that merely by describing an entity as a "person" one is formulating its capacities in law . . . [6]

Postulated in other terms, while it is possible to infer personality from capacity the opposite is not juridically feasible! Addressing the capacity of the United Nations to espouse an international claim, as a subject of international law and which was the gravamen of the determination of the World Court in the *Reparations Case*, George Schwarzberger submitted:

> As with more recent administrative international institutions, the Organisation has not been granted international personality in so many words. It is merely provided in the Charter that the Organisation shall enjoy in the territory of each of the member States such *legal capacity*, privileges and immunities as are necessary for the exercise of its functions and the fulfillment of its purposes. In a similar formulation, provision has been made for the diplomatic immunity of representatives of member States and officials of the United Nations.[7]

And here again the distinction between 'legal personality' and 'legal capacity' is pellucidly clear, the latter status being perceived to operate at the municipal plane. Other recognised international publicists like Starke and Ian Brownlie, concur in this submission.[8]

It is sometimes assumed that the legal personality and legal capacity of these bodies are assimilable. As concerns the assumption that to assimilate legal personality and legal capacity would be to comply with regional and international instruments of this class, attention may be drawn to some examples of treaties of both a regional and international character addressing legal personality and legal capacity. Thus Article 48 of the Agreement Establishing the Caribbean Development Bank reads as follows:

> Article 48
>
> Legal Status
>
> 1. The Bank shall possess full juridical personality, and, in particular, full capacity:
>
> (a) to contract;
>
> (b) to acquire, dispose of immovable and movable property; and
>
> (c) to institute legal proceedings.

Similarly, Article 31 of the Agreement Establishing the Caribbean Food Corporation; Article 29 of the Agreement Establishing a West Indies Shipping Corporation; Article 17 of the Intergovernmental Agreement on the Establishment of the CARICOM Foundation for Arts and Culture; Article 20 of the Agreement Establishing the Caribbean Community Climate Change Centre; Article 20 of the Agreement Establishing the Caribbean Regional Fisheries Mechanism; and Article VIII of the Agreement Establishing the Caribbean Examination Council.[9]

At the international plane, reference may be made to the relevant articles of the constituent instruments of the International Bank for Reconstruction and Development and the International Monetary Fund, to wit, Article VII sec. 2 and Article IX sec. 2 respectively, of these organisations, which read as follows:

> Article VII
>
> Section 2. Status of the Bank
>
> The Bank shall possess full juridical personality, and, in particular, the capacity:
>
> (a) to contract;
>
> (b) to acquire and dispose of immovable and movable property; and
>
> (c) to institute legal proceedings.

> . . .
>
> Article XI
>
> Section 2. Status of the Fund
>
> The Fund shall possess full juridical personality, and, in particular, the capacity:
>
> (a) to contract;
>
> (b) to acquire, dispose of immovable and immovable property; and
>
> (c) to institute legal proceedings.

Both of these formulations distinguish 'personality' and 'capacity'. In fact, the distinction between personality and capacity is recognised in municipal law where legal persons are recognised as having differing capacities depending on their constituent instruments. The constituent instruments of various intergovernmental organisations employ formulations on the issue which differ in form but not in substance. And no attempt is made to assimilate these juridically discrete phenomena. Consider in this context Articles 210 and 211 of the Rome Treaty. Relevant international instruments also endeavour to protect the integrity and functional independence of intergovernmental organisations and their personnel.

REINFORCING THE INDEPENDENCE OF THE COURT AND COMMISSION[10]

In the submission of Brownlie,

> (i)n order to function effectively, international organizations require a certain minimum of freedom and legal security for their assets, headquarters, and other establishments and for their personnel and representatives of member states accredited to the organizations . . . The minimum principle appears to be that officials of international organizations are immune from legal process in respect of all acts performed in their official capacity. In any case, the international immunities are highly specialized and inevitably vary a great deal . . . Naturally the immunity given to judges of the International Court and other holders of judicial offices is of special importance and is equated to diplomatic privileges . . .[11]

In this section it is proposed to look at the arrangements agreed by competent decision-makers of the Caribbean Community to reinforce the independence and integrity of the Court and Commission in addition to the institutional arrangements agreed in various constituent instruments.

The provision of privileges and immunities for the Caribbean Court of Justice and the Regional Judicial and Legal Services Commission confirms the importance of the Court as a judicial institution. The provisions are intended to uphold its dignity, to further protect and safeguard the independence, impartiality and integrity of the judges and officers of these institutions, and to facilitate them as well as Attorneys before the Court in the performance of their duties.

The Protocol on Privileges and Immunities of the Caribbean Court of Justice and the Regional Judicial and Legal Services Commission is made under the enabling provisions of Article VII of the Agreement Establishing the Caribbean Court of Justice ('the Agreement') and the Protocol to the Agreement Relating to the Legal Personality and Capacity of the Court. The provisions which are contained in the Protocol are based on the international law principles on privileges and immunities for institutions such as the Court.

Article II of the Agreement Establishing the Seat of the Court and the Offices of the Regional Judicial and Legal Services Commission confers upon the Court and the Commission full juridical personality. In particular, it accords to them full capacity to contract, acquire and dispose of property and to institute legal proceedings. The Registrar has been identified to represent these institutions in all legal proceedings. The provisions of Article IX accord to judges and officers of the Court, as well as members of the Commission certain privileges and immunities in their official capacities. They will have the benefit of these privileges and immunities when they are engaged in the business of the Court or Commission in the territory of a government which is a party to the Agreement and will enjoy immunity from all legal action for acts, and words spoken or written in their official capacities. This immunity will continue even after they leave office.[12] These officials will also be immune from arrest or detention for acts which they perform in their official capacities[13] and will also be immune from inspection and from the seizure of their personal and official baggage, except in cases of *flagrante delicto*. In those cases in which the baggage of any of these officials of the Court will be searched, the competent authorities must immediately inform the Registrar or other appropriate officer of the Court. The inspection must be conducted in the presence of the official or his authorised representative. In these cases, official baggage must be searched in the presence of an officer who is the authorised representative of the Registrar.[14] All papers, documents and materials which are related to the work of the Court or Commission will be inviolable.[15]

These officials are also exempted from several municipal obligations such as national service obligations. It also exempts them from direct taxation on their salaries, remuneration and allowances which will be paid by the Court or Commission, as well as from custom duties on anything which they import for personal use.[16] This latter exemption will not apply, however, with respect to imported articles which are sold within the territory into which they are imported, except where the sale is done under such conditions as are provided by the government of that territory.[17] The officials who are the beneficiaries under this Article will also be entitled to the same privileges and facilities with respect to currency and exchange restrictions, and the same protection and repatriation facilities in times of international crises, that are accorded to representatives of foreign governments on temporary official missions.[18] For the purpose of all communications with the Court or Commission, they will also be entitled to the right to use codes to despatch or receive papers, correspondence or other official material by courier or in sealed bags.

Counsel appearing before the Court will be entitled to certain personal immunities, while they are in the territory of a Government Party. These immunities, which will relate to the performance of their functions connected to the proceedings in which they will be involved before the Court, are provided in Article X. They are intended to assist Counsel in the efficient representation of their clients as well as ensuring that the judicial process is not compromised. Article X entitles Counsel to immunity from personal arrest or detention, as well as from legal process for words spoken or written, or acts which are performed in relation to these proceedings. They will be entitled to continue to enjoy immunity from legal process even after the proceedings before the Court have ended.[19] The Article also entitles Counsel who are appearing before the Court to the inviolability of papers, documents and other materials which relate to the proceedings. It will also entitle them to exemption from immigration restrictions, alien registration requirements and national service obligations. It will further entitle them, in relation to the proceedings, to the same privileges and facilities that are accorded to government representatives on temporary official missions with respect to currency and exchange restrictions.[20]

Contracting Parties will facilitate judges and officers of the Court, other persons performing missions for the Court, and members of their families who form part of their households, to enjoy uninterrupted passage within, and entry into and departure from their territory. The same facilities will also be accorded to members of the Commission, Counsel, their clients and other persons who will appear before the Court, as well as other persons invited to the Seat of the Court, and the officers of the Commission on official business.[21]

Article VII provides exemptions for the Court and the Commission in their institutional capacities. It exempts them from any form of taxation, including airport departure, travel, hotel and restaurant, value added and other indirect taxes. The exemption from indirect taxes will not exempt these institutions from charges for public utility services. They will also be exempted from customs and excise duties, prohibitions, restrictions and levies on the importation, export or sale of their publications, as well as on articles which they will import or export for their official use. They will however be prohibited from selling articles imported or exported for their official use within the territory of a Government Party, except under conditions agreed to with the government. Article VI provides exemptions for the Court and the Commission, in their institutional capacities, from restrictions with respect to financial controls, regulation or moratoria. These institutions will be permitted to purchase negotiable currencies from authorised dealers, to hold and use these currencies, operate foreign currency accounts and external accounts, and to purchase through authorised dealers, hold and use funds and securities. The Article further permits them to transfer funds, securities and foreign currencies freely to the territory of a Government Party, and to convert any currency which they hold into other currencies, freely. In obtaining the benefits of these exemptions, these institutions will be required to take into consideration and give effect to any requests which may be made by a Government Party, so far as those requests will not be detrimental to their interests.

The Court and the Commission will be entitled according to Article VIII, to enjoy the same treatment for their official communications, which a Government Party accords to any international organisation. The Article also confers upon these institutions immunity from censorship with respect to their official correspondence and communications. It further affords them the right to use codes, and to send and receive correspondence by courier in sealed bags. Correspondence and communications which they send or receive by these means will enjoy the same immunities and privileges as diplomatic couriers and bags. By virtue of the provisions of Article III, the property and assets of the Court and Commission will be accorded immunity from legal process, except in so far as the immunity is expressly waived. Immunity from legal process cannot be waived, however, with respect to any measure of execution. The article also renders any property of those institutions immune from search, requisition, confiscation, expropriation and any other interference by executive administrative or judicial action.

Article IV provides for the inviolability of the premises occupied by the Court and the Commission with the consent of a Government Party. The Article seeks to prohibit government officials from entering the premises to perform any official duties except with the consent of the President, and under conditions agreed to by him. This prohibition will of course apply, except where there is a fire or other emergency which requires prompt action, or where government officials have reasonable cause to believe that such an emergency has occurred. In these cases, the consent of the President for their entry into the premises will be presumed if the President cannot be contacted on time. The Article empowers the President to make regulations for the purpose of establishing conditions for the full execution of the functions of the Court or Commission with respect to their premises. Article V renders inviolable the archives and all documents which belong to, or are held by the Court or Commission.

Even in the instances in which privileges and immunities are conferred upon an official of the Court or Commission, they are intended for their benefit in their official capacities. Article XI will therefore give the Conference (in relation to the President) and the President (in relation to all other persons entitled to privileges and immunities) the right to waive them whenever they are of the view that they would impede the course of justice, and their waiver will not be inimical to the interests of the Court or Commission. The Article also urges the President and the Registrar to co-operate with the competent authorities in order to facilitate the proper administration of justice, secure the observance of the laws and prevent the abuse of the privileges or immunities. It also imposes upon the beneficiaries of the privileges and immunities a duty to respect the laws of Government Parties and to refrain from interfering in their internal affairs. The Article further seeks to put into place a mechanism for the resolution of disputes which may arise concerning alleged abuses of the privileges and immunities. It will provide that a government which alleges an abuse should notify the Registrar of it. The Registrar should then consult the relevant competent authority, in order to determine whether there has been an abuse. If the matter is not thereby resolved to the satisfaction of the Registrar and the government, the matter is to be settled in accordance with the procedures for the settlement of disputes provided in Article XIII.

Article XIII requires the President to make provisions for the settlement of disputes. It refers specifically to disputes of a private law character to which the Court or Commission may be party, and disputes which may involve a judge or officer of the Court or Counsel conducting proceedings before the Court, where the privileges or immunities to which they are entitled are not waived. Article XIII(2) also provides for the settlement of differences between governments and the Commission with respect to the interpretation or application of the Protocol. A matter which is not settled is to be referred to a tribunal of three arbitrators, by any Government Party. The government and the Registrar will each appoint one arbitrator. The two arbitrators will then appoint a third arbitrator who will chair the tribunal. The Chairperson will determine all questions of procedure. Where the Registrar or the government fail to appoint an arbitrator within six weeks of the decision to resort to arbitration, the Secretary-General will be entitled to make the appointment. He will also be entitled to appoint the third arbitrator, at the request of the government or Registrar, if the two arbitrators fail to agree upon the third arbitrator within three weeks.

A majority decision of the tribunal will be final and binding.

The Protocol on Privileges and Immunities of the Caribbean Court of Justice and the Regional Judicial and Legal Services Commission is cast in terms similar to those of the Agreement Establishing the Seat of the Caribbean Court of Justice and the Offices of the Regional Judicial and Legal Services Commission.

SUPRANATIONALITY AND THE CARIBBEAN COURT OF JUSTICE

The competing claims of supranationality and national sovereignty as the basis for the organisation and functioning of the international system have a longer history than is generally acknowledged. From its very nature, national sovereignty had to predate supranationality as a basis of governance. The collapse of the Holy Roman Empire and the birth of Protestantism in the sixteenth century to challenge the ideological monopoly of the Catholic Church, heralded the rise of the nation state as the dominant political unit in the emerging international system. The treaty of Westphalia in 1648 which brought closure to the wars of religion, also accorded a measure of legitimacy to the emergent international order and foreshadowed the continuing rivalry between supranationality and national sovereignty as institutionalised in the congress system of nineteenth century and culminated in abortive attempts at universal government with the creation of the League of Nations in 1919 and the United Nations in 1945.

An analysis of the status of regional integration courts[22] as supranational organisations must take as its point of departure the allocative disposition of competences in international law between these collectivities and their constituent political entities, as well as the resulting impact on their autonomy of decision-making on important issues of regional and national policy. Such an analysis would also appear to require a credible and lucid determination of the essential attributes of sovereignty and supranationality as international juridical constructs, since, in the ultimate analysis, their interface determines the allocative disposition and residuum of competences among the principal actors.

Sovereignty, in the present context, attests to the totality of rights, powers and privileges which international law, and in particular, customary international law, recognises a state as entitled to exercise in relation to an ascertainable area or territory, including its superjacent airspace, and the persons, assets and resources therein, subject to compliance with the obligations correlative to the exercise of those powers, rights and privileges.[23] The jurisdiction of the state also extends to ships and persons bearing its nationality wherever they may be, to the continental shelf and exclusive economic zone adjacent to the territorial seas of states and to the resources thereof in respect of which the coastal state is recognised as having sovereign rights of exploration and exploitation.[24] As an international constitutional law doctrine, sovereignty does not involve the unfettered employment of competences by the state,[25] but is constrained by applicable rules of international law, especially those set out in the United Nations Charter, by which the legality of state acts is determined.[26] Despite the foregoing submissions however, limitations on the sovereignty of states are not to be lightly presumed[27] but must be definitively established in every case by reference to applicable norms of international law. For example, the provisions of the United Nations Charter contain various restrictions on the sovereign competence of States and which were voluntarily assumed by them. Consider in this context the provisions of Chapter VII of the Charter.[28]

Supranationality, on the other hand, speaks to voluntary derogations of sovereignty and to the competence of a collectivity to undertake sovereign acts, such as to make laws with direct effect for persons, natural and juridical, within the territorial jurisdiction of constituent state entities, without confirmation or promulgation by the State.[29] The status of supranationality, in effect, is perceived to require in the ordinary course of events, the state in relation to which this competence is exercised voluntarily surrendering certain attributes of statehood or sovereignty to the relevant supranational entity. Of course, exceptionally, supranationality may be a function of coercion where, for example, a conquering state legitimately employing military coercion effects a transfer of sovereignty from the vanquished state. The classic examples of supranational jurisdiction, however, are to be found in the treaties establishing the European Coal and Steel Community (ECSC) and the Economic Community, now incorporated in the European Union since the Treaty of Maastrecht.[30] In the characterisation of the European Court of Justice,

> (b)y contrast with ordinary international treaties, the EEC treaty has created its own legal system which . . . . became an integral

> part of the legal systems of the Member States and which their courts are bound to apply.[31] By creating a Community of unlimited duration, having its own institutions, its own personality, its own legal capacity and capacity of representation on the international plane and, more particularly, real powers stemming from a limitation of sovereignty or a transfer of powers from the states to the Community, the Member States have limited their sovereign rights . . . and have thus created a body of law which binds both nationals and themselves . . . It follows from all these observations that the law stemming from the Treaty, an independent source of law, could not, because of its special and original nature, be overridden by domestic legal provisions, however framed, without being deprived of the character of Community Law and without the legal basis of the Community itself being called into question. The transfer by the States from their domestic legal system to the Community's legal system of the rights and obligations arising under the Treaty, carries with it a permanent limitation of their sovereign rights against which a subsequent unilateral act incompatible with the concept of the community cannot prevail.[32]

The European Court of Justice, in determining that the European Community had established a novel corpus of law, distinct from national law or traditional international law as it is generally known, found that the states of the European Community had voluntarily transferred attributes of their sovereignty to the collectivity; had established a legal order separate and apart from that of the Member States; had concurred in Community law having direct applicability for persons and bodies in the jurisdiction of the Member States and submitted to the primacy of Community law which could not be revoked or amended by national law of the Member States. In short, these features of Community law particularised the European Community as a supranational entity.[33] Accepting the validity of these findings of the European Court of Justice, it does appear to be in the nature of an ineluctable inference that collectivities of states, which are wanting in one or more of these attributes, would not qualify for the status of a supranational entity.[34] Postulated in other terms, whereas an essential attribute of sovereignty, in the present submission, is the inherent faculty to compromise it to the extent determined by the sovereign power,[35] supranationality, in the ordinary course of events, appears to require a voluntary surrender of sovereign powers to an authority other than the conferring entity.

SUPRANATIONALITY AND THE EUROPEAN COURT OF JUSTICE

It is against this background that an attempt will be made to determine the extent, if any, to which one or another regional court, and, in particular, the Caribbean Court of Justice, enjoys supranational jurisdiction in relation to the state entities participating in the regional integration movements concerned. In the case of the European Court of Justice and the European Court of First Instance[36] established to assist the European Court of Justice in the performance of its duties, these institutions constitute an integral part of the European Community to which the Contracting States have voluntarily surrendered attributes of statehood or sovereignty, the most important of which is the competence to make laws with direct effect for nationals and persons within their jurisdictions, that is, without the intervention of their national legislatures and the correlative right of private entities to have *locus standi* in proceedings before the Court. To this extent therefore, the European Court of Justice, as an integral part of the European Community and one of its principal institutions[37] may be perceived to enjoy, by association, attributes of supranationality. In one submission, '(t)he provisions relating to the Court clearly demonstrate the statelike institutional structure of the Community.'[38] In this context, it is important to bear in mind the role of the Court in interpreting and applying Community Law, and in so doing, upholding the primacy and supremacy of Community Law over national law which has been expressed to be incapable of revoking or amending Community law.[39] Further, the referral procedure of the Court as set out in Article 177 of the Treaty of Rome and in Article 234 of the Treaty of Maastricht, has been perceived to be one of the most potent catalysts for economic and social cohesion in the European Union.

This procedure allows the European Court of Justice to insinuate itself in important aspects of national law to ensure convergence of the applicable norms of national law and Community law. In the submission of Lord Denning, M.R., in *H.P. Bulmer Ltd. v. Bollinger SA* [1974] 2 All ER 1226,

> when it comes to matters with a European element, the Treaty is like an incoming tide. It flows into the estuaries and up the rivers. It cannot be held back. Parliament has decreed that the Treaty is henceforward to be a part of our law. It is equal in force to any statute. Any rights or obligations created by the Treaty are to be given legal effect in England without more ado.

Consider in this context, too, the competence of the Court to determine its own jurisdiction and the direct applicability of Community law in national jurisdictions of the European Union. The European Court of Justice has been accorded the power to impose sanctions for non-compliance with its determinations on both states and private entities within the contemplation of the European Union. Such a sanctioning process of prescription is generally perceived as partaking more of an attribute of statehood than a competence enjoyed by an association of state entities established by treaty. In this context, Article 171 of the Rome Treaty suggests itself for consideration since it expressly requires Members States to 'take the necessary measures to comply with the judgments of the Court' when the Court finds that there was failure to fulfill a Community obligation in or under the Treaty. Similarly, the Court is competent to review the legality of acts of the Council and the Commission, and any natural or legal person may institute proceedings in the European Court of Justice against a decision of those bodies directly affecting the person aggrieved.[40] And these bodies are required by the Treaty of Rome to take the measures necessary to comply with the judgments of the Court.[41] The *locus standi* accorded private entities in proceedings before the Court, and which must be seen as an aberration from the normal requirements of traditional international law, appears to be a reasonable incident of European Union nationality.[42] Such a right is extremely important for a finding of supranationality in the jurisdiction of the European Court of Justice where private entities adversely affected by determinations of Community organs with direct effect are entitled to institute proceedings before the Court where those determinations impact negatively on their private interests.

An examination of the Agreement creating the Court of Justice of the Cartegena Agreement would also appear to support an inference that the Andean Court of Justice possesses some attributes of supranationality. Article 19 of the aforementioned Agreement, for example, empowers national and juridical persons to bring actions of nullification against decisions of the Commission or resolutions of the Junta, which are applicable to them and directly affect them. Like private entities in the European Union, private entities in the Andean Community have, as a matter of right, *locus standi* in proceedings before the Andean Court of Justice in respect of acts of central organs with direct effect.[43]

In evaluating the supranational attributes of the European Court of Justice, it was submitted that the status of this institution may be assimilated to that of the European Community of which it was an integral component and whose status as a supranational entity appears to be incontrovertible. However, it is important to point out that the perception of supranationality as it relates to the status of the European Court of Justice is more a function of the relevant provisions of the constituent instrument of the European Community than an axiomatic rationalisation of its status as an institution of the Community. Consider in this context the indeterminate juridical status of the European Parliament which is an institution of the Community but which cannot, by reason of its limited competence to make legally binding rules for States and private entities in their jurisdictions, be regarded as possessing attributes of supranationality. By analogous reasoning, it is proposed to examine the extent, if any, to which the Caribbean Court of Justice possesses any attributes of supranationality, either in its own right or as an integral part of the Caribbean Community.

In this connection, it is important to appreciate that the Caribbean Community including the CARICOM Single Market and Economy, which was established by the Revised Treaty of Chaguaramas, and has not yet formally entered into force but which is being provisionally applied pending its definitive entry into force, is an association of Sovereign States. This status of the Caribbean Community finds concrete juridical expression in the unanimity rule, which governs decision-making in the Conference of Heads of Government – the supreme policy-making organ of the institution.[44]

In the present submission, therefore, even if it could be established that the Caribbean Court of Justice is an integral component of the Caribbean Community, this judicial institution, by that very fact, could not be regarded as partaking of attributes of supranationality. In this connection, it does appear to be an interesting juridical circumstance that although the provisions on disputes settlement of the Revised Treaty identifies the Caribbean Court of Justice as the principal instrument for the judicial settlement of disputes, the Court has not been accorded the status of an organ of the Community. In fact, important political considerations argued persuasively at the material time, against making the Caribbean Court of Justice an organ of the Community thereby subjecting it to the political direction and control of the Conference of Heads of Government, the supreme policy-making organ. Consequently, the Agreement Establishing the Caribbean Court of Justice is an autonomous juridical instrument, separate and apart from the Revised Treaty and the institution it creates, and though indispensable for the efficient functioning of the CARICOM Single Market and Economy, is not organically linked to the Caribbean community.

However, by including in the disputes settlement provisions of the Revised Treaty, articles of the Agreement Establishing the Caribbean Court of Justice relating to the original jurisdiction of the Court and which speak expressly to the settlement of disputes concerning the interpretation and application of the instrument,[45] states parties have submitted to the compulsory and exclusive jurisdiction of the Court *ipso facto* and without special agreement.[46] The Revised Treaty, moreover, does not accord the Court the status as an institution or organ of the Caribbean community.[47] This being the legal position, the question falling to be answered is whether the Court, as an autonomous institution, possesses attributes of supranationality in its own right. Resolution of this issue does appear to require careful examination of the Court's constituent instrument and the relevant provisions of the Revised Treaty in order to determine its competence and jurisdiction. Compare in this context the legal arrangements for other regional integration courts like the Central American Court of Justice, the Court of Justice of the Andean community, the Court of the European Free Trade Association, the Court of Justice of the Common Market for Eastern and Southern Africa.[48]

Given the connotation which the term supranationality attracts, it would appear that unless it can be established that the CCJ in the exercise of its jurisdictions, appellate and original, creates new law with legally binding effect on the Member States and entities public and private within their jurisdictions, without the intervention of their national legislatures, it would be difficult if not impossible, to infer attributes of supranationality in relation to the Court. In the exercise of its appellate jurisdiction, the CCJ will be required to interpret and apply the municipal law, both statute law and common law, of State parties to its constituent instrument. And, in so doing, it must be perceived to be discharging a function essentially similar to that performed by the Judicial Committee of the Privy Council (JCPC), its predecessor. But the JCPC, like any other common law court is constrained to confine its jurisdiction to the declaration and application of the law and to resist the temptation to usurp the functions of the legislature by innovative forays into judicial legislation. Indeed, all common law courts are required to respect the primordial principle of separation or balance of powers and to represent themselves as conforming to this constitutional requirement. In the characterisation of the World Court 'when mention is made of a court dispensing justice or declaring the law, what is meant is that the decision finds its objective justification in considerations lying not outside but within the rules . . . .'[49] Nevertheless, it must be recognised that the law in any given polity aspires to regulate an extremely volatile and dynamic environment and that, in the ultimate analysis, the law, to be effective, is required to be as dynamic as the environment of its control.[50]

However, it does appear to be the subject of an axiomatic postulate that the legislature, more often than not, lags behind technological, social, political and economic developments in the modern state and that the common law is persistently lethargic in encapsulating and reflecting, as it must, in the ultimate analysis, the collective social ethos of a people. In these circumstances, therefore, the legislature is invariably called upon to intervene, and the courts being required to determine issues of law without guidance from the legislature or the common law, are constrained to indulge a measure of innovation and inventiveness in arriving at determinations appearing to offer the most satisfactory resolution of the issue at hand. Advocates of judicial legislation like Cardozo and Greanawall discern gaps in the law and which are, more often than not, a function of the lethargy of the legislature in keeping normative prescriptions current with social, economic and technological changes in the controlling environment. Such gaps the judiciary may be required to fill.[51] To the extent, therefore, that the CCJ would be required in the exercise of its appellate jurisdiction to indulge a measure of judicial legislation, to this extent the Court may be perceived as exhibiting attributes of supranationality, given the requirement of Member States of the Community to enforce its decisions in their national jurisdictions.[52]

The supranational attributes of the CCJ, in the exercise of its original jurisdiction, however, appear to be open to considerably less doubt and speculation. In the first place, Article 217 (2) of the Revised Treaty and Article XVII (2) of the Agreement Establishing the Caribbean Court of Justice perceive the Court as competent to deliver judgments where there is obscurity in the law or where the parties to a matter before the Court agree that the Court may proceed *ex aequo et bono* to reach a determination.[53] In effect, where the Court is unable to discern any applicable rules for a resolution of the case at hand because the law on the issue is either uncertain, obscure, or simply does not exist, the Court is required to apply general principles of law to render a judgment. In such an eventuality, the Court would be able to rely on various decisions of international tribunals in determining and applying general principles of law. In this connection it is also useful to remember that the International Law Commission of the United Nations also supports the view that international tribunals should eschew declining to reach a judgment on the ground of silence or obscurity of the law to be applied.[54]

In terms of the practice of international tribunals in employing general principles of law, reference may be made to the *Chorzow Factory (Indemnity)* case[55] where the Permanent Court of International Justice applied the principles of *res judicata* and the entitlement of a person aggrieved by the breach of an engagement to be compensated. The general principles, which may be applied by international tribunals, are of both a substantive and evidentiary nature.[56] In the *Mavromatis Palestine Concessions* case, the World Court referred to subrogation as a general principle[57] while in the case of *Diversion of Water from the River Meuse*, the World Court, through Judge Manley Hudson, expressed the view that the equitable principles of the common law may be applied as general principles.[58] It does appear to be the subject of an ineluctable inference, therefore, that when the Caribbean Court of Justice, as an international tribunal, in the exercise of its original jurisdiction, is constrained to resort to the application of general principles of law in order to avoid declining to make a determination on the ground of obscurity in the law or the absence of applicable rules to reach a determination on the instant issue, the Court may be seen to indulge a measure of judicial legislation. And to the extent that the national courts of States parties are required to enforce the judgments of the Caribbean Court of Justice like judgments of their superior courts,[59] it may be argued that the Caribbean Court of Justice is indulging a measure of supranationality.

Similarly, it may be submitted that the CCJ, in applying equitable principles to arrive at determinations, subject to the agreement of the parties in proceedings before the Court, is indulging a measure of supranationality inasmuch as its decisions create legally binding decisions for States and private natural and judicial entities of parties to the Agreement establishing the CCJ. For in so doing it is clear that the Court is not invariably applying settled and determinate rules of law but is engaging in a measure of judicial legislation in order to arrive at an equitable solution acceptable to the parties. In the *North Sea Continental Shelf* case,[60] the World Court considered certain equitable principles of Anglo American Common law and applied its own in order to arrive at a just solution. In this context, there is much judicial precedent for international courts reaching determinations *ex aequo et bono* even though the relevant precedents are not always convergent. Thus, in the *Serbian Loans* case,[61] the World Court declined to apply the equitable doctrine of estoppel one of the most potent and innovative principles of the common law contributed by British Courts to the corpus of general principles of law recognised by civilised States.[62]

As applied by international tribunals, the equitable doctrine of estoppel is known as the doctrine of preclusion, which has been accepted and applied by the World Court in several of its judgments. Outstanding cases in point are the case concerning the *Temple of Preah Vihear*,[63] the *Barcelona Traction (Preliminary Objections)* case[64] and the *North Sea Continental Shelf* case. Similarly, in the *Eastern Greenland* case,[65] the World Court held that a declaration by a foreign Minister on matters within his competence established a right by way of estoppel or preclusion. Consider in this context, too, the decision of the Arbitral Tribunal in the *Argentina-Chile Boundary Arbitration Award* (1966)[66] where it was held that representations regarding the course of boundary lines created an estoppel constraining the interlocutor making the representation from disputing or challenging the legality of the course of those boundary lines. The competence of the Caribbean Court of Justice to render decisions *ex aequo et bono* is, in the present submission, a powerful tool of judicial legislation and reinforces the perception of a potential supranational competence attributable to the Caribbean Court of Justice.

Before definitively pronouncing on the status of the Caribbean Court of Justice as a supranational institution, however, it would be important to bear in mind that the European Court of Justice in reaching the determination that the constituent instrument of the European Union had established a new legal order, different from that normally created by an association of States established by treaty, had identified certain features among which was the faculty of permanence; in effect the relevant constituent instrument did not provide for a duration. In the case of the Caribbean Court of Justice, however, parties to the Agreement are free to withdraw from the regime after five years.[67]

In this context, it should also be borne in mind that where international instruments accord private entities a right of *locus standi* in proceedings before an international court, such a right appears to stand in axiomatic correlation to the competence of the relevant collectivity to establish norms with direct effect. This is the case both in the European Union and in the Andean Community as indicated above. Where private entities of the Caribbean Community are concerned, however, no such right is accorded in proceedings before the Caribbean Court of Justice. Consistently with traditional international law private entities aggrieved by non-compliance, or the threat thereof, with an obligation in or under the Revised Treaty or by the impairment or nullification of a right granted therein, must prosecute their claims through the competent state of nationality. However, the Caribbean Court of Justice, may, in its absolute discretion recognise a private entity as entitled to *locus standi* in proceedings before it.[68] Furthermore, although the Revised Treaty expressly incorporated the provisions of the Agreement Establishing the Caribbean Court of Justice as a part of its structure, there is no juridical nexus between the CCJ and the Caribbean Community as exists in the case of the European Court of Justice and the European Union. Viewed another way, the Caribbean Court of Justice unlike the ECJ, is not organically linked to the Caribbean Community and partaking of the attributes of a collectivity of States possessing supranationality as is the case with the ECJ. And there are sound historical reasons for this. Opposition to the Caribbean Court of Justice was virulent from the private Bar in the Caribbean Community and, in particular, the private Bar of Jamaica. This opposition was due in no small measure to suspicion of the political directorate whose attitude to the courts in one or two cases fuelled the perception that an attempt would be made to subject the Caribbean Court of Justice to political direction and control. The Revised Treaty of Chaguaramas, 2002, not unlike its predecessor, the Treaty of Chaguaramas 1973, installed the Conference of Heads of Government as the Supreme policy-making organ of the Community. In the premises, it was perceived that any attempt to make the Caribbean Court of Justice an organ of the Community would support the conviction about its control by and subordination to the regional political directorate. But, even if the Caribbean Court of Justice were perceived to be organically linked to the Caribbean Community, nothing in the legal arrangements of this institution reinforces the perception that it is a supranational body. In effect, a finding for a supranational competence for the Caribbean Court of Justice would have to be grounded on either the powers enjoyed by the Court in its own right and constituting a function of the legal arrangements agreed in its constituent instrument, or on its organic relationship with the Caribbean Community as a supranational body. However, it does appear that in both respects it cannot be persuasively submitted that the Caribbean Court of Justice is a supranational body, although it does appear to exhibit some attributes of supranationality similar to those of its predecessor, the Judicial Committee of the Privy Council in the exercise of its appellate jurisdiction.

INNOVATIONS IN THE CCJ'S REMIT

Paragraph 1 of Article XVII of the Agreement Establishing the Caribbean court of Justice required the Court in the exercise of its original jurisdiction to 'apply such rules of international law as may be applicable'. The language of commitment of this provision does not require the Court to apply only rules of international law in the exercise of its original jurisdiction. In fact, paragraphs 2 and 3 of the said Article XVII allow the Court to employ general principles of law and equitable principles in specified conditions. In the premises, the competence of the Court to apply rules of law in the exercise of its original jurisdiction appears to be similar to traditional international law tribunals. Consider in this context the competence of the International Court of Justice of the United Nations.[69]

However, competent decision-makers of the Caribbean Community in seeking to ensure certainty and conformity in the norms applicable to the conduct of economic activities in the CARICOM Single Market and Economy and to the settlement of disputes arising in connection with such activities, introduced certain innovations in the provisions of the Agreement Establishing the Caribbean Court of Justice in relation to its original jurisdiction. Among the most important of these is the doctrine of *stare decisis*. Article XXII of the Agreement Establishing the Caribbean Court of Justice expressly provides that the judgments of the Court 'shall be binding precedents for parties in proceedings before the Court unless such judgments have been revised in accordance with Article XX'. As Lord Denning forcefully submitted in *Trendtex Trading Corporation v. Central Bank of Nigeria*[70] 'International law knows no rule of *stare decisis*'. It operates on the basis of *jurisprudence constant* or a disposition on the part of international tribunals to follow decisions of similar bodies without being constrained by a requirement to do so as would be the case if the doctrine of *stare decisis* were applicable to their determinations. The rationale of the approach adopted by the competent decision-makers of the Caribbean Community has already been addressed.[71]

Another important innovation introduced into the remit of the Court in the exercise of its original jurisdiction is to invest the Court with power to prescribe interim measures to preserve the rights of parties pending resolution of a dispute where the Court is satisfied that the circumstances of the case so require. Such interim measures, it is submitted, may be prescribed by the Court, *propio motu*, or on application by an interested party to the dispute in that behalf. Article 42 of the Statute of the International Court of Justice empowers it to *indicate* interim measures in similar circumstances. Since, however, there appears to be some uncertainty about the requirement to comply with an indication of interim measures, competent decision-makers agreed to adopt the approach taken by the United Nations International Tribunal on the Law of the Sea (ITLOS) and to *prescribe* interim measures thereby placing the requirement to comply beyond all reasonable doubt.[72]

The emerging consensus among publicists that persons, natural and legal, are being regarded less as objects of international law than subjects of international law finds support among provisions of constituent instruments of various inter-governmental organisations according to their *locus standi* in proceedings before international tribunals. It appears, however, that where private entities are accorded *locus standi* in proceedings before international tribunals it is to allow them to seek remedies which arise in connection with grievances issuing from the provisions with direct effect of such constituent instruments. An excellent case in point is the Treaty of Rome.[73] The Agreement Establishing the Court of Justice of the Cartagena Agreement also accords private entities *locus standi* in proceedings before the Court. Similarly, the Court of Justice of COMESA accords *locus standi* to private entities appearing before it in specified conditions, subject to the exhaustion of local remedies.[74]

Article XXIV of the Agreement Establishing the Caribbean Court of Justice does not accord private entities *locus standi* in proceedings before the Court as a matter of right. Enjoyment of this privilege depends on the leave of the Court where specified conditions are satisfied and the Court is satisfied that the requirement of justice prescribe that the entity be allowed to espouse its claim directly in proceedings before the Court. As such the provisions of this Article cannot reasonably be perceived as an innovation in international law, except in the sense of an international tribunal being authorised to accord *locus standi* to private entities.

Similarly, Article XIV of the Agreement Establishing the Caribbean Court of Justice is crafted in language based on the provisions of Article 177 of the Treaty of Rome as amended by Article 234 of the Treaty of Maastricht. As earlier indicated the purpose of this provision is to ensure uniformity, certainty and stability in the applicable norms in the absence of which, structured development of the regional economic integration movement would be impossible of achievement. The application of this provision in the European Union had been credited with facilitating the European Court of Justice insinuating itself into the domestic law of Member States thereby constituting a potent force for economic and social cohesion in the European Union.

CARIBBEAN COMMUNITY LAW AND NATIONAL LAW

Although, in the present submission, it would be juridically misconceived to speak of Caribbean Community law in the sense of a body of norms issuing from a supranational entity and possessing a unique status by virtue of its directly applicability in terms of incidence for states and private entities within the national jurisdictions of Member States, there is a sense in which one can perceive of the existence of a body of law recognised as Caribbean Community law. In this sense, Caribbean Community law will be law applicable to the Member States of the Caribbean Community and their nationals, natural and legal, in their normal interface with one another. This corpus of law will necessarily have two dimensions corresponding with the dual jurisdiction of the Caribbean Court of Justice – a municipal law dimension and an international law element. The municipal law dimension will issue from the Caribbean Court of Justice as a tribunal of last resort for member States of the Caribbean Community.

As a tribunal of last resort, the Caribbean Court of Justice will be performing the role which superior appellate courts normally perform, that is correcting perceived errors in the law made by subordinate courts, and clarifying and developing the law by reference to the collective social ethos of the peoples of the Caribbean Community. In this connection, the Caribbean Court of Justice will be the judicial body to give institutional expression to the goal of the decision-makers who determined to establish the Council of Legal Education in 1970. Consistent with the need for uniformity and certainty in the applicable norms, attributes of a normative regime which recognises the importance of a stable and attractive investment climate, the Caribbean Court of Justice as a tribunal of last resort would be expected to follow decisions of the Judicial Committee of the Privy Council when this institution was the final court of appeal for Member States of the Caribbean Community, even though there is no such requirement in the constituent instrument of the Caribbean Court of Justice. However, this should not preclude the Court from regarding the doctrine of *stare decisis* more as a guide to future determinations than as a juridical shackle for the promotion of petrification in the normative framework. In the present submission, the Caribbean Court of Justice, in developing the jurisprudence of the Caribbean Community must have as its primary goal the achievement and maintenance of dynamic stability in the normative environment.

As submitted above, the Caribbean Court of Justice in exercising its original jurisdiction will be assimilated to an international tribunal required to employ rules of international law[75] in reaching its determinations. Conceding however, that the Court is competent to employ general principles of law and equitable principles[76] where circumstances so prescribe in order to reach a definitive resolution of disputes, it is submitted that there appears to exist some leverage for judicial legislation. And norms generated in this context might be peculiar to Member States of the Caribbean Community reflective of their peculiar circumstances and needs and contributing to the corpus of norms perceived to constitute the international law dimension of Caribbean Community law. However, the bulk of the international dimension of Caribbean Community law may be expected to derive from determinations of the Court relating to the settlement of disputes or the rendering of advisory opinions[77] touching on the interpretation and application of the provisions of the Revised Treaty. The international law dimension of Caribbean Community law must also draw on the various international agreements to be concluded by the Member States of the Caribbean Community among themselves[78] and between them and third parties.[79]

The intractable question falling to be resolved is: what is the relationship between Caribbean Community law as applied by the Caribbean Court of Justice and the national law of Member States? Resolution of the issue must take account of the dual jurisdiction of the Caribbean Court of Justice as well as the fact that the Member States of the Caribbean Community subscribe to both the common law and civil law systems of jurisdiction. In considering this issue it is proposed to adopt as the point of departure dicta of the European Court of Justice which determined that the Member States of the European Union had created their own legal system which became an integral part of their own legal systems and which their municipal courts were bound to apply. Further, because of its special nature, this system of law could not be overridden by the domestic law of the Member States.[80] It is submitted, however, that the position is qualitatively different in the Caribbean Community where the Caribbean Court of Justice would be performing the role of a court of last resort for Member States.

As successor to the Judicial Committee of the Privy Council, the Caribbean Court of Justice will be the final court of appeal for each Member State of the Caribbean Community as a collectivity. If the latter position were the case, then its determinations could not be unilaterally modified by any one Member State. Consequently, the Parliaments of the Member States must be perceived as juridically competent to enact legislation nullifying decisions of the Caribbean Court of Justice in its appellate jurisdiction. In fact and as a matter of law, the Member States of the Caribbean Community not having surrendered any attributes of sovereignty to the Caribbean Court of Justice are competent to deprive the Court of its appellate jurisdiction by act of Parliament in much the same way as they abolished the jurisdiction of the Judicial Committee of the Privy Council and invested the Caribbean Court of Justice with such jurisdiction.

In addressing the international dimensions of Caribbean Community law it is submitted that this element would consist of the Revised Treaty establishing the Caribbean Community including the CARICOM Single Market and Economy, protocols and other international legal instruments mandated to be elaborated, either expressly or by compelling inference, to complement the principal instrument, valid determinations of competent organs reached under the principal instrument, determinations of the Caribbean Court of Justice in the exercise of Caribbean Community law in relation to the municipal law of Member States of the Community.

In the case of the European Union, the European Court of Justice has determined that Community law is superior to the municipal law of the Member States. This determination was based on the finding that by concluding the Treaty of Rome, the Member States of the European Union had created a unique corpus of law which was neither international law, *simpliciter*, nor municipal law but which became an integral part of their domestic law but which could not be amended unilaterally by the Member States. Caribbean Community law as perceived cannot claim as lofty a status as European Community law but it may be argued that to the extent the former body of norms is largely international law intended to regulate the conduct of CARICOM Member States in their interface with one another,

Member States are precluded from pleading their domestic law as a bar to the performance of obligations imposed by Caribbean Community law.[81]

However, this statement of the juridical position should not be construed as espousing a claim for the supremacy of Caribbean Community law over the domestic law of Member States. To the extent that Member States of the Caribbean Community are in breach of Caribbean Community law by not enacting domestic legislation to bring them in compliance with obligations assumed under Caribbean Community law, Member States would be engaging their international responsibility entitling aggrieved persons, natural or legal, to espouse their claims in competent international tribunals, including the Caribbean Court of Justice in the exercise of its original jurisdiction as appropriate. In effect, resolution of any issue involving the incompatibility of the domestic law of Member States of the Caribbean Community with Caribbean Community law would not depend on the supremacy or otherwise of Caribbean Community law over domestic law[82] but would be determined by the applicable rules of international law.

NOTES

1. See Article 217(1) of the Treaty establishing the Caribbean Community, including the CARICOM Single Market and Economy and Article XVII of the Agreement Establishing the Caribbean Court of Justice.
2. Consider in this context section 2(1) of the British European Communities Act 1972 which requires British legislation to be construed so as to give effect to rights prescribed by the Rome Treaty.
3. At present, the Agreement Establishing the Caribbean Court of Justice Trust Fund is governed by international law while the Vesting Deed is governed by municipal law.
4. See, for example, Article 217 (2) of the Treaty establishing the Caribbean Community, including the CARICOM Single Market and Economy.

5. Protocol to the Agreement Establishing the Caribbean Court of Justice Relating to the Legal Personality and Capacity of the Court.
6. See *Cases and Materials on International Law*, 5th ed., (London: Sweet and Maxwell, 1998) 101.
7. *A Manual of International Law*, 5th ed., (London: Stevens & Sons, Ltd., 1967) 287.
8. See, for example, *Starke's International Law*, 11th ed., London: Butterworths, 1974), 58 and Ian Brownlie, *Public International Law*, (Oxford: Clarendon Press, 1998) 678-81.
9. See Duke Pollard, *The CARICOM System: Basic Instruments*, (Kingston: The Caribbean Law Publishing Co. Ltd., 2003) 153; 269; 743; 755 and 774 for these instruments.
10. Reprinted with permission from the Commonwealth Secretariat.
11. Ian Brownlie, *Principles of Public International Law*, 4th ed., (London: Clarendon Press, 1972).
12. See Article IX (1) (a) of the Agreement Establishing the Seat of the Court at Appendix V.
13. See Article IX (1) (b).
14. See Article IX (1)(h).
15. See Article IX (1)(c).
16. See Article IX (1)(d).
17. See Article IX (1)(b).
18. See Articles IX (1)(g) and IX (1)(e).
19. See Article X(2).
20. See Article X (1).
21. See Article XII of the Agreement.
22. Among the better-known regional integration courts are the European Court of Justice (ECJ), the Court of First Instance (CFI), the Central American Court of Justice, the Court of Justice of the Andean Community, the Court of the European Free Trade Association, and the Court of Justice of the Common Market for Eastern and Southern Africa.
23. See, for example, Brownlie, *Principles of Public International Law*, 291-2; also *Starke's International Law*, 11th ed., 90-94.
24. See Articles 56 and 77 of the United Nations Convention on the Law of the Sea (1982).

25. Contrast in this context, the Hobbesian and Austinian concepts of sovereignty in municipal law. For example, see G. Sabine, *History of Political Theory*, 4th ed. 433-4 and 620.
26. See, *Starke's International Law*, 91.
27. See, for example *the Lotus Case*, PCIJ, Series A, No. 10 (1927).
28. For example, Article 51 of the Charter is widely construed as imposing restrictions on the employment of force except in self-defense to an armed attack. In this connection, it is a moot point whether anticipatory self defense or a preemptive strike is within the contemplation of Article 51.
29. See J.T. Lang, *The Common Market and Common Law*, (Illinois: Chicago University Press, 1966) 10.
30. See, for example, The Treaty on Political Union adopted by the Heads of State and Government of the Community of December 10, 1972.
31. See, for example, Articles 189-92 which address the legal incidence of regulations, directives, decisions, recommendations for Member States and private entities within their jurisdiction.
32. *Costa v. ENEL* No. 6/64, 1964 CMLR 425.
33. See, Dr. Klaus-Dieter Borchardt, *The ABC of Community Law*, European Commission, 2000 p. 25.
34. See, Borchardt, 23-24.
35. D.E. Pollard, 'The Caribbean Court of Justice, Challenge and Response', *CARICOM Perspective*, Vol. 1, June 1999 pp. 24.
36. See Article 168a of the Treaty of Maastricht which reads: 'A Court shall be attached to the Court of Justice with jurisdiction to hear and determine at first instance, subject to a right of appeal to the Court of Justice on points of law only and in accordance with the considerations laid down by the statute, certain classes of action or proceedings defined in accordance with the conditions laid down in paragraph 2. The Court of First Instance shall now be competent to hear and determine questions referred for a preliminary ruling under Article 177'.
37. See Part V of the Rome Treaty and in particular Section 4 entitled The Court of Justice.
38. Lang, *The Common Market and Common Law*, 15.
39. See Borchardt, p. 24. This interpretation of the legal arrangements in the Community, if valid, would appear to have extremely important

implications for the doctrine of Parliamentary supremacy in British Constitutional law. The supremacy of Community law over national law was confirmed in the *Simmanthal Case* 106/77, (1978) ELR 629.

40. Articles 173 and 175 of Rome Treaty 1957.
41. Article 176 of Rome Treaty 1957.
42. The definitive attributes of European citizenship are spelt out in Articles 8 – 8(e) of the Treaty of Maastricht (1972).
43. See, Pollard, *The Caribbean Court of Justice*, 32.
44. See Article 28 of the Revised Treaty Chaguaramas Establishing the Caribbean Community including the CARICOM Single Market and Economy.
45. Consider in this context Article 211-223 of the Revised Treaty and Articles XII - XXIV of the Agreement Establishing the Caribbean Court of Justice.
46. See, Article 216 of the Revised Treaty of Chaguaramas and Article XVI of the Agreement Establishing the Caribbean Court of Justice.
47. See, Article 10 of the Revised Treaty which details the organs of the Caribbean Community.
48. P. Sands, R. Mackenzie and Y. Shany, *Manual on International Courts and Tribunals*, (London: Butterworths, 1999).
49. *North Sea Continental Shelf Case,* ICJ Reports, 1969, paragraph 88.
50. For an exposition on the relevance and sustainability of a social ethic in relation to its environment of control, See R.H. Tawney, *Religion and the Rise of Capitalism*, Peter Smith, Lexington Ave, MA. 1930.
51. Consider in this context, Carl Singh, 'The Experience of Regional Tribunals' in *Caribbean Issues and Perspectives*, Vol. 2, CARICOM Secretariat pp. 55 ff. See also A D'Amato, *Cardozo Law Review* 63 (1979) and Brian Harvey, 'Judicial Interpretation in Commercial Law – the People Limits of Judicial Inventiveness', Paper presented at the 8th Commonwealth Law Conference, Ocho Rios, Jamaica, 1986.
52. See Article XXVI of the Agreement Establishing the Caribbean Court of Justice.
53. See Article 217 (3) of the Revised Treaty and Article 17 (3) of the Agreement Establishing the Caribbean Court of Justice.

54. See Article II of the Draft Articles on Arbitral Procedure elaborated by the ILC.
55. (1928) PCIJ Series A, No. 17, p. 29.
56. See the *Corfu Channel Case*, ICJ, 1949, 4 at p.18.
57. 1924 PCIJ, Series A, No 2, p. 28.
58. See *Stark's International Law*, 11th ed., (London: Butterworths, 1994) 31.
59. See Article XXVI of the Agreement Establishing the Caribbean Court of Justice.
60. ICJ, 1969 p.3 et p. 26.
61. (1929) PCIJ, Series A Nos. 20-21, pp. 38-39.
62. Consider in this context the decision of Lord Denning in *Central London Property Trust Ltd. v. Hightrees House Ltd.* [1947] KB 130.
63. ICJ, 1962, p. 6.
64. ICJ 1964, 6.
65. (1933) PCIJ Series A/B No. 53.
66. See, *Argentina-Chile Boundary Arbitration Award* (1966) 38 ILM 10.
67. See Article XXXVII of the Agreement Establishing the Caribbean Court of Justice.
68. Agreement Establishing the Caribbean Court of Justice.
69. See, for example, Article 58 of the Statute of the Court.
70. [1977] QB 529 at p.554.
71. See chapter 4.
72. See Article 96 of the ITLOS
73. See Article 173 of the Rome Treaty.
74. Article 27 (2) of the COMESA Treaty.
75. See Article 217 (1) of the Revised Treaty.
76. Consider in this context the provisions of Article 217 (2) and (3) of the Revised Treaty.
77. See Article XIII of the Agreement.
78. A compendium of these instruments may be found in Pollard, *The CARICOM System: Basic Instruments*, (Kingston: The Caribbean Law Publishing Co., 2003).
79. These instruments include the Colombia/CARICOM Free Trade Agreement, the CARICOM/Venezuela Free Trade Agreement, the

CARICOM/Cuba Free Trade Agreement, the CARICOM/Costa Rica Free Trade Agreement.

80. See *Costa v. ENEL*, No.6/64, 1964, CMLR, 425.

81. See *UN Headquarters Agreement case*, ICJ, 1981 *Advisory Opinion on Treatment of Polish Nationals in Danziig* (1932) PCIJ, Series A/B No. 44; *Free Zones of Upper Savoy and Gex* (1932) PCIJ Series A/ B No.46.

82. Consider in this context the submissions of one commentator on the supremacy of the law of the Common Market of COMESA in relation to the domestic law of its member states: S.E. Kulusika, 'The Lawyer and the Challenges of Economic Integration', *Zambia Law Journal*, Vol. 3 No. 2 pp.20-50.

CHAPTER SEVEN

Closing the Circle of Independence

THE GESTATION PERIOD

The termination in 1945 by the leading free market economies of the world of the widespread destruction of private and social capital and the genocidal atrocities by the combatants, euphemistically referred to as the Second World War, and the commencement of the Cold War, as exemplified and institutionalised in the establishment of the North Atlantic Treaty Organisation (NATO) and the Warsaw Pact, coincided with an internecine struggle for the winning of the minds of the uncommitted political entities emerging from colonialism in the mid-twentieth century. In the extremely volatile international political atmosphere existing at this time, the Colonial Office in London was indisposed to grant political independence to the fragile economic entities of the Commonwealth Caribbean except in a federalised political system that promised plausible expectations of economic viability and sustainability – hence the disastrous federal experiment between 1958-1962 allegedly imposed by Whitehall. A changing attitude on the part of the Colonial Office, however, resulted in a successful bid for political independence by Jamaica and Trinidad and Tobago in 1962 which was followed by a mad rush for political independence by Guyana and Barbados a few years later, followed by the entities in the Windward and Leeward Islands which subsequently coalesced to create the Organisation of Eastern Caribbean States in 1981.[1]

However, independence for the political entities of the Commonwealth Caribbean stopped short at autonomous decision-making in political and economic affairs and did not include autonomy of decision in judicial matters. Indeed, this arrangement appeared to be acceptable for both the former colonial power which saw it as a means of continuing control, and the political leaders of the emergent independent states who regarded it as an emollient for the disquiet of political opponents. And so the Judicial Committee of the Privy Council continued to be the court of final appeal for the independent states of the Caribbean Community which came into being with the conclusion and ratification of the Treaty of Chaguaramas in 1973.[2] Growing confidence in their ability to manage their own affairs and the establishment of several regional institutions in the post-federation period, including the Council of Legal Education in 1970,[3] witnessed intermittent but earnest calls for the patriation of the court of final appeal to the Caribbean Community.

Commencing with a proposal in that behalf by the Jamaican delegation at the Sixth Meeting of the Conference of Heads of Government in 1970, the call for the establishment of a regional court of last resort in substitution for the Judicial Committee of the Privy Council was made in the Report of the Representative Committee of the Organisation of Commonwealth Caribbean Bar Associations (OCCBA) in 1972 and reiterated by the West Indian Commission in its report, *Time for Action*, which was published in 1992. Before this, the Commission on Constitutional Reform set up by the Government of Trinidad and Tobago under the chairmanship of Sir Hugh Wooding in 1974 recommended the establishment of a court of last resort in the Region.[4] A similar call was made by another constitution Commission of Trinidad and Tobago in 1987. In fact, every constitutional Commission appointed in any Commonwealth Caribbean country since 1974 has recommended severance of ties with the Privy Council.[5] Calls to close the circle of independence by asserting the right to autonomous judicial decision-making in the Caribbean Community were made by the various political, legal and academic personages in the Caribbean Community during the last three decades of the twentieth century.[6]

However, it would appear to be overly rash and simplistic to assume that calls to close the circle of independence were unopposed by important stakeholders of the justice sector in the Region. Indeed, the most resolute and enduring opposition to patriating the final court of appeal came from the regional private Bar, some of whom entertained legitimate and genuine concerns about the independence and financial sustainability of a regional court of last resort. Nevertheless, unsubstantiated allegations persist in some quarters of the Region that the most virulent detractors of the Caribbean Court of Justice have a private agenda which does not coincide with the lofty ideals of the staunchest supporters of the Caribbean Court of Justice. In the cut and thrust of the regional debate on this issue, however, the present commentators owe it to future generations of the Region to address the more important generalised perceptions on both sides of the institutional divide in order to validate a balanced and informed perspective of what promises to be one of the most innovative experiments in international institutional relations.

The decision of the Conference of Heads of Government on February 14, 2001, in Barbados, to conclude the Agreement Establishing the Caribbean Court of Justice must be perceived as a defining moment in the historical development of the Commonwealth Caribbean States. In the present submission, it ranks in importance with the conclusion of the Treaty of Chaguaramas on July 4, 1973, establishing the Caribbean Community and Common Market and the decision of the Conference of Heads of Government of the Caribbean Community reached in Grand Anse, Grenada, in 1989 to revise the Treaty of Chaguaramas in order to establish a CARICOM Single Market and Economy. For the decision to establish a Caribbean Court of Justice with an appellate jurisdiction in substitution for the Judicial Committee of the Privy Council was in effect a long-awaited determination to sever the last visible vestiges of the colonial link with Britain and to assert the inherent right of the Member States of the Caribbean Community to autonomy of decision in judicial matters. At the same time, the decision to vest the Caribbean Court of Justice with compulsory and exclusive jurisdiction in respect of disputes concerning the interpretation and application of the Revised Treaty of Chaguaramas attested to the commitment of Heads of Government of the Caribbean Community to enhance and deepen the regional economic integration movement; for, in the ultimate analysis, the Caribbean Court of Justice with authority to pronounce authoritatively and definitively on the Revised Treaty must be perceived as an institutional imperative of the CARICOM Single Market and Economy.

The decision of the Conference of Heads of Government to establish the Caribbean Court of Justice was the culmination of a protracted process of debate, deliberation and self-effacing introspection, and even, perhaps, self-vilification, dating back to 1901 when an editorial of the Daily Gleaner Newspaper in Jamaica lamented the umbilical nexus with the Judicial Committee of the Privy Council as being out of joint with the times. The issue of delinking from the Judicial Committee of the Privy Council was considered and deliberated by various official and unofficial bodies during the century, including a meeting of colonial governors in Barbados in 1947, a meeting of the Heads of Government of the Caribbean Community in 1970, a meeting of the Attorneys General of the Region in Georgetown, Guyana, a meeting of the Representative Committee of the OCCBA which produced a report in 1972, the meetings of the Commission on Constitutional Reform set up by the Government of Trinidad and Tobago under the distinguished chairmanship of Sir Hugh Wooding, Chief Justice, the meetings of every constitutional commission set up in the Commonwealth Caribbean since 1974 and the tenth Meeting of the Conference of Heads of Government of the Caribbean Community in Grand Anse, Grenada, in 1989. Hence the decision was reached to establish the West Indian Commission with a broad mandate 'to formulate proposals for advancing the goals of the Treaty of Chaguaramas which established the Caribbean Community and Common Market in 1973.'[7] The Commission reported in 1992 and recommended the establishment of a Caribbean Supreme Court with an appellate jurisdiction replacing the jurisdiction of the Judicial Committee of the Privy Council and an original jurisdiction, *inter alia*, to hear and determine disputes among Member States and nationals of the Community relating to the interpretation and application of a Revised Treaty of Chaguaramas.

At its Eleventh Meeting held in Kingston, Jamaica, the Conference of Heads of Government of the Caribbean Community considered a draft Inter-Governmental Agreement to establish the Caribbean Court of Appeal prepared by the CARICOM Secretariat and determined that the Standing Committee of Ministers responsible for Legal Affairs should consider it further at their Second Meeting in Nassau, The Bahamas, in September 1990. At this Meeting, the Standing Committee made revisions to the Draft Inter-Governmental Agreement establishing the Caribbean Court of Appeal. The Twelfth Meeting of the Conference of Heads of Government considered the Draft Inter-Governmental Agreement in caucus and 'noted that in the ongoing effort towards the establishment of the Caribbean Court of Appeal, a previously prepared Draft Inter-Governmental Agreement was being revised for presentation to Member States for their consideration'. In anticipation of the Report of the West Indian Commission, the Standing Committee of Ministers responsible for Legal Affairs at its third meeting in Barbados in September 1991 considered and discussed a revised Draft Inter-Governmental Agreement to establish a Caribbean Court of Appeal which took account of observations made by the Conference of Heads of Government at its Twelfth Meeting in Basseterre, St. Kitts from July 2-4, 1991.

At the Third Meeting of the Standing Committee of Ministers responsible for Legal Affairs held in Barbados, the establishment of a reserve fund for the Court was proposed. The CARICOM Secretariat considered the proposal and determined

> that a reserve fund must necessarily be established and maintained out of moneys from some identifiable source and that the rationale for the establishment and maintenance of a reserve fund would not be met if payments into the fund were dependent on contributions being made by participating Member States. Consequently, the text of the draft Inter-Governmental Agreement does not include provision for the establishment and maintenance of a reserve fund for the Court.[8]

At its Fifteenth Meeting held in Barbados from July 4-7, 1994, the Conference of Heads of Government was content to note 'the Secretariat's report on the status of matters relating to the proposed establishment of a CARICOM Supreme Court' and further 'that a special parliamentary majority was required, under the constitution of Trinidad and Tobago, for the enactment of legislation to establish the Caribbean Supreme Court as the final Appellate Court for Trinidad and Tobago'. By this time Member States of the Caribbean Community appeared to have accepted in principle that the seat of the Court would be located in Trinidad and Tobago. However, the problem appeared to be that while the incumbent administration of Trinidad and Tobago was prepared to sign on to the Court in its original jurisdiction and in its appellate jurisdiction for criminal matters, it entertained reservations about delinking from the Judicial Committee of the Privy Council in respect of civil matters. This attitude was apparently informed by the conviction that investors with considerable amounts of capital to invest in the exploitation of the extensive natural gas reserves of Trinidad and Tobago would be more comfortable with the Judicial Committee of the Privy Council as the court of last resort in civil matters than a regional court of last resort.

In the meantime, the Secretariat was caught up in trying to widen the integration movement and advance the revision of the Treaty of Chaguaramas and not much attention was devoted to the establishment of the Court which managed to earn honourable mention at the Seventeenth Meeting of the Conference of Heads of Government held in Barbados, 1996, when the Secretary-General in his welcoming address submitted that 'for some time now a Caribbean Court of Appeal has been under consideration ... (and) it is now near past time for action'.

At its Nineteenth Meeting held in Castries, Saint Lucia, the Conference of Heads of Government made two significant determinations relating to the Court. It determined that the Court would have an original jurisdiction in respect of the interpretation and application of the Revised Treaty of Chaguaramas and that the name of this institution should be the Caribbean Court of Justice to signify that it was more than an appellate court. Consequent on this determination, the CARICOM Secretariat set about engaging the services of a consultant to assist in the elaboration of the articles of the Agreement relating to the original jurisdiction of the Court and in elaborating the Draft Enabling Bill to implement the Agreement into domestic law and to prepare the draft rules of court for the original and appellate jurisdictions. Preparation of the foregoing instruments was undertaken with such expedition that the Conference of Heads of Government was in a position at its Twenty-first Meeting in Canouan, St. Vincent and the Grenadines to reach the following determinations:

> *Decided* that there should be a Special Ceremony for the signing of the Agreement Establishing the Caribbean Court of Justice (CCJ), before the end of the year 2000, to be held in Port-of-Spain, where the headquarters of the Court is to be located;
>
> *Agreed* that all Member States should sign the Agreement Establishing the CCJ, at the above-mentioned ceremony, it being understood that signing of the Agreement would not constitute an irrevocable commitment to ratify and implement the said Agreement until the required legal and constitutional measures to implement the said Agreement are in place;
>
> *Also agreed* that the Sub-Committee in its deliberations should be guided by the following decisions of the Conference:
>
> (i) that the age of retirement of judges of the Court, including the President, should be 72 years;
>
> (ii) that the composition of the Regional Judicial and Legal Service Commission should reflect the public interest; in this context, two members of the Commission should be appointed by the President on the joint recommendation of the Secretary-General of the Caribbean Community and

the Director-General of the Organisation of the Eastern Caribbean States (OECS);

(iii) that the Conference did not concur with the recommendation of the Legal Affairs Committee (LAC) that the regional Bar Association should nominate for appointment to the Regional Judicial and Legal Service Commission, three members, one of whom would be a lay person;

(iv) determined that the Public Education Programme should address, *inter alia,*

(a) the concern expressed in some parts of the Community regarding the need for the Court to be free of political interference/influence and, in that regard, should emphasise the steps which have been taken to insulate the Court from such influence;

(b) the peculiarities of the OECS sub-region where a Joint Supreme Court already exists;

(c) the "reversal" of the British position in relation to the continued access by CARICOM countries to the Judicial Committee of the Privy Council which should be placed in the following context -

(i) the issue of "judicial erosion" of existing laws in CARICOM, including laws providing for capital punishment;

(ii) commercial cases involving British companies in the Region;

(d) the reduced costs associated with accessing the Court as compared to the Privy Council.

The Agreement Establishing the Caribbean Court of Justice was signed in Barbados on February 14, 2001, and entered into force on July 23, 2003, with the deposit of the third instrument of ratification by Guyana in Port-of-Spain, Trinidad and Tobago. The inaugural meeting of the Regional Judicial and Legal Services Commission took place on August 21, 2003, and that of the Trustees of the Caribbean Court of Justice Trust Fund on August 22, 2003. But even at this late stage detractors of the Caribbean Court of Justice applied to the Supreme Court in Trinidad and Tobago on August 22, 2003, for a declaration that the appointment of the members of the Regional Judicial and Legal Services Commission was invalid, null and void.

REGIONAL PERSPECTIVES ON THE COURT

Received perspectives of stakeholders of the Caribbean Court of Justice about the high quality of the administration of justice in Britain, coupled with subtly implanted notions about the role of the Judicial Committee of the Privy Council in maintaining a desirable balance of power among the executive, legislature and judiciary in the emergent independent states of the Commonwealth Caribbean probably played an important and, perhaps, determinative role in informing some self-effacing and derogatory perceptions of the Caribbean Court of Justice. However, on the basis of an informed, dispassionate evaluation of the institutional arrangements established to date by competent decision-makers in the Caribbean Community, it is difficult to avoid the conclusion that the Court is a unique innovative judicial body in international institutional relations in terms of its structure, composition and financing arrangements. More importantly, the establishment of the Caribbean Court of Justice is seen in some quarters as an historic, momentous and defining development in the history of the Caribbean Community.

The establishment of the Caribbean Court of Justice in its appellate jurisdiction will not only sever the last remaining vestige of a colonial condition, but will signal the birth of autonomous judicial decision-making in Member States of the Caribbean Community and close the circle of independence which commenced as early as 1962. In a real sense, too, the establishment of the Court will mark the culmination of initiatives to create our own regional institutions to facilitate and promote the development of an indigenous jurisprudence reflective of the moral, political, social and economic imperatives of our Region and which commenced with the establishment of the Council of Legal Education in 1970. In the premises, the virulent and incessant attacks on the Caribbean Court of Justice by its detractors might be perceived as introducing a cacophonous note into what would otherwise have been a harmonious finale to the third movement of a regional symphony. As such, it is submitted that even though the circle of independence is about to be closed institutionally, there is a sound reason to believe that it remains open, psychologically, in influential legal circles.

It is because of a genuine concern that, psychologically, the circle of independence remains to be closed that consideration must be given to addressing *ad nauseum* certain negative perceptions which have dogged the progress of the current initiative to establish a regional court of last resort, particularly in its denouement when sitting judges on the Judicial Committee of the Privy Council perceive the Caribbean Court of Justice, in its institutional configuration, as providing a worthy precedent for judicial bodies worldwide. In the present submission, the line between perception and reality, is, in the ultimate analysis, indistinguishable since in the conduct of interpersonal relationships, people are necessarily constrained to react only to their perceptions of reality. And since the quality of those reactions is necessarily informed by the quality of perceptions, be they uninformed, inadequately informed or intentionally and mischievously misinformed, it does appear to follow *a fortiori,* that, ideally, perceptions should be accurately and adequately informed. Indeed, competent decision-makers of today, in the present submission, owe it to the generations of tomorrow to explain the rationale of decisions likely to affect their lives.

One incorrect perception enjoying wide currency in the Caribbean Community and which appears to be palpably misconceived and somewhat vexatious is that current initiatives to establish the Caribbean Court of Justice are being undertaken with indecent haste. Competent decision-makers however, have been at pains to demonstrate the protracted gestation period of the Caribbean Court of Justice. Although the idea of a regional court of last resort was mooted as early as 1901 and discussed again in 1947[9] at a meeting of colonial governors of the Region, the nexus between current initiatives and past efforts appears to have been established in 1970 and spanned the last three decades as described above. As such, this misperception need not detain us here and, in any event, it is of marginal importance for legitimising the establishment of the Court. More important, is the perception that the Member States of the Caribbean Community are incapable of producing judges with the required legal erudition to sit on the Bench of the Court.

In response, in the world of ideas, the Caribbean Community as a Region commands an audience way beyond its miniscule political and economic significance. Which other region in the world as small as the Caribbean has produced three Nobel Prize winners? Which other entity or group of entities in the Commonwealth has produced lawyers whose professional skills have been recognised by invitations to sit on the very Judicial Committee of the Privy Council which detractors of the Caribbean Court of Justice would wish upon the Region indefinitely? Which other region in the world, as small as the Caribbean has produced judges who have occupied benches in the International Court of Justice (ICJ), the International Tribunal on the Law of the Sea (ITLOS), and the International Tribunal for the Former Yugoslavia (ITFY)? In the submission of the West Indian Commission, why are we so full of self-doubt? Or is it that more sinister motivations conspire to inform the devaluation of our worth?

An even more invidious and gratuitous misconception is the notion that the smallness of our societies constrains attempts, however strenuous and well-intentioned, by our sitting judges to avoid frequent social intercourse with persons likely to appear in proceedings before them either as advocates or as their clients. Such social contacts, it is alleged, are likely to inform inarticulate biases one way or another in respect of such persons and compromise the ability of our judges to render judgments with required detachment, dispassionately, and impartially. From the tenor and thrust of the arguments in this particular, it does appear to be the subject of a compelling inference that the undesirable conditions perceived would only operate to compromise the performance of our judges at the highest appellate level, particularly since judges of the Judicial Committee of the Privy Council were wont to commend the quality of decisions in civil appeals issuing from our own appellate courts. In the premises, dubious and unworthy arguments were adduced by the Court's detractors to have the Judicial Committee of the Privy Council remain the court of last resort for Member States of the Caribbean Community, at least for the time being! This submission, of course, conveniently ignores the persuasive argument in favour of access to justice which the location of the Judicial Committee of the Privy Council renders difficult to attain.

In addressing this misconception this author has had reason to point out in another context[10] that the dispensation of justice from a distance also has an important downside in as much as it militates against familiarity with the values and norms of a society, a knowledge of which can only be perceived as enhancing the quality of justice emanating from the Bench. It was submitted in this context that the law was much more than a corpus of norms to be administered mechanically by dispassionate judges, studiously impervious to the moral, political, social and economic imperatives of the environment for which judicial determinations were being made. On the contrary, it was submitted that for the law to be effective and inspire voluntary compliance, it must be seen to reflect the collective social ethos of a people and administered, interpreted and applied by persons internalising the values informing the content of that collective social ethos. It is not known whether any sociological insights have been advanced to invalidate the foregoing submissions.

Of far more legitimacy and credibility is the perception that the political executive in the Caribbean Community are not always Caesar's wife in their interface with the judiciary. This perception finds support in the relatively exiguous allocations of budgetary resources for the administration of justice in the Caribbean Community and even the diffidence of the regional executive in complying with judgments of national courts against their members. In one celebrated case the Judicial Committee of the Privy Council had to order the executive to make adequate arrangements for the satisfaction of a judgment against the Hon. Attorney General.[11] But it is precisely because of the legitimacy of this concern that credible and imaginative arrangements have been established for the appointment of judges capable of performing their functions with independence, impartiality and integrity.

RESPONDING TO THE CHALLENGE[12]

> . . . the case for a Caribbean Supreme Court could be based on the need for a regional Court of last resort to apply laws incorporating a collective regional ethos, reflecting the moral imperatives of the Caribbean social reality and amenable to interpretation by judges who would have internalised the values informing the content of that social reality. (Duke Pollard, CARICOM Perspective, June 1998).

The Agreement Establishing the Caribbean Court of Justice must be perceived as constituting the measured institutional response of competent decision-makers in the Caribbean Community to a challenge which persisted in the Region for several decades. This challenge is multi-faceted, comprehending dimensions which include juridically misconceived appeals to sovereignty, genuine concerns about autonomous judicial decision-making, the legal erudition of potential incumbents, inaccessibility by the ordinary man to the court of last resort; subjection of the Court to influence or control of the regional political directorate, and the financial insecurity of an indigenous Court of last resort. All of these issues were ventilated by both members of the Judiciary and the private Bar at a symposium organised and sponsored by Caribbean Rights in Bridgetown, Barbados, on November 28, 1998, and will be employed as the point of departure for much of the discussion which follows.

Among the more ardent proponents of the argument that an indigenous Court of last resort is necessary to complete the independence of Member States of the Caribbean Community is Justice Telford Georges. In his characterisation, the learned judge maintained:

> (s)tarkly put, it appears to me that an independent country should assume the responsibility for providing a court of its own choosing for the final determination of legal disputes arising

> for decision in the country. It is a compromise of sovereignty to leave that decision to a court which is part of the former colonial hierarchy, a court in the appointment of whose members we have absolutely no say. The counter argument is that . . . on achieving independence the countries (of the Caribbean) had a choice of either allowing appeals to an external court to continue or of abolishing them. It is therefore not a derogation from sovereignty to allow appeals to continue. It was in effect an exercise of that right. I think this is the type of argument which the average person would call a lawyer's argument. It asserts that it is an exercise of sovereignty and of independence to choose a situation of dependency. In real life, any one who behaved in that way would evoke pity and exasperation, like the grown man who demonstrates his independence by continuing to live free at home.[13]

However, from the perspective of the norms applicable to State interaction in the international community, it appears to be in the nature of an axiomatic juridical postulate that the essence of sovereignty is the faculty to compromise it. And, as postulated, the sovereignty argument is based on the wrong conclusion for the wrong reason.

As the quotation at the commencement of this chapter suggests, the case for an indigenous Court of last resort may be persuasively advanced without an emotional appeal to popular sentiment informed by our colonial past. Nor should lawyers resile from employing a lawyer's arguments to demonstrate the relevance of legal rules. Indeed, the layman's inability to appreciate such arguments should not be more a cause of concern than the lawyer's inability to grasp the mathematical complexities of Einstein's theory of relativity or the scientific implications of Newton's corpuscular theory of light. And in this context, it does appear to be less a construct of Cartesian logic than an incident of special pleading to introduce at this juncture of the debate a simile whose pertinence for addressing socio-attitudinal phenomena appears to be unimpeachable, but which is unlikely to be accorded any persuasive value in analysing inter-state relations governed by generally accepted norms of international law. An issue of considerable and continuing concern to the private Bar in the Caribbean Community is the insulation of the

Caribbean Court of Justice (CCJ) from political manipulation. And with the inclusion of good governance on the international political agenda, this concern has assumed inordinate significance in polities the world over.

In the present submission, it would be disingenuous to attribute a greater disposition by the political directorate in the Caribbean Community to interfere with the Judiciary than exists among the political directorate of Member States of the European Union. In point of fact, the appointment of judges to the European Court of Justice and to the Court of First Instance of the European Community is made by the political directorate of the Member States of the European Union. Thus Article 167 of the Rome Treaty provides:

> The Judges and Advocates General shall be chosen from persons whose independence is beyond doubt and who possess the qualifications required for appointment to the highest judicial offices in their respective countries or who are jurisconsults of recognized competence; *they shall be appointed by common accord of the Governments of the Member States* for a term of six years ... and shall be eligible for reappointment...

In order to address this concern of the private Bar in the Caribbean Community, the political directorate of the Member States have agreed to remove the appointment of judges of the Caribbean Court of Justice from direct and indirect political control. Thus Article V (1) of the Agreement provides for the establishment of a Regional Judicial and Legal Services Commission, the majority of whose members are nominated by the private Bar; and Article V (3) (1) (a) charges the Commission with responsibility for the appointment of judges other than the President.

The President is to be appointed or removed from office by a qualified majority vote of the Contracting Parties on the recommendation of the Regional Judicial and Legal Services Commission.[14] The President of the European Court of Justice is elected by the members of the Court from among their number for a term of three years and may be re-elected.[15] Thus in both cases the appointment of the President is one stage removed from the political directorates of the European Union and the Caribbean Community respectively.

In either case, the temptation to compromise the independence of the Court is likely to be a function of the values informing the prevailing political culture and the viability of the perception of the positive and determinative role of the justice sector in the structured development of national economies. In this connection, it does appear to be pertinent to submit that, as a general rule the political directorate in the Caribbean Community appear to be egregiously unaware of the contribution of the judicial sector to national economic and social development. But, in the present submission, its contribution must be seen to be critical. Suffice it to comment that investment decisions by potential investors are not unrelated to perceptions of the expeditious delivery of judicial services, the effectiveness of judicial remedies in one or another jurisdiction and the adequacy of legal infrastructure supportive of national economic development.

As Justice Telford Georges remarked, it was distressing that the opposition of the private Bar in the Community to the establishment of an indigenous Court of last resort-based on the quality of judges before whom counsel are likely to appear. However, this perception of the private Bar has been vigorously contested in informed quarters of the Caribbean Community. The validity of this perception is brought into question by the fact that most appeals to the Judicial Committee of the Privy Council from the Caribbean are dismissed. And, in any event, it has been observed that there is no requirement established by the relevant provisions of the Agreement Establishing the Caribbean Court of Justice that members of the Court be appointed from among sitting incumbents. Moreover, the argument could be advanced that, more often than not, the quality of judicial pronouncements is a function of the quality of the submissions of counsel in the relevant case. Indeed, the West Indian Commission, in its celebrated Report, submitted that:

> On the matter of judicial talent for staffing the Court, there can be no room for doubt. Some of our own highest judicial officers

> have sat on the very Privy Council itself; the Caribbean has now provided a judge of the world's highest judicial tribunal - the International Court of Justice at the Hague; several of our lawyers have been in demand as Chief Justices and Judges of Courts of Appeal in jurisdictions like The Bahamas, Bermuda, the Seychelles and several countries of continental Africa. When Commonwealth countries look for legal talent, it is often to the Caribbean that they turn. What ails us that we lack the confidence to go forward.[16]

And competent decision-makers are in no doubt that the required expertise can be accessed from among qualified persons in the Caribbean Community and the wider Commonwealth.

Concerns expressed by the private Bar and one or two opposition political parties in the Region about the willingness and ability of Governments of the Community to provide the funding necessary to establish and maintain the Caribbean Court of Justice are not without considerable merit. In the characterisation of Justice Telford Georges:

> . . . if Great Britain had given a grant on the dissolution of the Federation for the construction of buildings and the provision of a basic library for a Caribbean final Court and had agreed for a period of ten years to make available judges paid by them, one may today have been looking forward for the celebrating of the 40th anniversary of that Court rather than being timid about setting it up if not downright opposed.[17]

In the submission of the West Indian Commission:

> . . . A CARICOM Supreme Court will require the provision of resources but, in one sense, this is like straining at a gnat when we have already swallowed a camel in terms of national expenditure on the judicial system. Even so, we should find ways of reducing costs. One way, we feel, is to locate the Court in one place. We have already referred to the generous offer by Trinidad and Tobago; that is a great help. Another device might be to allow some of the members of the Court to remain in their home locations – other perhaps than the Chief Justice. Communications have improved so greatly, both physical communications and telecommunications, that savings can be explored in new and imaginative ways. Where the resources will be most needed will be in attracting and retaining the very best of our judicial talent for service on the Court. On this we cannot skimp; but it will be one of the most productive investments the Region can make in the interest of making

> CARICOM work and in the wider cause of civil society throughout our Region.[18]

It does appear that the countries of the OECS have resolved the problem of the financial security of their Court by agreeing to an arrangement by which the Eastern Caribbean Central Bank (ECCB) is responsible for funding that institution, including the payment of the emoluments of judges. There was no guarantee, however, that an agreement by the other Member States of the Caribbean Community to have their central banks provide the funding for the Caribbean Court of Justice would yield the same result. The central banks of other Member States are not independent of their political directorates and any such arrangement was unlikely to afford greater comfort than the currently proposed arrangement to make the expenses of the Court a charge on the national consolidated fund. Consequently, the CARICOM Secretariat proposed, and competent decision-makers accepted, the mechanism of a Trust Fund already addressed in chapter 2.

As concerns the issue of jurisdiction, policy-makers have responded positively to the recommendation of the West Indian Commission to vest the Caribbean Court of Justice with original jurisdiction in respect of the interpretation and application of the Treaty of Chaguaramas as amended. In his excellent presentation mentioned above on the Caribbean Court of Justice, the learned Mr. Justice Telford Georges expressed doubt about such a course of action. In his submission, Articles 11 and 12 of the original Treaty were adequate to address the issue of disputes among Member States concerning the interpretation and application of the Treaty. In his submission, disputes arising between Member States on issues of unfair trading practices will be disputes similar to the one between the European Union and the United States on the scheme of preferences afforded bananas from ACP territories as contrasted with bananas from Central and South America:

> . . . and the sense of bitterness may be no less . . . (and) it would be unwise to permit the possibility of exposing a Caribbean Court still building its reputation to a divisive dispute of that sort among the members where there is an allegation of unfair trading.[19]

In the present submission, it would be imprudent and ungracious to disregard lightly the submissions of the learned Justice, especially in view of his acknowledged erudition and vast experience on the bench. This observation notwithstanding, it is pertinent to indicate some issues of considerable importance which might have been overlooked. Foremost among these is the fact that whereas the regional economic integration regime established by the original Treaty of Chaguaramas was relatively meagre on rights and weak on obligations, the new dispensation contemplated by the far-reaching revision of the Treaty creates a qualitatively different regime in which extremely important rights are being conferred and equally important obligations are being assumed by Member States. In this new dispensation, it cannot be business as usual and relevant decisions cannot remain unimplemented if the stated objectives of the CARICOM Single Market and Economy are to be realised. An immediate task confronting all Member States on the entry into force of the revised Treaty would be its implementation by the enactment of relevant legislation. A model Bill has already been drafted by the CARICOM Secretariat and Barbados has already enacted implementing legislation for proclamation at a later date.

The practical effect of such enactments would be to endow national courts with jurisdiction to interpret and apply the Revised Treaty thereby facilitating a Pandora's box of interpretations which are not required to be consistent with one another. The economic instability this state of legal uncertainties was likely to generate underscored the need for uniformity in the applicable norms.

The case for vesting the Court with original jurisdiction was persuasively argued by the West Indian Commission in its celebrated report Time for Action.[20]

The submissions of the West Indian Commission on this issue touch on three important issues which have been addressed by the Revised Treaty and the draft Rules of Court of the Caribbean Court of Justice relating to the original jurisdiction of the Court. These relate to the following:

- uniformity in the interpretation and application of the Treaty;
- *locus standi* for both public and private entities in matters of which the Court is seised;[21] and
- development of Community law pursuant to decisions taken within the CARICOM process (*stare decisis*).[22]

Before examining these issues, however, it is proposed to offer some clarification on the term 'Caribbean Community' and 'Community law' as they are employed in the CARICOM context. As a first step in any such examination, it is important to bear in mind that despite its misleading nomenclature, to wit, 'Caribbean Community', the regional integration movement from its very inception and, indeed, up to the present time, remains an association of sovereign States. This status was clearly reflected in the voting procedure established for the Conference of Heads of Government, the highest decision-making organ of the Caribbean Community, in both the original and Revised Treaty of Chaguaramas establishing the Caribbean Community. Article 9 of the original Treaty provides:

> The Conference shall make decisions and recommendations by the affirmative vote of all its members.

Article 28(1) of the Revised Treaty provides:

> Save as otherwise provided in this Treaty and subject to paragraph 2 of this Article and the relevant provisions of Article 27, the Conference shall take decisions by an affirmative vote of all its members and such decisions shall be binding.

Paragraph 2 of Article 28 provides that abstentions in an amount of not more than one-quarter of the Community's membership shall not operate to impair the validity of decisions of the Conference, while Article 27(3) provides that decisions of all Organs of the Community, including the Conference, on procedural issues shall be reached by a simple majority of the Member States.

In effect, the unanimity rule, which is ordinarily perceived by international lawyers as the legal expression of the sovereign equality of States, operates to deprive the highest organ of the Caribbean Community of any attributes of supranationality, which is a standard ingredient of 'communities' in the juridical sense. Further, the Caribbean Community possesses no organ like the European Union and the Andean Common Market, whose acts create legally binding rights and obligations directly for private entities, that is, without the intervention of national legislatures. In short, the term 'Community law' appearing in the West Indian Commission's submission quoted above is ordinarily employed to characterise norms arising from or under relevant international instruments and which create rights and obligations directly for private law entities. *Stricto juris*, therefore, the term 'Community law' appears to be inappropriate in its application to the Caribbean regional integration movement.

UNIFORMITY IN THE INTERPRETATION AND APPLICATION OF THE TREATY

The objective of uniformity in the application and interpretation of the constituent instrument of any integration movement would appear to be as axiomatic for its successful development as it would be for the efficient functioning of the CARICOM Single Market and Economy. Given that the Revised Treaty of Chaguaramas initially creates rights and obligations for Member States only and has to be implemented by national law before private entities can benefit from its provisions, it would be reasonable to conclude that, in the absence of an agreed mechanism for authoritatively and definitively interpreting and applying the Revised Treaty, the aphorism *quot homines tot sententiae* would prevail. Such an eventuality would, in the present submission, constitute a prescription for legal uncertainty in the macro-economic environment of the Community with dauntingly adverse consequences for foreign direct investment, and the structured development of the CSME. Postulated in other terms, not only should the Caribbean Court of Justice have jurisdiction to interpret and apply the Revised Treaty, but such jurisdiction must either be exclusive or final if legal certainty, which is indispensable for the successful development of the

CARICOM Single Market and Economy, is to attend the operation of the applicable norms.

The founding fathers of the European Union, buoyed by similar economic and juridical imperatives, crafted Article 177 of the Rome Treaty to read as follows:

> *Article 177*
>
> 1. The Court of Justice shall have jurisdiction to give preliminary rulings concerning:
>
> (a) the interpretation of this Treaty;
>
> (b) the validity and interpretation of acts of the institutions of the Community;
>
> (c) the interpretation of the statutes of bodies established by an act of the Council, where those statutes so provide.
>
> 2. Where such a question is raised before any court or tribunal of a Member State, that court or tribunal may, if it considers that a decision on the question is necessary to enable it to give judgment, request the Court of Justice to give a ruling thereon.
>
> 3. Where any such question is raised in a case pending before a court or tribunal of a Member State, against whose decisions there is no judicial remedy under national law, that court or tribunal shall bring the matter before the Court of Justice.[23]

It does appear from an ordinary reading of these provisions that the European Court of Justice is the final, though not the only, tribunal competent to rule on the interpretation and application of the Rome Treaty. The ultimate objectives of legal certainty and uniformity in the applicable norms are, however, the same. Similar considerations appear to have informed the establishment of the Court of Justice of the Cartagena Agreement, whose final preambular paragraph reads as follows:

> Certain that both the stability of the Cartagena Agreement and the rights and obligations deriving from it must be safeguarded by a juridical entity at the highest level, independent of the governments of the member countries and from the other bodies of the Cartagena Agreement with the authority to define communitarian law, resolve the controversies which arise under it, and to interpret it uniformly . . . [24]

Consistently with the foregoing, the provisions of the said Agreement on Advisory Opinions read as follows:

Article 28.

It shall correspond to the Court (sic) to interpret, through prior advisory opinions, the norms which comprise the juridical structure of the Cartagena Agreement, in order to assure uniform application in the territories of the member countries.

Article 29.

National judges who have before them a case in which any of the norms which comprise the juridical structure of the Cartagena Agreement must be applied may petition the Court for its interpretation of such norms, but provided that the ruling is subject to appeal within the national judicial system. In the event that it is necessary for the national court to issue its ruling before receiving the interpretation of the Court, the judge must proceed to decide the case.

In the event that the ruling is not subject to appeal within the national judicial system, the judge shall suspend the proceeding and petition the interpretation of the Court, *ex officio* in all cases, or upon the petition of an interested party, if so required by law.

Article 30.

The Court shall restrict its interpretation to defining the content and scope of the norms of the juridical structure of the Cartagena Agreement. The Court may not interpret the content and scope of domestic law nor judge the substantive facts of the case.

Article 31.

The judge hearing the case must adopt the interpretation of the Court.

The approach adopted by the Articles of the Agreement is to vest the Caribbean Court of Justice with compulsory and exclusive jurisdiction in respect of disputes concerning the interpretation and application of the Treaty. Indeed, this was the only rational approach open to the drafters if the objectives of legal certainty and uniformity in the applicable norms were to be secured. A decision of the Conference to vest the Caribbean Court of Justice with original jurisdiction, as distinct from exclusive jurisdiction, would not operate to deprive municipal courts within the Caribbean Community of concurrent jurisdiction in respect of the interpretation and application of the Treaty. In the premises, the objectives of legal certainty and uniformity in the applicable norms could only be secured if the Court were also vested with exclusive and compulsory appellate jurisdiction in respect of the interpretation and application of the Treaty.

The foregoing considerations appear to explain the thrust of the relevant Revised Treaty Articles which read as follows:

> *Article 211*
>
> Subject to the Treaty, the Court shall have compulsory and exclusive jurisdiction to hear and determine disputes on the interpretation and application of the Treaty including:
>
> (a) disputes by Member States parties to this Agreement;
>
> (b) disputes between the Member States parties to the Agreement and the Community
>
> (c) referrals from national courts of the Member States parties to the Agreement;
>
> (d) applications by persons in accordance with Article 222,
>
> concerning the interpretation and application of this Treaty.
>
> 2. For the purpose of this Chapter, 'national courts' includes the Eastern Caribbean Supreme Court.
>
> . . .
>
> *Article 214*
>
> Where a national court or tribunal of a Member State Party is seised of an issue whose resolution involves a question concerning the interpretation or application of the Treaty, the court or tribunal concerned shall, if it considers that a decision on the question is necessary to enable it to deliver judgment, refer the question to the Court.

Consequently, even though the Conference in relevant determinations did not pronounce on the exclusive jurisdiction of the Court, the Legal Affairs Committee advised the Conference that in the absence of such exclusivity, the exercise of an original jurisdiction by the Court would not operate to secure the objectives of legal certainty and uniformity in applicable norms, both of which were required for the efficient and successful development of the CSME.

LOCUS STANDI FOR BOTH PUBLIC AND PRIVATE ENTITIES

Since traditional international law only recognised States and State entities as subjects of international law, only such entities were regarded as competent to espouse a claim in an international forum. Consequently, there was no machinery in the international domain by which private entities, natural and juridical, aggrieved by a wrongful act could have asserted a claim against foreign States and their nationals in an international forum.[25] In the submission of the Permanent Court of International Justice (PCIJ), predecessor to the International Court of Justice (ICJ), the claimant State, in espousing the claim of its national, was in effect asserting a right with respect to a wrong committed against the State in respect of its national.[26]

When a State determines that an international delinquency has been committed against one of its nationals or his property, the foreign office of the State concerned normally makes a claim against the offending State, initially, by diplomatic representation designed to secure an *ex gratia* settlement, and ultimately, by judicial settlement if the parties so agree.[27] In the absence of consent, an international tribunal is not competent to determine the claim and would decline jurisdiction. For the claim to succeed, however, the claimant State must establish:

(a) the nationality of the claim, or its legal entitlement to espouse the claim;

(b) the exhaustion of local remedies in the jurisdiction of the delinquent State; and

(c) the jurisdiction of the tribunal to hear the claim.

And, in the absence of a contrary agreement, the State espousing a claim must establish continuous nationality, or show that the person aggrieved was its national at all material times, that is, both at the time of the incident grounding the claim and at the date of espousal of the claim. Where the claim is by a State for breach of treaty provisions respecting its nationals, the injury is considered to be a breach of good faith and an injury directly to the State itself.[28]

> Only in the rare instance where the treaty is intended to confer rights directly upon the individual can it be said that the individual is also injured.[29] Even where the national has rights directly under the treaty, the contracting State alone should have the competence to bring suit and this competence should be independent of any change in nationality.[30]

Where the national aggrieved is a company or corporation, the nationality of the claim will be determined by one or more genuine links such as the place of incorporation,[31] the place of domicile,[32] the place of the *siege social* or administrative direction, or the disposition of effective control.[33]

Consonant with traditional international law, the Statutes of the International Court of Justice (ICJ) accord *locus standi* to States only. Article 34(1) of the Statutes of the ICJ reads as follows: 'Only States may be parties in cases before the Court.' These provisions are in sharp contrast to the provisions of Article 173 of the Rome Treaty which read as follows:

> 1. The Court of Justice shall review the legality of acts of the Council and the Commission other than recommendations or opinions. It shall for this purpose have jurisdiction in actions brought by a Member State, the Council or the Commission on grounds of lack of competence, infringement of an essential procedural requirement, infringement of this Treaty or of any rule of law relating to its application, or misuse of powers.
>
> 2. Any natural or legal person may, under the same conditions, institute proceedings against a decision addressed to that person or against a decision which, although in the form of a regulation or a decision addressed to another person, is of direct and individual concern to the former.
>
> 3. The proceedings provided for in this Article shall be instituted within two months of the publication of the measure, or of its notification to the plaintiff or, in the absence thereof, of the day on which it came to the knowledge of the latter, as the case may be.

Similarly, the Court of Justice of the Cartagena Agreement accords *locus standi* to both public and private entities as provided in the following Articles of the Treaty creating the Court of Justice of the Cartagena Agreement:

Article 17

It shall correspond (sic) to the Court to decide the nullification of Decisions of the Commission and Resolutions of the Junta adopted in violation of the norms which comprise the juridical structure of the Cartagena Agreement, including *ultra vires* acts, when these are impugned by any member country, by the Commission, by the Junta, or by natural or juridical persons as provided in Article 19 of the Treaty.

Article 18

The member countries may only bring an action of nullification against the Decisions approved without their affirmative vote.

Article 19

Natural and juridical persons may bring actions of nullification against Decisions of the Commission or Resolutions of the Junta which are applicable to them and cause them harm.

It is important to note, however, that in both cases where private entities are accorded *locus standi* as of right in proceedings before the courts, such entities are directly affected by the acts of competent organs of the integration movement. In both integration movements, provision has been made for legislation with direct effects. Thus, Article 189 of the Rome Treaty which addresses Community legislation, provides as follows:

In order to carry out their task, the Council and the Commission shall, in accordance with the provisions of this Treaty, make recommendations or deliver opinions.

A regulation shall have general application. It shall be binding in its entirety and directly applicable in all Member States.

A directive shall be binding, as to the result to be achieved, upon each Member State to which it is addressed, but shall leave to the national authorities the choice of form and methods.

A decision shall be binding in its entirety upon those to whom it is addressed.

Recommendations and opinions shall have no binding force.[35]

Similarly, the relevant provisions of the Agreement creating the Court of Justice of the Cartagena Agreement provide as follows:

Article 2

Decisions are obligatory for the member countries as of the date they are approved by the Commission.

> *Article 3*
>
> Decisions of the Commission are directly applicable in the member countries from the date of their publication in the Official Gazette of the Cartagena Agreement, unless the decision provides for a later date.

The question which fell to be examined and determined by competent decision-makers of the Caribbean Community was whether, given the broad objectives of the CARICOM Single Market and Economy as set out in the Revised Treaty and the role the private sector was required to play in this new paradigm of economic development, private entities should not have been accorded *locus standi* in proceedings before the Caribbean Court of Justice. At its Second Ordinary Meeting held in The Bahamas from September 7-10, 1998, the Legal Affairs Committee, *inter alia*, 'noted the recommendation that a procedure should be considered to afford individuals, institutions or other private entities, the opportunity to appear before the Court in special circumstances'. This recommendation came from the CARICOM Secretariat but did not commend itself in its entirety to the regional Attorneys General.

The Agreement Establishing the Caribbean Court of Justice, consonant with traditional international law, does not accord private entities *locus standi* as a matter of right in matters before the court. Consequently, a private entity aggrieved by a Member State or any of its nationals in the enjoyment of rights accorded by or under the Revised Treaty must have its claim espoused by the State of nationality. Alternatively, the party aggrieved may institute legal proceedings in the national courts properly seised of the issue against the delinquent party and secure a ruling of the Caribbean Court of Justice on any issue relating to the interpretation or application of the Treaty through a reference by the competent national court to the Caribbean Court of Justice. In both instances, therefore, access to the Caribbean Court of Justice by private entities would be indirect either by espousal of the claim through the state of nationality or by way of a reference pursuant to Article 214 of the Treaty. The issue which fell to be determined was whether, in the considered view of the Legal Affairs Committee, such access should not be direct.

Unlike the Treaty of Rome, which legislates directly and derivatively for private entities in the European Union with direct effect, the Treaty Establishing the Caribbean Community, as revised, does not create rights and obligations directly for private entities within the Caribbean Community. Nor does any Organ of the Caribbean Community like the Council and the Commission of the European Union or the Commission and Junta of the Andean Common Market, have the competence to create rights and obligations for private entities within the domestic jurisdiction of Member States by legislation, without the intervention of national legislatures. The rights and obligations created by the Revised Treaty of Chaguaramas are both primary and derivative, issuing either from the Revised Treaty itself or from determinations of competent organs established by the Revised Treaty *and which have legal incidence for Member States only*. Preeminent among such organs is the Conference of Heads of Government of the Caribbean Community. Of secondary importance are the Community Council of Ministers, the Council for Finance and Planning (COFAP), the Council for Trade and Economic Development (COTED), the Council for Foreign and Community Relations (COFCOR) and the Council for Human and Social Development (COHSOD).

Rights and obligations enjoyed or assumed by private entities in the Caribbean Community and expressed in the Revised Treaty have legal incidence for such entities only where the relevant Revised Treaty provisions have been enacted into local law. It would appear to follow, therefore, that all claims of private entities arising in connection with the Revised Treaty would have to be espoused by the country of nationality or made the subject of a reference to the Court by national courts seised of the issue. For example, where the Revised Treaty, as set out in chapter III, provides for the removal of restrictions on the right of establishment, the provision of services or the movement of capital in the Caribbean Community, enjoyment of such rights by private entities is contingent on:

(a) the enactment of the relevant provisions of Chapter III of the Revised Treaty into local law by Member States;

(b) the establishment of the required programme for the removal of relevant restrictions by the Council for Trade and Economic Development (COTED) or the Council for Finance and Planning (COFAP) as appropriate;

(c) compliance by Member States with the programmes established for the purpose by taking appropriate legislative or administrative measures as the case may require.

The requirement for Member States of the Caribbean Community to enact treaty provisions into domestic law before they create rights and obligations for private entities is a function of the dualist doctrine of international law to which CARICOM Member States with common law systems subscribe.

On the basis of the foregoing submissions, the Attorneys General of the Region have determined that private entities should be accorded *locus standi* in proceedings before the Caribbean Court of Justice only by special leave of the Court and on the satisfaction of specified conditions. Consonant with this determination, Article XXIV of the Agreement Establishing the Caribbean Court of Justice reads as follows:

> *Article XXIV - Locus Standi of Private Entities*
>
> Nationals of a Contracting Party may, with the special leave of the Court, be allowed to appear as parties in proceedings before the Court where:
>
> (a) the Court has determined in any particular case that the Treaty intended that a right conferred by or under the Treaty on a Contracting Party shall inure to the benefit of such persons directly; and
>
> (b) the persons concerned have established that such persons have been prejudiced in respect of the enjoyment of the benefit mentioned in sub-paragraph (a) of this Article; and
>
> (c) the Contracting Party entitled to espouse the claim in proceedings before the Court has:
>
> (i) omitted or declined to espouse the claim, or
>
> (ii) expressly agreed that the persons concerned may espouse the claim instead of the Contracting Party so entitled; and

(d) the Court has found that the interest of justice require that the persons be allowed to espouse the claim.

DEVELOPMENT OF COMMUNITY LAW PURSUANT TO DECISIONS TAKEN WITHIN THE CARICOM PROCESS

> Although no international decision is binding on subsequent tribunals, there is a natural reluctance to depart from principles and rules which have proved satisfactory in the past for the settlement of legal issues. Hence a tendency towards *stare decisis* is most marked.

This submission of O'Connell eloquently adumbrates the current position in international law where decisions of international tribunals create rights and obligations only for the parties to the dispute and constitute a *res inter alios acta* in respect of a third State or party. And it does appear to follow ineluctably from the doctrine of sovereignty that decisions of an international tribunal involving third parties cannot operate to establish rights and obligations for a State in the absence of the State's consent. In effect, the doctrine of *stare decisis* is perceived to have no place in international law,[36] but is a doctrine of municipal law associated with common law jurisdictions. The foregoing submissions notwithstanding, publicists like Hersh Lauterpact detect in the practice of international tribunals a *jurisprudence constant*, or a tendency for such tribunals to be influenced by previous judicial decisions on the issue even though adherence to such decisions is not considered a legal requirement. Under Article 59 of the Statute of the International Court of Justice, decisions of the Court have 'no binding force except between the parties and in respect of the particular case'. But although the Court did not treat its prior decisions as binding, it used them as a guide as to the applicable law and for distinguishing the application of particular rules.[37]

Since, therefore, it is provided that the Caribbean Court of Justice shall apply international law in the exercise of its original jurisdiction, the Court, in the absence of a contrary intention, would ordinarily have been precluded from being constrained in its determinations by the doctrine of *stare decisis*. But given, as mentioned above, that legal certainty was perceived to be required for the successful operation of the CARICOM Single Market and Economy, the question falling to be decided was whether such legal certainty was possible of achievement in the absence of the application of the doctrine of *stare decisis* in the Court's determinations. The draft Articles have opted for the application of the doctrine of *stare decisis* in the determinations of the Court. Proposed draft Article IX(e) considered by the Legal Affairs Committee reads as follows:

> Member States parties agree that decisions of the Chamber shall create legally binding precedents for parties in proceedings before the Chamber, unless such judgments have been revised in accordance with Article IX(j).[38]
>
> Alternate Formulation
>
> Decisions of the Court are binding on the parties in respect of the particular case; they constitute binding precedents for parties in subsequent proceedings before the Chamber unless such judgments have been revised in accordance with Article IX(j).

The Legal Affairs Committee was required to examine and formulate a recommendation on this issue to the Conference and reached a firm determination on the issue. The provisions of the Agreement finally adopted are set out in Article 221 of the Revised Treaty.

CONSIDERATIONS ON DELINKING FROM THE PRIVY COUNCIL

In closing the circle of independence the political directorate of the Caribbean Community were determined to put in place institutional arrangements which satisfactorily addressed the legitimate concerns of stakeholders, particularly those relating to the judicial independence and financial sustainability of the Caribbean Court of Justice. In order to give stakeholders a credible and plausible assurance about the independence of the judges of the Court, competent decision-makers adopted mutually supportive measures. Firstly, they agreed to establish an independent body for the appointment and disciplinary control of judges of the Court – the Regional Judicial and Legal Services Commission. Secondly, they agreed that the method of making appointments to the Commission must be seen to generate public confidence in the independence of its members from political direction and control. Thirdly, the arrangements for financing the operations of the Court must not support an inference of indirect political control by the regional executive.

At the Second Meeting of Attorneys General and Presidents of the Bar and Law Associations of Member States of the Caribbean Community which convened in Castries, Saint Lucia on November 13, 2000, the position of the regional private Bar on the Draft Agreement Establishing the Caribbean Court of Justice may be adumbrated in the following submissions:

- there was general agreement in principle on the establishment of a regional court of last resort, but the time was not propitious for such an initiative;
- currently, the regional judiciary was in a state of near crisis as evidenced in the quality of delivery of judicial services and resources identified for the establishment of the Caribbean Court of Justice could be employed in improving the judiciary;
- given the important role of the Judicial Committee of the Privy Council in the administration of justice in the Region, there was need for much more information on the proposed Caribbean Court of Justice, especially among the general public in the Organisation of Eastern Caribbean States where delinking from the Privy Council required the holding of referenda;
- the embarrassing situation surrounding the appointment of the Chief Justice of the OECS Court of Appeal, Sir Norris Davis, underscored the need for the Caribbean Court of Justice to be insulated from political control or manipulation and in this context, the terms and conditions of service of judges of the Court should be assimilated to international standards;
- the Agreement Establishing the Caribbean Court of Justice should not provide for withdrawal from the Court and the constitutions of Member States participating in the regime should provide for entrenchment of the Caribbean Court of Justice not

unlike the Privy Council in several national constitutions;

- the Members of the Regional Judicial and Legal services Commission were not sufficiently insulated from political control, especially since the President, who was also Chairman of the Commission, was appointed by the Contracting Parties; the preferred position was for the judges to elect the President whose removal from office should not be initiated by only one Head of Government; and finally,
- arrangements for financing the operations of the Court for the first five years of its existence did not generate much confidence among stakeholders in the Region, especially in view of the appalling record of regional governments in supporting regional institutions.

Several of these concerns were subsequently addressed by competent decision-makers.

An examination of submissions in the relevant debates of stakeholders in Australia and New Zealand about delinking from the jurisdiction of the Judicial Committee of the Privy Council would reveal an uncanny similarity with the submissions of detractors of the Caribbean Court of Justice. Similarly, the submissions of proponents of national courts of last resort in those jurisdictions exhibited a remarkable degree of convergence. The official positions adopted in all jurisdictions leaned heavily on the inconsistency of national sovereignty and independence with continued reliance on determinations of an extra-territorial court of last resort. Similarly, heavy reliance was placed on the primordial requirement of public access to justice and the denial of this principle by the remoteness of the Judicial Committee of the Privy Council. In all these jurisdictions opponents of severing the nexus with the Judicial Committee of the Privy Council pointed to the international prestige of this body, the high quality of its determinations and the comfort it afforded foreign investors whose direct investment was required for national economic development. In this connection, reservations were expressed about the quality of judgments by national courts. Finally, supporters of national courts of last resort were reminded that the Judicial Committee of the Privy Council constituted a charge on the British taxpayer and that establishment of an indigenous court of last resort would require substantial outlays of expenditures if such a court were to be properly structured and adequately financed. In the present submission, therefore, all the arguments advanced against the establishment of the Caribbean Court of Justice may elicit the response of *deja vu.*

Article V of the Agreement Establishing the Caribbean Court of Justice and which addresses the composition of the Commission reads as follows:

> 1. There is hereby established a Regional Judicial and Legal Services Commission which shall consist of the following persons:
>
> (a) the President who shall be the Chairman of the Commission;
>
> (b) two persons nominated jointly by the Organisation of the Commonwealth Caribbean Bar Association (OCCBA) and the Organisation of Eastern Caribbean States (OECS) Bar Association;
>
> (c) one Chairman of the Judicial Services Commission of a Contracting Party selected in rotation in the English alphabetical order for a period of three years;
>
> (d) the Chairman of a Public Service Commission of a Contracting Party selected in rotation in the reverse English alphabetical order for a period of three years;
>
> (e) two persons from civil society nominated jointly by the Secretary-General of the Community and the Director-General of the OECS for a period of three years following consultations with regional non-governmental organisations;
>
> (f) two distinguished Caribbean jurist nominated jointly by the Dean of the Faculty of Law of the University of the West Indies, the Deans of the Faculties of Law of any of the Contracting Parties and the Chairman of the Council of Legal Education; and
>
> (g) two persons nominated jointly by the Bar or Law Associations of the Contracting Parties.
>
> 2. Where any person or body required to nominate a candidate for appointment to the Regional Judicial and Legal Services Commission in accordance with paragraph 1, fails to make such nomination within thirty (30) days of a written request in that behalf, the nomination shall be made jointly by the heads of the judiciaries of the Contracting Parties.

3. (1) The Commission shall have responsibility for:

(a) making appointments to the office of Judge of the Court, other than that of President;

(b) making appointments of those officials and employees referred to in Article XXVII and for determining the salaries and allowances to be paid to such officials and employees;

(c) the determination of the terms and conditions of service of officials and employees; and

(d) the termination of appointments in accordance with the provisions of this Agreement.

(2) The Commission shall, in accordance with the Regulations, exercise disciplinary control over Judges of the Court, other than the President, and over officials and employees of the Court.

4. The term of office of members of the Commission, other than the Chairman shall be three years, but such members shall be eligible for reappointment for another term of office.

5. The members of the Commission referred to in paragraph 1(b), (c), (d), (f) and (g) shall be appointed by letter under the hand of the President.

6. If the office of a member of the Commission, other than the Chairman is vacant or the holder thereof is unable to perform the functions of his office, a person may be appointed to perform the functions of that office for the unexpired term of the holder of the office or until the holder resumes office.

7. Subject to paragraph 13 of this Article, the Commission shall not be:

(a) Disqualified from the transaction of business by reason of any vacancy in its membership and its proceedings shall not be invalidated by the presence or participation of any person not entitled to be present or to participate in those proceedings;

(b) Disqualified from the transaction of business nor its proceedings invalidated by reason of the nonreceipt by a member of the Commission, of a notice for a meeting of the Commission.

8. The Commission may, by directions in writing and subject to such conditions as it thinks fit, delegate any of its powers under paragraph 3(1)(b) and (c) of this Article to any one or more of its members or to the Registrar.

9. A member of the Commission, other than the Chairman may, by writing under the hand of that member, addressed to the Chairman of the Commission, resign from the Commission.

10. The Commission shall, no later than March 31 in every year, submit to the Heads of Government, an Annual Report of its work and operations during the previous year.

11. The Registrar of the Court shall perform the functions of Secretary of the Commission and shall be the chief administrative officer of the Commission.

12. In the exercise of their functions under this Agreement, the members of the Commission shall neither seek nor receive instructions from any body or person external to the Commission.

13. A quorum for the transaction of business by the Commission shall consist of not less than six members of the Commission including the Chairman or, where the Deputy Chairman is presiding, the Deputy Chairman.

14. Subject to this Article, the Commission shall have power to regulate its own procedure.[39]

Careful perusal of the persons and bodies entitled to make nominations for membership of the Commission would confirm that the majority of the Commissioners are likely to be persons nominated by the regional private Bar comprising the most resolute opponents to the establishment of the Caribbean Court of Justice. However, the Heads of Government of the Caribbean Community and regional Attorneys General considered the establishment of the Caribbean Court of Justice an inclusive process in which the regional private Bar must be seen to be important stakeholders. Despite their recognition of the importance of the private Bar in regional judicial institution building, competent decision-makers were careful to point out that the Caribbean Court of Justice was intended to serve the peoples of the Region and should not be regarded as a lawyers' court in the establishment of which the regional Bar was entitled to have an exclusive or determinative role. Consequently, it was determined that civil society must be seen to have an important say in the selection of the judges of the Court – hence the formulation of Article V of the Agreement Establishing the Caribbean Court of Justice.

In order to buttress the independence of judges from political control or influence, it was agreed that, unlike procedures in similar institutions, the judges of the Court would not be appointed on the recommendation of Governments[40] but on the basis of open competition. Furthermore, credible arrangements were put in place to ensure that the tenure of judges of the Court was placed on a sound and generally acceptable footing. Thus, the Agreement provides that the office of a judge shall not be abolished while there is a substantive holder of the post.[41] Similarly, the age of retirement of judges was established at 72 years thereby avoiding the procedure of extending the period of service of judges thereby making them vulnerable to political manipulation.[42] Security of tenure of judges was also enhanced by the procedures for their removal from office. In this context it is important to note that judges may only be removed from office by the Commission for misbehaviour or inability to perform their functions. But before a judge may be removed from office, there must be a recommendation in that behalf from a tribunal of inquiry established to investigate the conduct of the judge.[43] And the tribunal's proceedings must be regulated in the same manner as commissions of inquiry in the place where the tribunal is carrying out its functions.[44]

The removal of the President from office is addressed separately in the Agreement in order to underscore the extreme importance competent decision-makers attached to this issue. There, it was provided that the President shall be removed from office by the heads of Government on the recommendations of the Commission,

> if the question of the removal of the President has been referred by the Heads of Government to a tribunal; and the tribunal has advised the Commission that the President ought to be removed from office for inability or misbehaviour referred to in paragraph 3.[45]

The provisions of Article VIII (6) of the Agreement Establishing the Caribbean Court of Justice regulate the establishment of the tribunal. In providing for the appointment and removal of the President, competent decision-makers were influenced by the impasse involving the appointment of the Chief Justice of the OECS Court of Appeal whose appointment requires a unanimous vote. As such the voting procedures normally employed by the Conference of Heads of Government were not utilised in the appointment and dismissal of the President.[46]

In responding to the challenge posed by financing of the operations of the Caribbean Court of Justice on a credible and sustainable basis, competent decision-makers agonised over the choice of institutional arrangements. In the earliest draft Inter-Governmental Agreement consideration was given to establishing a reserve fund. Another mechanism which was considered involved the posting of a bond by participants in the regime establishing the CCJ and which could be negotiated for cash in the event of Member States defaulting in their contributions to the budget of the Court. It was also proposed that Contracting Parties should be required to pay their contributions to the budget of the Court for five years in advance. However, in both cases, funding for the Court would not have been secured on a sustainable basis after the lapse of five years. In the end, however, it was agreed that the establishment of a trust fund to finance the operations of the Court was the most desirable and feasible option. In the first place, if the Caribbean Development Bank (CDB) were to raise the amount required in international capital markets, which were known to be quite liquid at the material time, the amount could be on-lent to the Contracting Parties which could repay it over the medium or long term without too much inconvenience. Further, the interest from investment of the capital could be utilised to defray the expenses of the Court, capital and current, on a sustainable basis. Consequently, competent decision-makers opted for the establishment of a trust fund. The major concern in this context was the willingness of the non-borrowing Members of the Board of Governors of the Caribbean Development Bank to approve the raising of the estimated US$100 million required, given their known doctrinal positions on the death penalty and the generally known positions of the political directorate of the Caribbean

Community on this issue. At the end of the day, and to their credit, the Board of the CDB gave their consent and the President was authorised to raise the capital for on-lending to the Contracting Parties subject to their concluding satisfactory arrangements for the establishment of the Trust Fund and for repayment to the Bank.

The financial arrangement for funding the operations of the Court placed beyond all reasonable doubt the commitment of competent decision-makers to the CARICOM Single Market and Economy whose structured development was perceived to depend on putting in place adequate institutional arrangements for the settlement of relevant disputes and for enforcement of relevant rights and obligations. In this connection, the Prime Minister of Saint Lucia, who is charged with the portfolio of Justice and Governance in the quasi-Cabinet of the Conference, appeared to have played a determinative role both in terms of concurring in the capital outlay required and in persuading his colleagues of the OECS Member States to support the proposal.

Based on the foregoing description and analysis of events surrounding the establishment of the Caribbean Court of Justice, it does appear that the quality of the response by competent decision-makers of the CARICOM to the challenge of establishing a regional court of last resort and whose structure, composition and financing arrangements were acceptable to the various stakeholders was unique and innovative.

The uniqueness of the CCJ is to be found not only in its jurisdiction being that of a municipal court of final appeal and a court of first instance in respect of issues involving the settlement of disputes concerning the interpretation and application of the Treaty Establishing the Caribbean Community including the CARICOM Single Market and Economy. The CCJ, as an international judicial body is also unique in terms of the procedures for the appointment of its judges. No other such institution has its judges appointed by persons other than ministers of Government or political representatives of Contracting Parties participating in the relevant regime. Finally, arrangements for the financing of the capital and recurrent expenditure of the Court are both unique and innovative. The institutional arrangements agreed in this connection would secure the independence of the judiciary both from administrative control of the Attorneys General or the political manipulation by the executive through the control of salaries. In this regard it is important to remember that the salaries of the judges are to be established by the Commission with the Agreement of the Heads of Government of the Contracting Parties. Security of tenure of judges of the Court is also enhanced by arrangements for their appointment, removal and retirement. In respect of their retirement, judges are entitled to serve until they are 72 years of age. Provision is not made for extensions and control. In effect, the arrangements agreed for the CCJ constitute a new and significant development in international institutional relations and are likely to provide a worthy precedent for judicial bodies of both a municipal and international status.

Before addressing prevailing perceptions in the Caribbean Community about delinking from the Judicial Committee of the Privy Council, it is proposed to examine briefly national perceptions current in Australia and New Zealand about this issue at the material time. Such an examination would support a finding that many of the arguments adduced by proponents and opponents of retaining the nexus with the Judicial Committee of the Privy Council in these jurisdictions were not dissimilar to the arguments employed in the Member States of the Caribbean Community. In this context, however, it is also important to note that unlike New Zealand and the Member States of the Caribbean Community,

> Australia already had in place a final court of appeal which took over the remaining role of the Privy Council . . . What is perhaps a relevant lesson from the Australian experience, however, is that political agreement is often a necessary precondition and must go hand in hand with legal changes in bringing Privy Council appeals to an end.[47]

In the case of New Zealand and all other Commonwealth countries, the Judicial Committee of the Privy Council was not being replaced by a multinational court of appeal like the Caribbean Court of Justice, but by a Supreme Court of domestic vintage. Further, Member States of the Caribbean community already had experience with a multinational appeal court in the form of the Court of Appeal of the Organisation of Eastern Caribbean States (OECS) which was not perceived as compromising the independence of participants.

The similarity of several of the arguments in favour of retaining the nexus with the Judicial Committee of the Privy Council in Australia, New Zealand and the Caribbean Community, despite their known cultural differences, appears to be more a function of the potency and resilience of colonialism as a cultural phenomenon than the debility of the indigenous social ethos aspiring to replace it. All these jurisdictions identified above have evolved cultural values peculiar to their own national circumstances differing significantly from the cultural values of the erstwhile colonial power; yet, when required to choose, relevant stakeholders tended to exercise the colonial option.

In the Commonwealth of Australia, the most compelling argument adduced in favour of rupturing the nexus with the Judicial Committee of the Privy Council, was the perceived incompatibility of that country's status as a sovereign independent state and retention of the Judicial Committee of the Privy Council as the court of final appeal, thereby compromising autonomous judicial decision-making. Opponents supporting retention of the linkage came largely from the legal profession, including chief justices of the state courts, who questioned the legal erudition of Australian judges, and the mercantile community which believed that retention of the link would be good for foreign investment in particular and business generally.

In New Zealand, too, strong support for delinking came from the political community which perceived autonomous judicial decision-making an indispensable attribute of sovereignty. Consequently, retention of the Privy Council as the final court of appeal was inconsistent with New Zealand's status as an independent, sovereign state.[48] But the most forceful argument adduced by the Government of New Zealand in favour of delinking from the Judicial Committee of the Privy Council was 'access to justice by improving the accessibility of New Zealand's highest court, broadening the range and increasing the volume of appeals considered by New Zealand's highest court, and using greater understanding of local conditions of the judges of New Zealand's highest court.'[49] Opponents to delinking from the Judicial Committee of the Privy Council, pointed to the credibility of its judges and the fact that it was maintained by the British taxpayer. Reservations were also expressed about the low quality of determinations issuing from the New Zealand Court of Appeal. Furthermore, retention of the link would operate to secure 'the irreplaceable benefits of conformity, tradition, informed detachment and expertise of an older and larger society. Arguments for the retention of this link are not for sentimental reasons; they are based on realism and efficiency and a desire to share in a wider legal heritage'.[50]

In the Caribbean Community, proponents of delinking from the Judicial Committee of the Privy Council leaned heavily on the 'sovereignty argument'. In the submission of Sir David Simmons, Chief Justice of Barbados:

> But over and above the preceding considerations there is one overarching reason why the time for the Caribbean Court of Justice has come. It has to do with the assertion of our sovereignty and the "completion of our independence" – legal and psychological. For if Commonwealth Caribbean countries can legitimately claim political independence, it must be the case that they are not fully independent while their highest court sits outside the Region and is staffed by persons from outside the Region. To continue the association with the Privy Council is inconsistent with independence and is an affront to sovereignty.[51]

Although this author is a staunch supporter of delinking from the Judicial Committee of the Privy Council, it is important to point out that the sovereignty argument as expressed to be exemplified in the establishment of the Caribbean Court of Justice appears to be juridically misconceived. For although the Caribbean Court of Justice is to be located in the Region and hopefully to be staffed ultimately by judges of the Region familiar with local conditions and sharing local values, in the final analysis, the Caribbean Court of Justice is an international court set up by treaty, and to whose jurisdiction participants in the relevant regime have submitted as an act of sovereignty, in the same way as they have submitted to the jurisdiction of the Judicial Committee of the Privy Council and that of the OECS Court of Appeal. In all of these cases, it does appear that the final appellate court is outside the jurisdictions of participating states which cannot legitimately claim autonomous judicial decision-making. Postulated in other terms, if submission to the jurisdiction of the Judicial Committee of the Privy Council as an attribute of sovereignty is, juridically, to compromise national sovereignty, submission to the jurisdiction of the Caribbean Court of Justice is, *aequo vigore*, a compromise of national sovereignty.

In this context, the submissions of one interlocutor, in referring to the position of the anti-abolitionists, appear to be eminently relevant:

> That the motivation of the Court is power driven by the governments of the day who have been stung by their reversals before the Privy Council in the death penalty cases. They see the argument of nationalism and sovereignty as a blind, lacking in consistency since in relation to the independent nations of the Region the Caribbean Court of Justice will be a non-national Court both in constitutional terms as well as in composition, and would therefore be in no different position that the Privy Council.[52]

Selwyn Ryan also indicated as follows:

> Opposition was fostered not only by insular nationalism, but also by deep seated fears that the political executives of the Region would make a mess of a regional judiciary, just as they had with other regional institutions. All that had been done or not done over the past four decades with respect to the relationship between political and judicial elites informed the debate and emotional postures that various groups took on the issue.[53]

The national sovereignty argument apart, proponents of severing the link with the Judicial Committee of the Privy Council also point to increased access to justice which regionalising the final court of appeal would provide. 'The sheer distance of the Privy Council from the states of the Caribbean Community has, undoubtedly, denied litigants access to justice'.[54] The Caribbean Court of Justice has been designed to be an itinerant court like the OECS Court of Appeal and significant reduction in costs can be expected to enhance access to the final court of appeal. Abolitionists also perceive the Caribbean Court of Justice as promoting the development of an indigenous jurisprudence – a process begun some decades ago with the establishment of the Council of Legal Education. Supporters of the CCJ also point to the exclusive jurisdiction of the Court in respect of the interpretation and application of the Revised Treaty of Chaguaramas in the absence of which the structured development of the CARICOM Single Market and Economy is likely to be severely compromised.

In the characterisation of Bernice Lake,

> the issue is public confidence both for the proponents as well as those who stand in opposition to the Court. For the former, confidence is important for the foreign investor, and for the latter, it is paramount for his own protection. There is need, therefore, to ensure that we enjoy a judicial culture in which the requisite climate of confidence exists before we embark on this unchartered voyage. If it does not exist, then we must find a mechanism to create and secure that confidence. It would be foolhardy to proceed to the adoption of the Court without that confidence being assured. Without that confidence, nothing else matters.[55]

After elaborating on the structure of constitutional arrangements, the role of the legislature, executive and judiciary in those arrangements, which are predicated on the fundamental rights and freedoms of the individual which are to be promoted by the state and protected by the judiciary, the author proceeds to question public confidence in the ability of municipal courts in the Region to 'deliver the constitutional protection of our rights and secure our democratic way of life in order to determine whether at this point in time we ought to chance upon indigenising our final appellate court?'[56] The writer proceeded to cite several instances where the courts were ready to sanction and exculpate unlawful state intrusion upon the constitutional rights of the citizen[57] by reference to the so-called presumption of constitutionality in respect of actions of the executive and legislature. Public confidence in the regional judiciary was allegedly compromised by the public stand-off between the Chief Justice and Attorney General of Trinidad and Tobago over administrative control of the judiciary which led to the setting up of a Commission of Inquiry, the appointment of Sir David Simmons, a former Attorney General to the position of Chief Justice of Barbados and the nomination of the late Lee Moore, former Prime Minister of St. Kitts and Nevis for appointment to the position of Chief Justice in the Eastern Caribbean.

Cases were referred to by the interlocutor to demonstrate how the OECS Court of Appeal applied the presumption of constitutionality in respect of acts of the executive and rules against the plaintiffs. The rulings of the Court in those cases allegedly did nothing to enhance public confidence in the readiness and willingness of regional courts to protect the fundamental rights of citizens from capricious and arbitrary intrusions by the executive. In that submission, the powers of the legislature and the executive must be made subordinate to the overriding supremacy of the constitution and the judiciary must be empowered to determine whether the provisions of the constitution have been respected. But, if the judiciary is the guardian of the constitution, what checks must be available to ensure that the judiciary does not overstep the permissible limits of constitutional interpretation? The answer should be sought in credible arrangements for judicial responsibility and judicial integrity, as well as societal and public accountability of the judiciary. The presumption of constitutionality, which by a curious twist of irony, was introduced into Caribbean jurisprudence by the Judicial Committee of the Privy Council, was eventually laid to rest in *Brown v. Scott* [2001] 2 All ER 1997.

The argument has been advanced that the composition of the Regional Judicial and Legal Services Commission was not structured to generate public confidence in the independence of the judges for the Bench of the Court. In this perception 'The Agreement now provides that there shall be 11 members of the Commission six of whom will be appointed by the Bar Associations and Academia and the remaining five including the President will be subject to appointment by the political directorate. Further, the three-year term of membership itself brings the life of membership well within the five-year lives of Parliament and affords review of membership in accordance with changes of Government.'

In the present submission, it is difficult to see how the regional political directorate is credited with responsibility for the appointment of five Commissioners. For even though the President is appointed by the Contracting Parties to the Agreement, his appointment has to be on the recommendation of the Commission. Further, event though the head of the Judicial Services Commission or Public Service Commission of a Contracting Party is likely to be a nominee of the political directorate, the same cannot be said for the two Commissioners appointed jointly by the Secretary-General of the Caribbean Community and the Director General of the OECS from civil society. The composition of the Commission, by any dispassionate measure of assessment, must be seen to be weighted against the nominees of the regional political directorate, as was intended by competent decision-makers in order to generate public confidence in the mechanism for the appointment of the judges of the Caribbean Court of Justice.

Commenting further on public confidence in the judiciary, Bernice Lake submitted:

> In short, you must have confidence in the appeals process as a mechanism of accountability. In the period 2000 to 2001 out of the eighteen (18) appeals considered by the Privy Council from the Eastern Caribbean Court of Appeal, fourteen (14) were reversed and only four (4) upheld. All of those concerned with freedom of expression were reversed.[58]

Other regional perceptions of an indigenous court of last resort relate to the lack of erudition of potential candidates for appointment to the Bench of the Caribbean Court of Justice, inability of the regional political directorate to provide funding for the Court on a sustainable basis, and the Olympian detachment which distance of the Privy Council generates and ensures dispassionate consideration of matters before the Court as a basis for delivering a fair and unbiased judgment.

On the question of legal erudition of prospective candidates for positions on the Bench of the Court, it is submitted that the legal erudition discerned in the recent judgments of the Judicial Committee of the Privy Council should hold no terror for the average product of the Law Schools of the Caribbean Community. In fact, submissions of regional counsel in the famous case of *Pratt and Morgan v. Attorney-General of Jamaica* (1993) 30 JLR 473 appear to exhibit a greater depth of legal reasoning than the judgment itself. So why is there so much self-doubt about the Caribbean's competence to produce judges with the required legal erudition to deliver judgments of the required quality? Intellectual brilliance is an attribute transferable from any one discipline to another. So why should a region as small as the Caribbean, which has three Nobel Prize winners within a relatively short span harbour any reservations about intellectuality in any area of expertise? Again, the perception of dispassionate dispensation of justice being impossible of attainment by judges hailing from small societies like those in the Caribbean Community appears to be misconceived. As mentioned by this author in another context, the law to be meaningful and effective as a mechanism of social engineering must embody the collective social ethos of a people and be interpreted and applied by judges who would have internalised the values informing the value content of that collective social ethos. Similar sentiments were expressed by Michael de La Bastide, former Chief Justice of Trinidad and Tobago, who maintained:

> Decisions which require the weighing of the individual's interests against those of the society are sometimes similar to the legislative function of Government. The judges who are called upon to carry out that exercise should have an intimate

> knowledge acquired first hand of the society for whom the decision is made.[59]

The abolitionists of the judicial linkage with the Judicial Committee of the Privy Council from Australia and New Zealand also argue for judges in their final appellate court knowledgeable about local conditions. Indeed, it speaks volumes that the Judicial Committee of the Privy Council tends to reverse cases from regional courts of appeal that contain a large element of subjectivity touching on the mores of our societies. Is it because the judges occupying the Bench of the Judicial Committee of the Privy Council are out of joint with the times? Or is it that the normative imperatives issuing from different social conditions nurturing them are not assimilable to values to be employed in solving problems of social engineering in our Region?

Issues addressing the independence of prospective candidates for the Bench of the Court and the financial sustainability of the Court have already been addressed. However, it is useful to address briefly the importance of perceptions. Much of the debate about a court of last resort in the Caribbean Community is based on the perceptions of various stakeholders about one or another aspect of the Court, be it the independence of judges of the Court; their legal erudition; their personal integrity and so forth. Many of these perceptions have operated to inform the attitudes of various stakeholders of the Court. But it is important to appreciate that perceptions like human beings from which they emanate are not infallible. Perceptions may be fully and accurately informed, in which case they may provide a sound basis for rational decision-making and intelligent choices. On the other hand, perceptions may be uninformed, inadequately informed or entirely misinformed, in which case they do not constitute a sound, rational, reliable guide to human conduct. More importantly, however, since persons may only react to their perceptions of reality, the line of distinction between perception and reality is invariably blurred and perception and reality tend to synonimity. And it is for this reason that perceptions about the Caribbean Court of Justice should be comprehensively and accurately informed. The CCJ will be an institution with an awesome potential to affect the lives of nationals of the Caribbean Community in one way or another. And it therefore behoves us to get it right!

THE CURTAIN FALLS

As is the case with other final appellate courts of the Commonwealth which have replaced the Judicial Committee of the Privy Council, the Caribbean Court of Justice will no longer be bound by decisions of the former body past and future. However, the CCJ will have to determine at an early date what construction is to be placed on the doctrine of *stare decisis* which governs its determinations in both its appellate and original jurisdictions. As concerns the appellate jurisdiction of the Caribbean Court of Justice it is interesting to note that Article III (2) of the Agreement is crafted in language ominously reminiscent of the language employed by Lord Salisbury in *London Street Tramways Co. Ltd. v. London County Council* [1898] AC 375 where he opined that decisions of the House of Lords were conclusive – hence their legally binding status. Prior to the Practice Statement issued by the House of Lords in 1966, the doctrine of *stare decisis* was construed as requiring the House of Lords to follow faithfully its previous decisions. Since then, there was some relaxing in the application of the doctrine to allow for a dynamic stability in the normative environment rather than a petrification of the applicable norms. The Caribbean Court of Justice will be required to clarify how the doctrine of *stare decisis* will be construed and applied in both its appellate and original jurisdictions. In this context the CCJ may be guided by the Practice Statement of the House of Lords in 1966 and relevant decisions of British courts on the subject like *Young v. Bristol Aeroplane Co. Ltd.* [1944] KB 718.

The establishment of the Caribbean Court of Justice and its determinations in the exercise of its original jurisdiction will probably constitute a rude awakening for several Member States of the Community which are unaccustomed to complying with obligations assumed under international instruments and are blissfully unaware of the applicability of sanctions for politically deviant conduct. There appears to be no culture in the Caribbean Community impelling compliance with international obligations. Consequently, many a treaty is ratified without being enacted into domestic law, and even when enacted into domestic law, there is no assurance that the enabling legislation will adequately address the obligations of the enacting States. A case in point is the Agreement Establishing the Council of Legal Education where the Government of Trinidad and Tobago was remiss in enacting its obligations into domestic law, resulting in persons legally entitled being deprived of the opportunity to enter the Law School at St. Augustine. In fact, several Member States of the Caribbean Community have omitted to enact into domestic law the original Treaty of Chaguaramas of 1973. This general disregard for international obligations assumed by Member States in international instruments concluded *inter se* was encouraged by the reluctance of States Parties aggrieved by non-compliance on the part of Member States to espouse claims at the international level against delinquent Member States. And this reluctance could have been explained in large measure by the absence of a mechanism for the compulsory judicial settlement of disputes. The establishment of the Caribbean Court of Justice with exclusive and compulsory jurisdiction in relation to disputes concerning the application and interpretation of the Revised Treaty of Chaguaramas will change all of this. Member States of the Caribbean Community will soon realise that it is a new dispensation and it cannot be business as usual. The 'Banana Case' in the World Trade Organization is but one example of the requirements of a rules-based regime.

In this context, it will be necessary for the political directorate of the Caribbean Community to accept that several, if not most, Member States lack the required capabilities to discharge the responsibilities of sovereign states in terms of establishing the national legislative and administrative infrastructure to comply with obligations assumed at the international plane.

Consequently, immediate attention will have to be given to sensitising Member States about their responsibilities in order to provide the required enabling mechanisms and institutions. In some preliminary measure, the CARICOM Secretariat has begun to address this issue by putting in place the CARICOM Legislative Drafting Facility (CLDF)[60] and the Technical Assistance Services Unit (TASU). The former is concerned with the drafting of model legislation for Member States to put in place the required legislative infrastructure for the CARICOM Single Market and Economy, to treat with justice, security and terrorism issues and the HIV/AIDS pandemic in the sub-region. The latter addresses deficiencies in the administrative infrastructure of Member States. However, much more remains to be done.

The establishment of the Caribbean Court of Justice also constitutes a belated wake-up call for competent decision-makers to address the provision of relevant legal skills and services in the area of international law. Liberalisation of legal services under the Free Trade Area of the Americas may find a surfeit of international lawyers from third country jurisdictions practising before the CCJ in its original jurisdiction, due to the paucity of relevant skills by regional legal practitioners. Similarly, the Council of Legal Education will have to take appropriate measures to ensure that Caribbean Community nationals are trained in the various areas of international law. Already it appears that British legal practitioners are eyeing the professional opportunities in the Region and have formed the British/Caribbean Jurists Association to facilitate a right of audience for British lawyers in the courts of the Caribbean Community on a non-reciprocal basis.

Undoubtedly, there is much speculation concerning how the Caribbean Court of Justice will address the issue of the death penalty in the Caribbean Community. However, it is not proposed to address this issue here out of deference for the Court. Speculation is also rife about the workload of the Court in its appellate and original jurisdictions. But this is a matter of seminal concern for the Regional Judicial and Legal Services Commission which has to decide on the appointment of judges of the Court and the Trustees of the Trust Fund whose resources are required to defray the operating expenses of the Caribbean Court of Justice. In the present submission, however, the enhanced access to justice likely to ensue from the establishment and peripatetic operations of the Court are likely to result in a heavy workload for the Court in its appellate jurisdiction. And the experience of the Court of First Instance of the European Union should provide a reliable guide in relation to the workload of the Caribbean Court of Justice in its original jurisdiction. Indeed, the former court was established to deal exclusively with economic and commercial disputes arising under the Treaty of Rome (1957).

The prospects of success of the Caribbean Court of Justice will depend in large measure on the quality of judges attracted and appointed to the bench by the Regional Judicial and Legal Services Commission, as well as on the success of the CCJ Trust Fund in providing resources for capital and recurrent expenditures of the Court through prudential management of its assets. In this connection competent decision-makers should make every effort to ensure adequacy of administrative staff and infrastructure and that economic charges are imposed for judicial and legal services rendered by the Caribbean Court of Justice. Undoubtedly, the regional political directorate have recorded several failures in the area of regional institutions like the CARICOM Multilateral Clearing Facility, the CARICOM Enterprise Regime, the Caribbean Food Corporation and the Caribbean Shipping Corporation. At the same time, the regional political directorate can point to several successful regional institutions like the University of the West Indies, the Council of Legal Education and the Caribbean Examinations Council. And the Caribbean Court of Justice is likely to fall in the last mentioned group of regional institutions if every effort is made to generate public confidence in this institution.

CONCLUSION

From conception to actualisation, the Caribbean Court of Justice took approximately 100 years. In the premises, the detractors of the Caribbean Court of Justice who are disposed to express reservations about the haste with which this judicial institution is being established appear to be ignorant of its history. And the formal inauguration of the Court, as intimated above, will constitute a defining moment in the history of the Caribbean Community. In this protracted period of soul-searching debate and institutional development, the political fortunes of national administrations in several Member States of the Caribbean Community have vacillated with the vicissitudes of political life. Despite this, the idea of establishing a regional court of last resort was kept alive with varying degrees of enthusiasm. The idea of a regional court of last resort, however, allegedly took hold when perceptions in the Region were rife that the Judicial Committee of the Privy Council by virtue of turning the hallowed doctrine of *stare decisis* on its head was generating unacceptable levels of instability in the administration of criminal justice in the Region, and this, at a time of social instability and escalating criminal violence in several Member States of the Caribbean Community.

The validity of these perceptions was borne out by the submissions of Robin Cooke, the erstwhile member of the Judicial Committee of the Privy Council and which gave considerable credence to the assumption that contortions of determinations of the Board were less a function of modifications of its legal policy than fortuitous changes in its composition. In this context, Robin Cooke maintained:

> One occasion of dissent may be worth mentioning, partly because it illustrates an agonizing type of decision which judges sitting in this country are spared but which confronts the Privy Council all too often. I refer to death row appeals from the Caribbean. In the countries concerned the death penalty is constitutional but unacceptable delays in carrying it out seems to be endemic. In *Pratt v. Attorney-General for Jamaica*, the Privy Council held that a delay of more than five years after

sentence could not be tolerated and that the sentence must be commuted to life imprisonment. In *Higgs v. Minister of National Security*, from the Bahamas, two men properly convicted of murder had been held in prison in appalling conditions only marginally removed from solitary confinement for more than five and more than six years respectively. In one case systemic delays in the trial process had exacerbated the delay (a failure of a committing magistrate to certify the record of evidence; excessive interruptions by the trial judge, necessitating a second trial). But the inhuman confinement had begun on arrest, not on conviction. The five years had not quite run from the convictions. The main issue was whether that made all the difference. Lord Hoffmann and Lord Hobhouse thought that it did; Lord Steyn and I thought otherwise. It turned out that we were in the minority. I am sorry to have to say that the fifth member of the Board felt impelled by his legal conscience to support execution. He was a respected New Zealand Court of Appeal Judge, now retired, who shall be nameless.

When it became clear that such would be the result, I said to Lord Steyn that I would join in his dissenting judgment. He suggested that it might be more effective if I were to write separately. I said that I had not understood that two dissenting judgments were permissible. He replied that he was in the chair and would recognize no such rule. At the end of the second dissenting judgment, I risked the proposition that the less rigorous view would ultimately prevail.

And so it surely will – ultimately. Immediately it did not. One of the men was hanged; the other saved the hangman the trouble by committing suicide. But in another way there has been a breakthrough. In *Lewis v. Attorney-General of Jamaica*, a differently constituted Board (the majority consisted of Lord Slynn, Lord Nicholls, Lord Steyn and Lord Hutton), revisiting the question of atrocious death row conditions and treatment, have accepted that prolonged confinement in such circumstances could indeed make an ultimate execution unconstitutional; cumulatively the punishment may be ruled out as inhuman and degrading. A way of bringing this out is that, while allowing capital punishment, the Constitution also prohibits inhuman and degrading treatment. A sentence of five years extremely rigorous imprisonment to be followed by execution could not be accepted as civilized. The majority judgment is also important as recognizing both a right to natural justice when the prerogative of mercy is being considered and the bearing of international norms and treaty obligations on the requirements of natural justice. These rights, norms and

> obligations are relevant even when not expressly incorporated in domestic law. Lord Hoffman, adhering to his former view, was a lone and caustic dissentient. Despite all the horrors of the present-day world, I believe that progress towards universal human rights does very slowly take place.[61]

On reflection however, the official reaction to the allegedly destabilising determinations of the Judicial Committee of the Privy Council in the line of cases commencing with *Pratt and Morgan* is a function of the failure to appreciate the significance of the interface between international law and municipal law, especially at a time of burgeoning influence of international humanitarian law.

Support for the Caribbean Court of Justice also came from an extremely influential and persuasive quarter, the West Indian Commission, established by the Conference of Heads of Government of the Caribbean Community at its Tenth Meeting in Grand Anse, Grenada, in 1989. Not only did the West Indian Commission firmly recommend the establishment of a Caribbean Supreme Court with an appellate jurisdiction to replace the jurisdiction of the Judicial Committee of the Privy Council, but also recommended vesting the Court with an original jurisdiction in respect of the interpretation and application of the Revised Treaty of Chaguaramas. Fortunately for the advocates of the Court, the CARICOM Secretariat diligently set about revising the original Treaty of Chaguaramas to establish the CARICOM Single Market and Economy. The completion of this exercise towards the end of the millennium gave added impetus to the establishment of the Caribbean Court of Justice. For one thing, it enabled supporters of the Court to point to the need for this institution to make the CSME a reality. For another, it enabled members of the regional political directorate to come out in support of the Court when they would have otherwise been extremely reluctant to do so only as a replacement for the Judicial Committee of the Privy Council.

Political developments supportive of the establishment of the Caribbean Court of Justice also played a determinative role in the process. In Jamaica, the People's National Party, which was always supportive of this institution, won an unprecedented four consecutive terms in office, thereby allowing continuous support at the governmental level during the most critical years of the Court's establishment. In Barbados, Prime Minister Owen Arthur, an unqualified supporter of this CSME and the CCJ perceived as its institutional centrepiece, won an unprecedented three consecutive terms of office during the critical formative years of the Court. In Saint Lucia, Prime Minister, Dr. Kenny Anthony, a product of the Caribbean Community's School of Law, came to office and exerted his considerable skills and influence to persuade his OECS colleagues to support the establishment of the Caribbean Court of Justice. In Trinidad and Tobago, the Peoples National Movement, both in opposition and government, supported the establishment of the Court at the most critical times. And in Guyana, even a change of national administrations in 1992 did not appear to dampen support for the establishment of the Court, which received strong endorsement from the private Bar. And it is also important to note the critical support which came from the CARICOM Secretariat at this time.

Despite the foregoing, it is extremely doubtful if the initiative to establish the Caribbean Court of Justice would have succeeded in the absence of a credible, affordable mechanism to finance the Court on a sustainable basis. The economies of Member States of the Caribbean Community were considerably less buoyant during the last decade of the millennium than earlier. Bananas, the lifeblood of several OECS Member States, became a casualty of the World Trade Organization multilateral trading system. Tourism was hard hit by the event of September 11, 2001 and offshore financial services of several Member States came under attack by the Organisation of Economic Cooperation and Development (OECD) in its initiative against harmful tax jurisdictions. Consequently, the various proposals advanced to finance the operations of the Court did not generate public confidence in the Region, given the parlous financial circumstances of several Member States and the history of regional administrations in this context – payments out of national consolidated funds, five years' assessed contributions payable in advance, the posting of a bond to be forfeited for non-payment of contributions, and even the establishment of a reserve fund for the Court. None of these modalities offered plausible assurances of financial viability and sustainability, nor removal of the Court from the political control or influence of the regional political directorate through the power of the purse.

Fortunately, however, the CARICOM Secretariat proposed the establishment of a Trust Fund and Mia Mottley, Chairperson of the Preparatory Committee for the Establishment of the Caribbean Court of Justice concurred in the proposal as one viable mechanism to be considered. Even more fortunate for supporters of the Court, Dr. Kenny Anthony held the portfolio for Justice and Governance in the Community's quasi-Cabinet and on him fell the important determination of initial acceptance or rejection of the proposal to establish a Trust Fund. Not only did the Prime Minister of Saint Lucia concur in the establishment of the Trust Fund, but he even insisted on its adequate capitalisation in order to yield sufficient income to finance the operations of the Court on a sustainable basis.

The institutional arrangements agreed for the Trust fund appeared to have satisfied the concerns of most skeptics about the willingness of the regional political directorate to subscribe to the budget of the Court on a sustainable basis and to allow the Court to function independently of political control or influence. The capital to be contributed to the Trust Fund was to be borrowed in the international financial markets by the Caribbean Development Bank on behalf of Member States and on-lent to them by the Bank for repayment over the medium and long-term at rates of repayment that were both acceptable and manageable. The Trust Fund was to be beyond political control and managed by independent Trustees identified by the CARICOM Secretariat and assisted by a professional manager. Default in repayments to the Bank would not affect the operations of the Trust or the Court and would attract its own peculiar sanctions normally imposed by international financial institutions. As such, one of the most critical supportive measures for the establishment of the Court was successfully put in place.

In terms of institutional independence, arrangements for the appointment and removal of the judges and President of the Court appeared to be credible and satisfactory. The Commission is comprised of a majority of members institutionally beyond the political influence of the regional political directorate and who are in a position to determine members of the Bench, including the President. Consequently, the success of the Court is likely to depend heavily on their choice of judges for the Bench. Responsibility in this context cannot be seen to rest with the regional political directorate. The Commission must now assiduously set about to appoint judges with the required professional qualifications, independence and personal integrity. These qualities more than any other are required to insure public confidence in the Caribbean Court of Justice.

NOTES

1. See Duke Pollard, *The CARICOM System: Basic Instruments* (Kingston: The Caribbean Law Publishing Co.) 366.
2. *Ibid.*, 184.
3. *Ibid.*, 3 and 96.
4. See, Sir David Simmonds, *The Caribbean Court of Justice – an Historic Necessity*, Paper presented to the Expert Group to Examine the Removal of the Appellate Jurisdiction from the Judicial Committee of the Privy Council, 2.
5. *Ibid.*
6. See Hugh Rawlins, *The Caribbean Court of Justice: the History and Analysis of the Debate*, CARICOM Secretariat. 2000, p.44-47.
7. See *Time for Action: Report of the West Indian Commission*, Black Rock, Barbados, 1992, 4.
8. See Savingram No. 97/1998 dated May 20, 1992 at p.2.
9. See Rawlins, The Caribbean Court of Justice, 5.
10. See *The Caribbean Court of Justice: what it is, what it does.* CARICOM Secretariat, 2000.

11. See *Gairy v. Attorney General of Grenada* [2002] AC 167.
12. Originally published in a slightly different form in *Caribbean Perspective*, Vol. 1, June 1991.
13. See *Report of the Caribbean Rights Symposium*, Barbados, 28 November 1998, p.13.
14. See Article IV (6) of the Agreement Establishing the Caribbean Court of Justice.
15. See Rule 7 (1) of the Rules of Procedure of the ECJ. Compare Rule 7 (1) of the Rules of Court of CFI; also Article 21 of the Statute of the International Court of Justice.
16. See *Time for Action*, p.499.
17. See *Report of Caribbean Rights Symposium*, Barbados, 28 November 1998, p.15.
18. See *Time for Action*, 501.
19. See *Report of Caribbean Rights Symposium, Barbados*, 28 November 1998, p.21.
20. See *Time for Action*, 500.
21. See Article 222 of the Revised Treaty.
22. See Article 221 of the Revised Treaty.
23. The Articles relating to the European Court of Justice are set out at 298 UNTS 3.
24. The Agreement Creating the Court of Justice of the Cartagena Agreement is set out at 8 ILM 910 (1969).
25. D.P. O'Connell, *International law, Vol. II*, 2nd ed., 1970, 1029.
26. *The Mavromatis Concession Case (Jurisdiction)*, PCIJ, Sec. A, No.2, 1924.
27. For international responsibility and the property of aliens, see D.E. Pollard, *Law and Policy of Producers' Associations* (Oxford: Oxford University Press, 1982) 283.
28. O'Connell, *International Law*, 1036-7.
29. *Ibid.*
30. *Ibid.*
31. *Standard Oil Co. of New York (U.S.) v. Germany*. U.N. Reports, Vol VII, p.61 (1926).
32. *F.W. Flack (G.B.) v. United Mexican States*, U.N. Reports, Vol V, p.61 (1929).
33. *Daimler Co. v. Continental Tyre and Rubber Co.* [1916] 2 AC 307.

34. See Articles relating to the International Court of Justice at 298 UNTS 3.
35. See *Treaty Establishing the European Economic Community*, Rome, 25 March 1957, London, HM Stationery Office. (See Appendix IV). Also Richard Plender, *A Practical Introduction to European Community Law*, (London: Sweet & Maxwell, 1980) 7.
36. See Lord Denning in *Trendtex Trading Corp. v. Central Bank of Nigeria,* at p.554.
37. See *Starke's International Law*, 11th ed., (London: Butterworths, 1974) 41.
38. See the Draft Agreement set out in Compendium of CCJ Instruments, Revision No. 7, prepared by the CARICOM Secretariat (2000).
39. See Article V of the Agreement.
40. See Article IV (7) of the Agreement Establishing the Caribbean Court of Justice.
41. See Article IX (1) of the Agreement Establishing the Caribbean Court of Justice.
42. See Article IX (3) of the Agreement Establishing the Caribbean Court of Justice. Consider in this context, too, the document entitled *Constitutional Reform: A Discussion* prepared by the Unity Labour Party of Prime Minister Ralph Gonsalves which said, *inter alia*, that extension of services of a High Court Judge 'ought purely to be a matter for the Judicial and Legal Services Commission'. Quoted by Justice Henry S.R. Moe in *The Pros and Cons of the Caribbean Court of Justice* unpublished Paper dated 1 June 2002.
43. See Article IX (5) (2) of the Agreement Establishing the Caribbean Court of Justice.
44. See Article IX (7) of the Agreement Establishing the Caribbean Court of Justice.
45. It is important to note here that due to a lapse in drafting it is not clear that Heads of Government of the Contracting Parties are intended and for 'paragraph 3' read 'paragraph 4'. See Article IX (8) of the Agreement Establishing the Caribbean Court of Justice.
46. Compare Article 28 (1) of the Treaty.
47. *Australia's Experience in Abolishing Privy Council Appeals.* Paper presented by the Commonwealth of Australia for the Commonwealth Expert Group Meeting on Replacement of Appeals to the Privy Council with Appeals to Regional Courts of Appeal, hereinafter the 'Commonwealth Expert Group', at p.11.

48. See Margaret Wilson, *Preparatory Steps to be Taken so as to Achieve a Smooth Transition in Removing the Jurisdiction of the Judicial Committee of the Privy Council*: Paper presented to the Commonwealth Experts Group, p.13.

49. *Ibid.*, 1.

50. Noel Cox, 'The Abolition or Retention of the Privy Council as the Final Court of Appeal for New Zealand: Conflict Between National Identity and Legal Pragmatism', *The Commonwealth Lawyer*, November 2002, pp.32-4.

51. See Sir David Simmons, 'The Caribbean Court of Justice: An Historic Necessity'. Paper presented to the Commonwealth Meeting of the Expert Group to Examine the Removal of the Appellate Jurisdiction of the JCPC, Marlborough House, London, June 10-13, 2003, p.5.

52. See Bernice Lake, *The Caribbean Court of Justice – Public Confidence and the Role of the Media*, Paper presented at the Fifth Annual Caribbean Media Conference, held in St. John's, Antigua and Barbuda, on May 16, 2002, at p.6.

53. *Ibid*, 9.

54. Simmons, 'The Caribbean Court of Justice', 3.

55. *Ibid.*, 9.

56. *Ibid.*, 11.

57. Reference was made to *Revere Jamaica Alumina Ltd. v. Attorney General* (1977) 15 JLR 114; (1977) 26 WIR 486.

58. Lake, *The Caribbean Court of Justice*, 30.

59. See, Justice H.R. Moe, 'The Pros and Cons of the Caribbean Court of Justice' unpublished paper dated 1 June 2002.

60. The CARICOM Legislative Drafting Facility is a project funded by USAID, and commenced operations in January 2003.

61. See Robin Cooke, 'Final Appeal Courts: Some Comparisons', *Journal of Commonwealth Lawyers Association*, 2001, 49.

APPENDIX I

AGREEMENT ESTABLISHING THE CARIBBEAN COURT OF JUSTICE

The Contracting Parties,

Convinced that the Caribbean Court of Justice, (hereinafter referred to as "the Court"), will have a determinative role in the further development of Caribbean jurisprudence through the judicial process;

Convinced also of the desirability of entrenching the Court in their national Constitutions;

Aware that the establishment of the Court is a further step in the deepening of the regional integration process;

Recognising the sovereignty of Members of the Caribbean Community;

Hereby Agree as follows:

Article 1
Use of Terms

In this Agreement, unless the context otherwise requires:

'*Commission*' means the Regional Judicial and Legal Services Commission established by Article V;

'*Conference*' means the Conference of Heads of Government of Member States of the Caribbean Community;

'*Contracting Party*' means an entity referred to in Article II which has satisfied the requirements of membership and in relation to which this Agreement is in force;

'*Heads of Government*' means the Heads of Government of the Contracting Parties;

'*President*' means the President of the Court;

'*SecretaryGeneral*' means the SecretaryGeneral of the Caribbean Community;

'*Treaty*' means the Treaty establishing the Caribbean Community signed at Chaguaramas on 4 July 1973 and any amendments thereto which take effect either provisionally or definitively.

PART I

Membership, Establishment of the Court, the Commission and Related Matters

Article II
Membership

This Agreement shall be open to –

(a) Member States of the Caribbean Community;

(b) Any other Caribbean country, which is invited by the Conference to become a Party to this Agreement.

Article III
Establishment and Seat of the Caribbean Court of Justice

1. The Court is hereby established with:

(a) Original jurisdiction in accordance with the provisions of Part II, and

(b) Appellate jurisdiction in accordance with the provisions of Part III.

2. The decisions of the Court shall be final.

3. The Seat of the Court shall be in the territory of a Contracting Party as determined by a qualified majority of the Contracting Parties but, as circumstances warrant, the Court may sit in the territory of any other Contracting Party.

4. The Government of the Contracting Party in whose territory the Seat of the Court is situated shall provide suitable accommodation for the Seat of the Court and the offices of the Commission and shall conclude with the Court and the Commission an Agreement relating to the Seat of the Court and the offices of the Commission.

5. The Court shall have and use, as occasion may require, a seal having a device or impression with the inscription 'The Caribbean Court of Justice'.

Article IV
Constitution of the Court

1. Subject to paragraph 2 of this Article, the Judges of the Court shall be the President and not more than nine other Judges of whom at least three shall possess expertise in international law including international trade law.

2. The number of Judges, excluding the President, may be increased by the Heads of Government, upon the recommendation of the Commission.

3. The Court shall be duly constituted as set out in Parts II and III and may sit in such number of divisions as may be directed by the President but every Judge of the Court may sit in any division.

4. The determination of any question before the Court shall be according to the opinion of the majority of the Judges of the Court hearing the case.

5. Notwithstanding the provisions of this Article, the President may appoint one or more judges to determine interlocutory matters.

6. The President shall be appointed or removed by the qualified majority vote of threequarters of the Contracting Parties on the recommendation of the Commission.

7. The Judges of the Court, other than the President, shall be appointed or removed by a majority vote of all of the members of the Commission.

8. The President shall take precedence over all other Judges of the Court and the seniority of the other Judges of the Court shall be determined in accordance with the dates of their appointment.

9. The appointment of the President shall be signified by letter under the hand of the Chairman for the time being of the Conference acting on the advice of the Heads of Government and the appointment of any other Judge of the Court shall be signified by letter under the hand of the Chairman of the Commission.

10. A person shall not be qualified to be appointed to hold or to act in the office of Judge of the Court, unless that person satisfies the criteria mentioned in paragraph 11 and –

(a) is or has been for a period or periods amounting in the aggregate to not less than five years, a Judge of a court of unlimited jurisdiction in civil and criminal matters in the territory of a Contracting Party or in some part of the Commonwealth, or in a State exercising civil law jurisprudence common to Contracting Parties, or a court having jurisdiction in appeals from any such court and who, in the opinion of the Commission, has distinguished himself or herself in that office; or

(b) is or has been engaged in the practice or teaching of law for a period or periods amounting in the aggregate to not less than fifteen years in a Member State of the Caribbean Community or in a Contracting Party or in some part of the Commonwealth, or in a State exercising civil law jurisprudence common to Contracting parties, and has distinguished himself or herself in the legal profession.

11. In making appointments to the office of Judge, regard shall be had to the following criteria: high moral character, intellectual and analytical ability, sound judgment, integrity, and understanding of people and society.

12. The Commission may, prior to appointing a Judge of the Court, consult with associations representative of the legal profession and with other bodies and individuals that it considers appropriate in selecting a Judge of the Court.

Article V
Establishment of the Regional Judicial and Legal Services Commission

1. There is hereby established a Regional Judicial and Legal Services Commission which shall consist of the following persons:

(a) The President who shall be the Chairman of the Commission;

(b) Two persons nominated jointly by the Organisation of the Commonwealth Caribbean Bar Association (OCCBA) and the Organisation of Eastern Caribbean States (OECS) Bar Association;

(c) One chairman of the Judicial Services Commission of a Contracting Party selected in rotation in the English alphabetical order for a period of three years;

(d) The Chairman of a Public Service Commission of a Contracting Party selected in rotation in the reverse English alphabetical order for a period of three years;

(e) Two persons from civil society nominated jointly by the SecretaryGeneral of the Community and the Director General of the OECS for a period of three years following consultations with regional nongovernmental organisations;

(f) Two distinguished jurists nominated jointly by the Dean of the Faculty of Law of the University of the West Indies, the Deans of the Faculties of Law of any of the Contracting Parties and the Chairman of the Council of Legal Education; and

(g) Two persons nominated jointly by the Bar or Law Associations of the Contracting Parties.

2. Where any person or body required to nominate a candidate for appointment to the Regional Judicial and Legal Services Commission in accordance with paragraph 1, fails to make such nomination within thirty (30) days of a written request in that behalf, the nomination shall be made jointly by the heads of the judiciaries of the Contracting Parties.

3. (1) The Commission shall have responsibility for:

(a) making appointments to the office of Judge of the Court, other than that of President;

(b) making appointments of those officials and employees referred to in Article XXVII and for determining the salaries and allowances to be paid to such officials and employees;

(c) the determination of the terms and conditions of service of officials and employees; and

(d) the termination of appointments in accordance with the provisions of this Agreement.

(2) The Commission shall, in accordance with the Regulations, exercise disciplinary control over Judges of the Court, other than the President, and over officials and employees of the Court.

4. The term of office of members of the Commission, other than the Chairman shall be three years, but such members shall be eligible for reappointment for another term of office.

5. The members of the Commission referred to in paragraph 1(b), (c), (d), (f) and (g) shall be appointed by letter under the hand of the President.

6. If the office of a member of the Commission, other than the Chairman is vacant or the holder thereof is unable to perform the functions of his office, a person may be appointed to perform the functions of that office for the unexpired term of the holder of the office or until the holder resumes office.

7. Subject to paragraph 13 of this Article, the Commission shall not be:

(a) Disqualified from the transaction of business by reason of any vacancy in its membership and its proceedings shall not be invalidated by the presence or participation of any person not entitled to be present or to participate in those proceedings;

(b) Disqualified from the transaction of business nor its proceedings invalidated by reason of the nonreceipt by a member of the Commission, of a notice for a meeting of the Commission.

8. The Commission may, by directions in writing and subject to such conditions as it thinks fit, delegate any of its powers under paragraph 3(1)(b) and (c) of this Article to any one or more of its members or to the Registrar.

9. A member of the Commission, other than the Chairman may, by writing under the hand of that member, addressed to the Chairman of the Commission, resign from the Commission.

10. The Commission shall, no later than 31 March in every year, submit to the Heads of Government, an Annual Report of its work and operations during the previous year.

11. The Registrar of the Court shall perform the functions of Secretary of the Commission and shall be the chief administrative officer of the Commission.

12. In the exercise of their functions under this Agreement, the members of the Commission shall neither seek nor receive instructions from any body or person external to the Commission.

13. A quorum for the transaction of business by the Commission shall consist of not less than six members of the Commission including the Chairman or, where the Deputy Chairman is presiding, the Deputy Chairman.

14. Subject to this Article, the Commission shall have power to regulate its own procedure.

Article VI
The First Appointment of the President and Members of the Commission

1. For the purposes of the first appointment of the President and Commissioners and notwithstanding the provisions of paragraph 6 of Article IV, the members of the Commission appointed pursuant to the Agreement shall make a recommendation for the appointment of the President.

2. Notwithstanding the provisions of paragraphs 4 and 5 of Article V:

(a) the term of office of the members of the Commission appointed in accordance with paragraph 1 of this Article shall be one year; and

(b) the members of the Commission mentioned in subparagraph (a) of this paragraph shall be appointed by letter under the hand of the heads of the judiciary of the Contracting Parties.

Article VII
Legal Status of the Commission

1. The Commission shall possess full juridical personality including, in particular, full capacity to contract.

2. The privileges and immunities to be accorded the Commission and its members in the territories of the Contracting Parties shall be laid down in a Protocol to this Agreement.

3. The Contracting Parties undertake to make provision to ensure that the proceedings of the Commission shall not be enquired into in any Court.

Article VIII
Acting Appointments

1. If the office of President is vacant, or if the President is for any reason unable to perform the functions of that office, then, until some other person has been appointed to and has assumed the functions of that office or, as the case may be, until

the President has resumed those functions, they shall be performed by the Judge of the Court who is most senior according to the date of his appointment and he shall be appointed by letter under the hand of the Chairman for the time being of the Conference.

2. When none of the other Judges is senior by appointment, the functions of President shall be performed by such one of the other Judges of the Court appointed by letter.

3. An appointment referred to in paragraph 2 shall be made in accordance with the advice of the Heads of Government tendered after consultations with the President and such other persons or bodies of persons as the Heads of Government may think fit.

4. If one of the Judges of the Court is acting as the President of the Court or if the office of a Judge of the Court, other than the President, is vacant or if such a Judge is for any reason unable to perform the functions of that office, then, until some other person has been appointed to act and has assumed the functions of that office or, as the case may be, until the Judge has resumed those functions, they shall be performed by a person qualified for appointment as a Judge of the Court to be appointed by the Commission by letter under the hand of the Chairman of the Commission.

5. The person appointed in accordance with paragraph 4 shall continue to perform the functions of the office until a person is appointed to the office and has assumed the functions thereof or, as the case may be, until the holder resumes office.

Article IX
Tenure of Office of Judges

1. The office of a Judge of the Court shall not be abolished while there is a substantive holder thereof.

2. Subject to the provisions of this Article, the President shall hold office for a non renewable term of seven years or until he attains the age of seventytwo years, whichever is earlier, except that the President shall continue in office, if necessary, for a further

period not exceeding three months to enable him to deliver judgment or to do any other thing in relation to any proceedings partheard by him.

3. Subject to the provisions of this Article, a Judge of the Court shall hold office until he attains the age of seventytwo years, except that he shall continue in office, if necessary, for a further period not exceeding three months to enable him to deliver judgment or to do any other thing in relation to any proceedings partheard by him.

4. A Judge may be removed from office only for inability to perform the functions of his office, whether arising from illness or any other cause or for misbehaviour, and shall not be so removed except in accordance with the provisions of this Article.

5. (1) Subject to Article IV, paragraph 5, the President shall be removed from office by the Heads of Government on the recommendation of the Commission, if the question of the removal of the President has been referred by the Heads of Government to a tribunal and the tribunal has advised the Commission that the President ought to be removed from office for inability or misbehaviour referred to in paragraph 4.

(2) Subject to Article IV, paragraph 6, a Judge other than the President shall be removed from office by the Commission if the question of the removal of the Judge has been referred by the Commission to a tribunal; and the tribunal has advised the Commission that the Judge ought to be removed from office for inability or misbehaviour referred to in paragraph 4.

6. If at least three Heads of Government in the case of the President jointly represent to the other Heads of Government, or if the Commission decides in the case of any other Judge, that the question of removing the President or the Judge from office ought to be investigated, then

(a) the Heads of Government or the Commission shall appoint a tribunal which shall consist of a chairman and not less than two other members, selected by the Heads of Government or the Commission, as the case may be, after such consultations as may be considered expedient, from among persons who hold or have held office as a Judge of a court of unlimited jurisdiction in civil and criminal matters in some part of the Commonwealth, or in a State exercising civil law jurisprudence common to Contracting Parties, or a court having jurisdiction in appeals from any such court; and

(b) The tribunal shall enquire into the matter and advise the Heads of Government or the Commission, as the case may be, whether or not the President or the Judge ought to be removed from office.

7. The provisions of any law relating to the holding of commissions of inquiry in the Member State of the Caribbean Community where the inquiry is held shall apply as nearly as may be in relation to tribunals appointed under paragraph 6 of this Article or, as the context may require, to the members thereof as they apply in relation to Commissions or Commissioners appointed under that law.

8. If the question of removing the President or any other Judge of the Court from office has been referred to a tribunal under paragraph 6 of this Article, the Heads of Government in the case of the President, or the Commission, in the case of any other Judge of the Court, may suspend such Judge from performing the functions of his office, and any such suspension may at any time be revoked by the Heads of Government or the Commission, as the case may be, and shall in any case cease to have effect if the tribunal advises the Heads of Government or the Commission that the Judge ought not to be removed from office.

9. (1) The President may at any time resign the office of President by writing under the hand of the President addressed to the Chairman for the time being of the Conference.

(2) Any other Judge of the Court may at any time resign the office of Judge of the Court by writing under the hand of the Judge addressed to the Chairman of the Commission.

Article X
Oath of Office

1. A Judge of the Court shall not enter upon the duties of that office unless he has taken and subscribed the oath of office as set out in Appendix I to this Agreement.

2. The oath of office shall be taken and subscribed before the Head of State of any Contracting Party.

PART II

ORIGINAL JURISDICTION OF THE COURT

Article XI
Constitution of the Court

1. The Court, in the exercise of its original jurisdiction, shall be duly constituted if it consists of not less than three judges being an uneven number of judges.

2. The judges referred to in paragraph 1 shall possess the expertise necessary for the Court to adjudicate the matter

3. The deliberations of the Court shall be under the authority and control of a Chairman, who shall be the most senior of the judges appointed by the President.

4. Notwithstanding paragraph 1, the original jurisdiction of the Court may be exercised by a sole judge appointed by the Chairman.

5. The decision of a sole judge exercising jurisdiction under paragraph 4 may, on application of a Party aggrieved, be reviewed by a panel comprising not more than five judges.

Article XII
Jurisdiction of the Court in Contentious Proceedings

1. Subject to the Treaty, the Court shall have exclusive jurisdiction to hear and deliver judgment on:

(a) disputes between Contracting Parties to this Agreement;

(b) disputes between any Contracting Parties to this Agreement and the Community;

(c) referrals from national courts or tribunals of Contracting Parties to this Agreement;

(d) applications by nationals in accordance with Article XXIV,

concerning the interpretation and application of the Treaty.

2. For the purposes of this part, 'national courts' includes the Eastern Caribbean Supreme Court.

Article XIII
Advisory Opinions of the Court

1. The Court shall have exclusive jurisdiction to deliver advisory opinions concerning the interpretation and application of the Treaty.

2. Advisory opinions shall be delivered only at the request of Contracting Parties or the Community.

Article XIV
Referral to the Court

Where a national court or tribunal of a Contracting Party is seized of an issue whose resolution involves a question concerning the interpretation or application of the Treaty, the court or tribunal concerned shall, if it considers that a decision on the question is necessary to enable it to deliver judgment, refer the question to the Court for determination before delivering judgment.

Article XV
Compliance with Judgments of the Court

Member States, Organs, Bodies of the Community or persons to whom a judgment of the Court applies, shall comply with that judgment.

Article XVI
Compulsory Jurisdiction of the Court

1. Contracting Parties agree that they recognise as compulsory, *ipso facto* and without special agreement, the original jurisdiction of the Court provided for in Article XII.

2. In the event of a dispute as to whether the Court has jurisdiction, the matter shall be determined by decision of the Court.

Article XVII
Law to be Applied by the Court in the Exercise of its Original Jurisdiction

1. The Court, in exercising its original jurisdiction under Article XII (b) and (c), shall apply such rules of international law as may be applicable.

2. The Court may not bring in a finding of *non- liquet* on the ground of silence or obscurity of the law.

3. The provisions of paragraphs (1) and (2) shall not prejudice the power of the Court to decide a dispute *ex aequo et bono* if the parties so agree.

Article XVIII
Intervention by Third Parties

1. Should a Member State, the Community or a person consider that it has a substantial interest of a legal nature which may be affected by a decision of the Court in the exercise of its original jurisdiction, it may apply to the Court to intervene and it shall be for the Court to decide on the application.

2. Whenever the construction of a convention to which Member States and persons other than those concerned in the case are parties, is in question, the Registrar shall notify all such States and persons forthwith.

3. Every State or person so notified has the right to intervene in the proceedings; but if the right is exercised, the construction given by the judgment will be equally binding on all parties.

Article XIX
Application for Interim Measures

The Court shall have the power to prescribe if it considers the circumstances so require, any interim measures that ought to be taken to preserve the rights of a Party.

Article XX
Revision of Judgments of the Court in the Exercise of its Original Jurisdiction

1. An application for the revision of a judgment of the Court in the exercise of its original jurisdiction may be made only when it is based upon the discovery of some fact of such a nature as to be a decisive factor, which fact was, when the judgment was given, unknown to the Court and to the party claiming revision: provided always that such ignorance was not due to negligence on the part of the applicant.

2. Proceedings for a revision shall be opened by a judgment of the Court expressly recording the existence of the new fact, recognising that it has such a character as to lay the case open to revision, and declaring the application admissible on this ground.

3. The Court may require previous compliance with the terms of the judgment before it admits proceedings in revision.

4. The application for revision shall be made within six months of the discovery of the new fact.

5. No application for revision may be made after the lapse of five years from the date of the judgment.

6. Nothing in this Article shall affect the rights of third parties accrued since the delivery of the judgment mentioned in paragraph 1.

Article XXI
Rules of Court Governing Original Jurisdiction

1. The President shall, in consultation with five other Judges of the Court selected by him, establish rules for the exercise of the original jurisdiction of the Court.

2. Without prejudice to the generality of the preceding subparagraph, Rules of Court may be made for all or any of the following purposes –

(a) Regulating the sittings of the Court, the selection of Judges for any purpose, and the period to be observed as a vacation in the Court and the transaction of business during any such vacation;

(b) Regulating the pleading, practice, procedure, execution of the process of the Court and the duties of the officers of the Court;

(c) Regulating matters relating to practice in the Court by AttorneysatLaw, Legal Practitioners or advocates and the representation of persons concerned in any proceedings in the Court;

(d) Providing for the summary determination of any matter which appears to the Court to be frivolous or vexatious or to be brought for the purpose of delay;

(e) Regulating matters relating to the costs and the taxation thereof, of proceedings in the Court;

(f) Providing for the delivery of judgments in an expeditious manner;

(g) Prescribing forms and fees in respect of proceedings in the Court;

(h) Prescribing the time within which any requirement of the rules of Court is to be complied with;

(i) Regulating or prescribing or doing any other thing which may be regulated, prescribed or done by rules of Court.

Article XXII
Judgment of the Court to Constitute Stare Decisis

Judgments of the Court shall be legally binding precedents for parties in proceedings before the Court unless such judgments have been revised in accordance with Article XX.

Article XXIII
Alternative Dispute Resolution

1. Each Contracting Party shall, to the maximum extent possible, encourage and facilitate the use of arbitration and other means of alternative dispute resolution for the settlement of international commercial disputes.

2. To this end, each Contracting Party shall provide appropriate procedures to ensure observance of agreements to arbitrate and for the recognition and enforcement of arbitral awards in such disputes.

Article XXIV
Locus Standi of Private Entities

Nationals of a Contracting Party may, with the special leave of the Court, be allowed to appear as parties in proceedings before the Court where:

(a) The Court has determined in any particular case that the Treaty intended that a right conferred by or under the Treaty on a Contracting Party shall ensure to the benefit of such persons directly; and

(b) The persons concerned have established that such persons have been prejudiced in respect of the enjoyment of the benefit mentioned in subparagraph (a) of this Article; and

(c) The Contracting Party entitled to espouse the claim in proceedings before the Court has:

 (i) Omitted or declined to espouse the claim, or

 (ii) Expressly agreed that the persons concerned may espouse the claim instead of the Contracting Party so entitled; and

(d) The Court has found that the interest of justice requires that the persons be allowed to espouse the claim.

PART III

Appellate Jurisdiction of the Court

Article XXV
Appellate Jurisdiction of the Court

1. In the exercise of its appellate jurisdiction, the Court is a superior Court of record with such jurisdiction and powers as are conferred on it by this Agreement or by the Constitution or any other law of a Contracting Party.

2. Appeals shall lie to the Court from decisions of the Court of Appeal of a Contracting Party as of right in the following cases:

(a) Final decisions in civil proceedings where the matter in dispute on appeal to the Court is of the value of not less than twentyfive thousand dollars Eastern Caribbean currency (EC$25,000) or where the appeal involves directly or indirectly a claim or a question respecting property or a right of the aforesaid value;

(b) Final decisions in proceedings for dissolution or nullity of marriage;

(c) Final decisions in any civil or other proceedings which involve a question as to the interpretation of the Constitution of the Contracting Party;

(d) Final decisions given in the exercise of the jurisdiction conferred upon a superior court of a Contracting Party relating to redress for contravention of the provisions of the Constitution of a Contracting Party for the protection of fundamental rights;

(e) Final decisions given in the exercise of the jurisdiction conferred on a superior court of a Contracting Party relating to the determination of any question for which a right of access to the superior court of a Contracting Party is expressly provided by its Constitution;

(f) such other cases as may be prescribed by any law of the Contracting Party.

3. An appeal shall lie to the Court with the leave of the Court of Appeal of a Contracting Party from the decisions of the Court of Appeal in the following cases:

(a) Final decisions in any civil proceedings where, in the opinion of the Court of Appeal, the question involved in the appeal is one that by reason of its great general or public importance or otherwise, ought to be submitted to the Court; and

(b) Such other cases as may be prescribed by any law of the Contracting Party.

4. Subject to paragraph 2, an appeal shall lie to the Court with the special leave of the Court from any decision of the Court of Appeal of a Contracting Party in any civil or criminal matter.

5. Nothing in this Article shall apply to matters in relation to which the decision of the Court of Appeal of a Contracting Party is, at the time of the entry into force of the Agreement pursuant to the Constitution or any other law of that Party, declared to be final.

6. The Court shall, in relation to any appeal to it in any case, have all the jurisdiction and powers possessed in relation to that case by the Court of Appeal of the Contracting Party from which the appeal was brought.

7. (1) The President shall in consultation with five other Judges of the Court selected by him, make Rules of Court for regulating the practice and procedure of the Court in exercise of the appellate jurisdiction conferred on the Court and, in relation to appeals brought before the Court, the practice and procedure of any court in respect of such appeals.

(2) Without prejudice to the generality of the preceding sub paragraph, Rules of Court may be made for all or any of the following purposes –

(a) Regulating the sittings of the Court, the selection of Judges for any purpose, and the period to be observed as a vacation in the Court and the transaction of business during any such vacation;

(b) Regulating the pleading, practice, procedure, execution of the process of the Court and the duties of the officers of the Court;

(c) Regulating matters relating to practice in the Court by AttorneysatLaw or Legal Practitioners and the representation of persons concerned in any proceedings in the Court;

(d) Prescribing the cases in which, and the conditions upon which an appellant in a criminal appeal to the Court shall be entitled to be present at the hearing of the appeal;

(e) Providing for the summary determination of any appeal which appears to the Court to be frivolous or vexatious or to be brought for the purpose of delay;

(f) Regulating matters relating to the costs and the taxation thereof, of proceedings in the Court;

(g) Providing for the delivery of judgments in an expeditious manner;

(h) Prescribing forms and fees in respect of proceedings in the Court;

(i) Prescribing the time within which any requirement of the rules of Court is to be complied with;

(j) Regulating or prescribing or doing any other thing which may be regulated, prescribed or done by rules of Court.

PART IV

Enforcement, Financial and Final Provisions

Article XXVI
Enforcement of Orders of the Court

The Contracting Parties agree to take all the necessary steps, including the enactment of legislation to ensure that:

(a) all authorities of a Contracting Party act in aid of the Court and that any judgment, decree, order or sentence of the Court given in exercise of its jurisdiction shall be enforced by all courts and authorities in any territory of the Contracting Parties as if it were a judgment, decree, order or sentence of a superior court of that Contracting Party;

(b) The Court has power to make any order for the purpose of securing the attendance of any person, the discovery or production of any document, or the investigation or punishment of any contempt of court that any superior court of a Contracting Party has power to make as respects the area within its jurisdiction.

Article XXVII
Officials and Employees of the Court

1. There shall be a Registrar of the Court, Deputy Registrars and other officials and employees of the Court as the Commission may consider necessary. The holders of those offices shall be paid such salaries and allowances and shall have such other terms and conditions of service as may, from time to time, be determined by the Commission.

2. With the concurrence of the competent authority of a Contracting Party, the Commission may appoint the Registrar of a superior court in the territory of that Contracting Party to be a Deputy Registrar of the Court.

3. The Commission may, by directions in writing and subject to such condition as it thinks fit, delegate any of its powers under

paragraph 1 to any one or more of its members or to the Registrar of the Court.

4. For the purposes of paragraph 2 of this Article, "competent authority" means the authority vested with power to make appointments to the office of Registrar of a superior court and to exercise disciplinary control over persons holding or acting in that office.

Article XXVIII
Financial Provisions

1. The expenses of the Court and of the Commission, including the cost of the maintenance of the Seat of the Court and the remuneration and allowances and other payments referred to in Article XXVII and this Article, shall be borne by the Contracting Parties in such proportions as may be agreed by the Contracting Parties. The assessed contributions to be paid by a Contracting Party shall be charged by law on the Consolidated Fund or public revenues of that Contracting Party.

2. (1) Subject to this Agreement and with the approval of the Conference, the Commission shall determine the terms and conditions and other benefits of the President and other Judges of the Court.

(2) The salaries and allowances referred to in subparagraph 1 shall be set out in Appendix II to this Agreement.

(3) Notwithstanding the provisions of Article XXXII, the Commission may, with the approval of the Conference, make regulations to amend Appendix II.

3. The salaries and allowances payable to the President and the other Judges of the Court and their other terms and conditions of service shall not be altered to their disadvantage during their tenure of office. For the purposes of this paragraph, in so far as the terms and conditions of service of any Judge of the Court depend upon the option of that Judge, the terms for which that Judge opts shall be taken to be more advantageous to that Judge than any other terms and conditions for which the Judge might have opted.

4. There shall be paid to members of the Commission, other than the Chairman, the actual travelling expenses and subsistence allowance at such rate per day as the Heads of Government may, from time to time, decide for the purpose of performing official duties as a member of the Commission.

Article XXIX
Right of Audience

AttorneysatLaw, legal practitioners or advocates duly admitted to practice law in the courts of a Contracting Party shall, subject to the powers of the Court, not be required to satisfy any other condition in order to practice before the Court wherever the Court is sitting in exercise of its jurisdiction and they shall enjoy the privileges and immunities necessary for the independent exercise of their duties.

Article XXX
Privileges and Immunities

The privileges and immunities to be recognised and granted by the Contracting Parties to the Judges and officers of the Court necessary to protect their independence and impartiality shall be laid down in a Protocol to this Agreement.

Article XXXI
Regulations

The Commission may make Regulations –

(a) governing the appointment, discipline, termination of employment and other terms and conditions of service and employment for –

   (i) Judges, other than the President; and

   (ii) officials and employees of the Court;

(b) prescribing the procedure governing the conduct of disciplinary proceedings;

(c) generally giving effect to this Agreement.

Article XXXII
Amendment

1. This Agreement may be amended by the Contracting Parties.

2. Every amendment shall be subject to ratification by the Contracting Parties in accordance with their respective constitutional procedures and shall enter into force one month after the date on which the last Instrument of ratification or accession is deposited with the SecretaryGeneral (hereinafter in this Agreement referred to as "the Depositary").

Article XXXIII
Signature

This Agreement is open for signature by any of the States or countries referred to in Article II.

Article XXXIV
Ratification

This Agreement shall be subject to ratification by the signatory countries in accordance with their respective constitutional procedures. Instruments of ratification shall be deposited with the Depositary who shall transmit certified copies to the Government of each Contracting Party.

Article XXXV
Entry Into Force

This Agreement shall enter into force upon the deposit of Instruments of Ratification or Accession in accordance with Article XXXIV, by at least three Member States of the Caribbean Community.

Article XXXVI
Accession

1. Any country to which paragraph (b) of Article II applies may accede to this Agreement and become a Contracting Party on such terms and conditions as the Conference may decide.

2. Instruments of Accession shall be deposited with the Depositary.

Article XXXVII
Withdrawal

1. A Contracting Party may withdraw from this Agreement by giving three years' notice in writing to the Depositary who shall promptly notify the other Contracting Parties accordingly and the withdrawal shall take effect five years after the date on which the notice has been received by the Depositary, unless the Contracting Party before the withdrawal becomes effective notifies the Depositary in writing of the cancellation of its notice of withdrawal.

2. A Contracting Party that withdraws from this Agreement undertakes to honour any financial or other obligations duly assumed as a Contracting Party; this includes any matter relating to an appeal filed before withdrawal becomes effective.

Article XXXVIII
Implementation

The Contracting Parties shall take all necessary action, whether of a legislative, executive or administrative nature, for the purpose of giving effect to this Agreement. Such action shall be taken as expeditiously as possible, and the Secretary General shall be informed accordingly.

Article XXXIX
Reservations

A reservation may be entered to Article XXV of this Agreement with the consent of the Contracting Parties.

IN WITNESS WHEREOF the undersigned duly authorised in that behalf by their respective Governments have executed this Agreement.

Done at St. Michael, Barbados on the 14th day of February 2001.

Signed by Lester Bird for the Government of Antigua and Barbuda on the 14th day of February 2001 at St. Michael, Barbados

Signed by Owen Arthur for the Government of Barbados on the 14th day of February 2001 at St. Michael, Barbados

Signed by Said Musa for the Government of Belize on the 14th day of February 2001 at St. Michael, Barbados

Signed by for the Government of the Commonwealth of Dominica on the day of 2001 at

Signed by Keith Mitchell for the Government of Grenada on the 14th day of February 2001 at St. Michael, Barbados

Signed by Clement Rohee for the Government of the Co operative Republic of Guyana on the14th day of February 2001 at St. Michael, Barbados

Signed by for the Government of Haiti on the day of 2001 at

Signed by Percival J. Patterson for the Government of Jamaica on the 14th day of February 2001 at St. Michael, Barbados

Signed by for the Government of Montserrat on the day of 2001 at

Signed by Denzil Douglas for the Government of St. Kitts and Nevis on the 14th day of February 2001 at St. Michael, Barbados

Signed by Kenny D. Anthony for the Government of Saint Lucia on the 14th day of February 2001 at St. Michael, Barbados

Signed by for the Government of St. Vincent and the Grenadines on the day of 2001 at

Signed by R. Venetiaan for the Government of The Republic of Suriname on the 14th day of February 2001 at St. Michael, Barbados

Signed by Basdeo Panday for the Government of The Republic of Trinidad and Tobago on the14th day of February 2001 at St. Michael, Barbados

APPENDIX I

I .... do hereby swear (or solemnly affirm) that I will faithfully exercise the office of President/Judge of the Caribbean Court of Justice without fear or favour, affection or illwill and in accordance with the Code of Judicial Conduct.

(So help me God (to be omitted in affirmation)).

APPENDIX II

Annual Salary

1. (a) The President of the Court [EC$]

   (b) Any other Judge of the Court [EC$]

2. Judges of the Court shall be paid super-annuation benefits in respect of their service as Judge of the Court as follows –

(a) Less than 5 years' service a gratuity of 20 per cent of the Judge's pensionable emoluments at the time of retirement for every year of service;

(b) 5 to 10 years' service a monthly pension equivalent to twothirds of the Judge's monthly pensionable emoluments at the time of retirement.

(c) More than 10 years' service a monthly pension equivalent to the Judge's monthly pensionable emoluments at the time of retirement.

3. Every Judge of the Court shall be paid a monthly allowance for housing to be determined by the Heads of Government of the Contracting Parties in respect of the Judge's occupation of a fully furnished residence.

4. Every Judge shall be paid a monthly allowance to be determined by the Heads of Government of the Contracting Parties to meet the expenses incurred by the Judge in respect of the employment of a chauffeur.

5. Every Judge shall be paid a travelling allowance to be determined by the Heads of Government of the Contracting Parties in respect of the use by the Judge of a motor car owned by the Judge on official duty, subject to the conditions of payment as determined by the Heads of Government of the Contracting Parties.

6. Every Judge of the Court shall be provided with telephone services at the Judge's residence, without charge, except for unofficial overseas telephone calls.

7. Every Judge of the Court shall be paid a subsistence allowance to be determined by the Heads of Government of the Contracting Parties for each day on which the Judge is on official duty in the territory of a Contracting Party other than that of the seat of the Court.

APPENDIX II

PROTOCOL TO THE AGREEMENT ESTABLISHING THE CARIBBEAN COURT OF JUSTICE RELATING TO THE JURIDICAL PERSONALITY AND LEGAL CAPACITY OF THE COURT

The Contracting Parties:

Noting that the Agreement Establishing the Caribbean Court of Justice (hereinafter referred to as "the Agreement") entered into force on 23 July 2002;

Conscious that Article VI of the Agreement confers on the Regional Judicial and Legal Services Commission (hereinafter referred as "the Commission") full juridical personality, including, in particular, full capacity to contract;

Aware that the Government of Trinidad and Tobago, the Contracting Party in whose territory the Seat of the Caribbean Court of Justice (hereinafter referred to as "the Court") is situated, in accordance with Article III (4) of the Agreement, intends to conclude an Agreement relating to the Seat of the Court and the Headquarters of the Commission;

Desirous of conferring on the Court full juridical personality and legal capacity,

Have agreed as follows:

Article I
Juridical Personality and Legal Capacity of the Court

1. The Court shall have full juridical personality.

2. Each Contracting party to the Agreement shall, in its territory, accord to the Court the most extensive legal capacity accorded to legal persons under its municipal law.

3. In any legal proceedings, the Court shall be represented by the Registrar of the Court.

4. Each Contracting Party to the Agreement shall take such action as is necessary to make effective in its territory the provisions of this Article and shall promptly inform the Secretary-General of the Caribbean Community of such action.

Article II
Privileges and Immunities of the Court and the Commission

The President of the Court shall conclude with the Government of Trinidad and Tobago an Agreement relating to the Seat of the Court and the Headquarters of the Commission setting out, *inter alia*:

(a) the terms respecting the facilitation of the administration and operation of the Court and the Commission; and

(b) the privileges and immunities to be accorded to the Commission and its members, the Court, the Judges and officers of the Court, parties, their counsel and other persons required to appear before the Court.

Article III
Relationship Between this Protocol and the Agreement

This Protocol shall be read as one with the Agreement.

Article IV
Signature

This Protocol shall be open for signature by the Contracting Parties to the Agreement.

Article V
Entry Into Force

This Protocol shall enter into force on signature by the Contracting Parties to the Agreement.

Article VI
Accession

1. Any Contracting Party to the Agreement may accede to this Protocol.

2. Instruments of accession shall be deposited with the Secretary-General who shall transmit certified copies to the Governments.

IN WITNESS WHEREOF the undersigned representatives, being duly authorised by their respective Governments or Institutions, have signed this Protocol.

Done at on the day of 2003

Signed by for the Government of Antigua and Barbuda on the day of 2003 at

Signed by for the Government of Barbados on the day of 2003 at

Signed by for the Government of Belize on the day of 2003 at

Signed by for the Government of the Commonwealth of Dominica on the day of 2003 at

Signed by for the Government of Grenada on the day of 2003 at

Signed by for the Government of the Cooperative Republic of Guyana on the day of 2003 at

Signed by for the Government of Jamaica on the day of 2003 at

Signed by for the Government of Montserrat on the day of 2003 at

Signed by for the Government of St. Kitts and Nevis on the day of 2003 at

Signed by for the Government of Saint Lucia on the day of 2003 at

Signed by for the Government of St. Vincent and the Grenadines on the day of 2003 at

Signed by for the Government of the Republic of Suriname on the day of 2003 at

Signed by for the Government of Trinidad and Tobago on the day of 2003 at

APPENDIX III

PROTOCOL ON THE STATUS, PRIVILEGES AND IMMUNITIES OF THE CARIBBEAN COURT OF JUSTICE AND THE REGIONAL JUDICIAL AND LEGAL SERVICES COMMISSION

Preamble

The Contracting Parties

Noting that the Agreement Establishing the Caribbean Court of Justice entered into force on 23 July 2002;

Recognising that paragraph 2 of Article VII of the Agreement Establishing the Caribbean Court of Justice (hereinafter referred to as *'the Agreement')* provides that the privileges and immunities to be accorded the Regional Judicial and Legal Services Commission shall be laid down in a Protocol to the Agreement;

Conscious that Article XXX of the Agreement also provides that the privileges and immunities to be recognised and granted by the Contracting Parties thereto to the judges and officers of the Court necessary to protect their independence and impartiality, shall be laid down in a Protocol to the Agreement; and

Desirous of establishing conditions to safeguard the independence and integrity of the judges and officers of the Caribbean Court of Justice (hereinafter referred to as 'the Court') and the Members of the Regional Judicial and Legal Services Commission,

Have agreed as follows:

Article I
Use of Terms

In this Protocol, unless the context otherwise requires:

'archives of the Court or the Commission' includes the records, correspondence, documents, manuscripts, photographs, slides, films, sound recordings and electronic storage devices belonging to or held by the Court or the Commission;

'Commission' means the Regional Judicial and Legal Services Commission established by Article V of the Agreement;

'competent Authorities' means national, regional or local authorities of the Contracting Parties as may be appropriate in the context and in the laws of the Contracting Parties;

'Conference' means the Conference of Heads of Government of the Member States of the Caribbean Community;

'Contracting Party' means a state in relation to which this Protocol is in force;

'counsel' means a person qualified to conduct proceedings before the Court on behalf of another;

'the Court' means the Caribbean Court of Justice established by Article III of the Agreement;

'the Government' means the Government of a Contracting Party to this Protocol;

'officers of the Court' means the Registrar of the Court and the Deputy Registrar;

'the President' means the President of the Court;

'property' means all forms of property, including funds and assets belonging to or held or administered by the Court or the Commission and all income accruing to the Court or the Commission;

'Registrar' means the Registrar of the Court;

'SecretaryGeneral' means the SecretaryGeneral of the Caribbean Community.

Article II
Property Funds and Assets of the Court and the Commission

1. The Court, the Commission, their property and assets, wherever located and by whomsoever held, shall enjoy immunity from every form of legal process except in so far as in any particular case such immunity has been expressly waived in accordance with Article X. No waiver of immunity shall extend to any measure of execution.

2. The property of the Court and the Commission, wherever located and by whomsoever held, shall be immune from search, requisition, confiscation, expropriation and any other form of interference whether by executive, administrative or judicial action.

Article III
Premises of the Court and the Commission

1. The premises occupied by the Court or the Commission shall be inviolable.

2. The President may make regulations relating to the premises mentioned in paragraph 1 of this Article for the purpose of establishing therein conditions necessary for the full execution of the functions of the Court or the Commission, as the case may be.

3. Officials of the Government shall not enter the premises referred to in this Article to perform any official duties therein except with the consent of and under conditions agreed by the

President. However, in case of fire or other emergency requiring prompt protective action or in the event that officials of the Government have reasonable cause to believe that such an emergency has occurred, the consent of the President to entry on the premises by the officials of the Government shall be presumed if the President cannot be reached in time.

Article IV
Archives of the Court and the Commission

The archives of the Court and the Commission, and in general all documents belonging to or held by the Court or the Commission, shall be inviolable wherever located.

Article V
Exemption From Foreign Exchange Controls

1. Without being restricted by financial controls, regulations or moratoria of any kind, the Court and the Commission shall be entitled for their official use only:

(a) to purchase from authorised dealers, hold and make use of negotiable currencies, operate foreign currency and external accounts and purchase through authorised dealers, hold and make use of funds and securities;

(b) to freely transfer their funds, securities and foreign currencies to or from the territory of any Contracting Party and to convert any currency held by them into any other currency.

2. The Court and the Commission, in exercising their rights under paragraph 1 of this Article, shall pay due regard to any representations made by the Government and shall give effect to such representations so far as this is possible without detriment to the interests of the Court or the Commission.

Article VI
Exemption from Taxes, Customs Duties and Import or Export Duties

1. The Court and the Commission shall be exempt from:

(a) any form of direct or indirect taxation, but the Court or the Commission shall not claim exemption from taxes which are, in fact, no more than charges for public utility services;

(b) customs duties and prohibitions and restrictions on imports in respect of articles imported or exported by the Court or the Commission for their official use, subject to the condition that articles imported under such exemption shall not be sold within the territory of the Contracting Party except under conditions agreed to with the Government;

(c) customs duties and other levies and prohibitions and restrictions in respect of the import, sale and export of their publications.

2. For the purposes of this Article, 'indirect taxation' means airport departure or travel tax, travel ticket tax, hotel and restaurant taxes, customs and excise duties, consumption tax, stamp duties, withholding tax on interest, value added tax, finance charges and imposts with equivalent effect.

Article VII
Facilities in Respect of Communications

1. The Court and the Commission shall, in relation to their official communications, enjoy in the territory of the Contracting Party, treatment no less favourable than that accorded by the Government to any other international organisation.

2. The Court and the Commission shall be immune from censorship of their official correspondence and official communications.

3. The Court and the Commission shall have the right to use codes and to despatch and receive correspondence whether by courier or in sealed bags, which shall have the same immunities and privileges as diplomatic couriers and bags.

4. Nothing in this Article shall be construed so as to preclude the adoption of appropriate security measures in the interest of the Government concerned.

Article VIII
Judges and Officers of the Court and Members of the Commission

1. Judges and officers of the Court and members of the Commission engaged in the business of the Court or the Commission, as the case may be, in the territory of a Contracting Party, shall enjoy:

(a) immunity from legal process in respect of words spoken or written and all acts done by them in their official capacity; such immunity shall continue notwithstanding that the persons concerned have ceased to exercise their functions with the Court or the Commission;

(b) immunity from personal arrest or detention in relation to acts performed by them in their official capacity;

(c) inviolability of all papers, documents and materials related to the work of the Court or the Commission as the case may be;

(d) exemption from immigration restrictions, alien registration requirements and national service obligations;

(e) the same protection and repatriation facilities in times of international crisis as are accorded representatives of foreign governments on temporary official missions;

(f) the right, for the purpose of all communications with the Court or the Commission, as the case may be, to use codes and to despatch or receive papers, correspondence or other official material by courier or in sealed bags;

(g) the same privileges and facilities in respect of currency and exchange restrictions as are accorded to representatives of foreign governments on temporary official missions;

(h) immunity from inspection and seizure of personal and official baggage except in cases where the person is caught *in flagrante delicto*. In such cases, the competent authorities shall immediately inform the Registrar or other appropriate official of the Court. Inspection of personal baggage shall be conducted in the presence of the person concerned or his authorised representative, and in the case of official baggage, in the presence of a duly authorised representative of the Registrar;

(i) exemption from any form of direct taxation on salaries, remuneration and allowances paid by the Court or the Commission and from customs duties on imports in respect of articles imported for personal use, subject to the condition that articles imported under such exemption shall not be sold within the territory of the Contracting Party except under conditions determined by the Government.

Article IX
Counsel Appearing in Proceedings Before the Court

1. Counsel appearing in proceedings before the Court while present in the territory of a Contracting Party shall, in the performance of their functions connected with such proceedings, enjoy:

(a) inviolability of all papers, documents and materials relating to the proceedings before the Court;

(b) immunity from personal arrest or detention and legal process in relation to words spoken or written or acts performed by them in relation to proceedings before the Court;

(c) exemption from immigration restrictions, alien registration requirements and national service obligations;

(d) the same privileges and facilities in respect of currency and exchange restrictions in relation to proceedings before the Court as are accorded to representatives of foreign governments on temporary official missions.

2. The immunity mentioned in paragraph 1(a) and (b) shall continue although the person entitled is no longer conducting proceedings before the Court.

3. The privileges, immunities and facilities mentioned in this Article are only intended to assist Counsel in the efficient

representation of clients in proceedings before the Court and shall not be employed to circumvent applicable laws and regulations of the Government.

Article X
Co-operation with Competent Authorities

1. Privileges and immunities are recognised and granted by this Protocol in the interest of the Court and the Commission and not for the personal benefit of persons entitled thereto. The Conference in the case of the President and the President in the case of other persons entitled thereto, shall have the right to waive such privileges and immunities whenever in their opinion the enjoyment of the privileges and immunities would impede the course of justice and could be waived without prejudice to the interests of the Court or the Commission.

2. The President and the Registrar, as the case may be, shall co operate at all times with the competent authorities to facilitate the proper administration of justice, secure the observance of the laws and regulations of the Government and to avoid the occurrence of any abuse in connection with the privileges, immunities and facilities mentioned in this Protocol.

3. Without prejudice to the privileges and immunities accorded by this Protocol, it is the duty of all persons enjoying such privileges and immunities to respect the laws and regulations of the Government and not to interfere in the internal affairs of the Contracting Party.

4. If the Government considers that an abuse has occurred in the enjoyment of any privilege or immunity conferred by this Protocol, the Registrar shall, at the request of the Government, consult with the competent authorities to determine whether such an abuse has occurred. If such consultations fail to achieve results satisfactory to the Registrar and the Government, the issue shall be settled in accordance with the procedure laid down in Article XII.

Article XI
Facilitation of Travel

1. Subject to the laws or regulations restricting entry or movement for reasons of national security, the Contracting Party shall extend all facilities for the uninterrupted passage within its territory as well as for the entry and departure therefrom of the categories of persons mentioned below:

(a) judges of the Court and members of their families forming part of their households;

(b) officers of the Court and members of their families forming part of their households;

(c) members of the Commission;

(d) counsel and their clients appearing in proceedings before the Court;

(e) persons appearing in proceedings before the Court;

(f) persons other than officers of the Court performing missions for the Court and members of their families forming part of their households; and

(g) other persons invited to the Seat of the Court or the offices of the Commission on official business.

2. The Registrar shall communicate to the Government the names of the persons mentioned in paragraph 1 of this Article.

3. This Article shall not be applicable in case of a general interruption of transportation and shall not impede the effective application of laws in force nor waive the reasonable application of quarantine and health regulations.

4. Visas required by persons referred to in paragraph 1 of this Article shall be granted by the Government expeditiously and free of charge.

Article XII
Settlement of Disputes

1. The President shall make appropriate provisions for the settlement of:

(a) disputes arising out of contracts and other disputes of a private law character to which the Court or the Commission is a party;

(b) disputes involving any judge or officer of the Court or Counsel conducting proceedings before the Court enjoying immunity if such immunity has not been waived by the persons empowered in that behalf.

2. Any difference between the Government and the Court or the Commission arising out of the interpretation or application of this Protocol and which is not settled by negotiation or other agreed mode of settlement, shall be referred for final decision to a Tribunal of three arbitrators at the instance of any Contracting Party to this Protocol: one to be appointed by the Government, one to be appointed by the Registrar, and the third, who shall be the Chairman of the Tribunal, to be chosen by the first two arbitrators.

3. If any of the parties fails to appoint an arbitrator within six weeks of the decision to resort to arbitration, an arbitrator or arbitrators, as the case may be, shall be appointed for such purposes by the SecretaryGeneral.

4. If the first two arbitrators within three weeks of their appointment fail to agree upon the third arbitrator, the Government or the Registrar shall request the SecretaryGeneral to appoint the third arbitrator.

5. A majority vote of the arbitrators shall be sufficient to reach a decision which shall be final and binding.

6. The Chairman shall be empowered to settle all questions of procedure in any case where there is disagreement between the other arbitrators in respect thereto.

Article XIII
Signature

This Protocol shall be open for signature by the Contracting Parties to the Agreement.

Article XIV
Entry Into Force

This Protocol shall enter into force immediately upon signature by at least three Contracting Parties to the Agreement.

Article XV
Accession

1. Any Contracting Party to the Agreement may accede to this Protocol.

2. Instruments of accession shall be deposited with the Secretary-General who shall transmit certified copies to the Governments.

Article XVI
Amendments

1. Consultations in respect of any amendment to this Protocol may be initiated either by the Government or the Registrar.

2. Amendments shall enter into force upon their acceptance by all of the Contracting Parties.

Article XVII
Depositary

This Protocol and any amendment thereto shall be deposited with the Secretary-General who shall transmit certified copies thereof to the Contracting Parties.

Article XVIII
Implementation

Each Contracting Party shall promptly inform the Conference of the action which it has taken to make effective the provisions of this Protocol in its territory.

Article XIX
Withdrawal

1. A Contracting Party which withdraws from the Agreement, may also withdraw from this Protocol by giving notice in writing to the Depositary who shall promptly notify the other Contracting Parties accordingly.

2. Withdrawal shall take effect five years after the date on which the notice was received by the Depositary, unless the Contracting Party before the withdrawal becomes effective notifies the Depositary in writing of the cancellation of its notice of withdrawal.

3. A Contracting Party withdrawing from this Protocol shall honour all obligations assumed by it before the effective date of its withdrawal.

IN WITNESS WHEREOF the undermentioned representatives duly authorised in that behalf have executed this Protocol for their respective Governments.

Done at ....on the............... day of 2003

Signed by for the Government of Antigua and Barbuda on the day of 2003 at

Signed by for the Government of Barbados on the day of 2003 at

Signed by for the Government of Belize on the day of 2003 at

Signed by for the Government of the Commonwealth of Dominica on the day of 2003 at

Signed by for the Government of Grenada on the day of 2003 at

Signed by for the Government of the Cooperative Republic of Guyana on the day of 2003 at

Signed by for the Government of Jamaica on the day of 2003 at

Signed by for the Government of Montserrat on the day of 2003 at

Signed by for the Government of St. Kitts and Nevis on the day of 2003 at

Signed by for the Government of Saint Lucia on the day of 2003 at

Signed by for the Government of St. Vincent and the Grenadines on the day of 2003 at

Signed by for the Government of The Republic of Suriname on the day of 2003 at

Signed by for the Government of The Republic of Trinidad and Tobago on the day of 2003 at

APPENDIX IV

AGREEMENT ESTABLISHING THE DRAFT ENABLING BILL TO IMPLEMENT THE CARIBBEAN COURT OF JUSTICE

A Bill entitled

An Act to implement the Agreement Establishing the Caribbean Court of Justice and for related matters.

Enacted by

ort title d nmencement]

1. (1) This Act may be cited as The Caribbean Court of Justice Act, 200.....

(2) [The Act shall come into force on a date to be proclaimed by the .....].

erpretation edule

2. In this Act,

'*Agreement*' means the Agreement Establishing the Caribbean Court of Justice, the text of which is set out in the Schedule;

'*appeal*' means an appeal to the Court;

'*appellant*' means the party appealing from a judgment;

'*Commission*' means the Regional Judicial and Legal Services Commission established by Article V of the Agreement;

'*Contracting Party*' means a Contracting Party within the meaning of Article I of the Agreement;

'*Court*' means the Caribbean Court of Justice established by the Agreement;

'*Court of Appeal*' means the Court of Appeal of [ ];

'*judgment*' includes conviction, decree, ruling, sentence order or decision;

'*party*' means any party to proceedings before the Court;

'*record*' means the aggregate of documents relating to proceedings before the Court, including the pleadings, evidence and judgments and exhibits required by *this Act* to be filed or laid before the Court;

'*relevant judgment*' means the judgment which is the subject of an appeal;

'*Rules of Court*' means the Rules of Court made under the authority of this Act:

'*Treaty*' means the Treaty establishing the Caribbean Community signed at Chaguaramas as on 4 July 1973 and amendments thereto which take effect either provisionally or definitively.

Force of La

3. The Agreement and the Rules of Court made thereunder shall have the force of law.

4. The jurisdiction conferred on the Judicial Committee of the Privy Council by [Section] of the Constitution is hereby abolished.

5. The Court shall have:

1. original jurisdiction in accordance with the provisions of Part II of the Agreement; and
2. appellate jurisdiction in accordance with the provisions of Part III of the Agreement.

Jurisdiction the Court ir contentious proceedings

6. The Court [in the exercise of its original jurisdiction] shall have exclusive jurisdiction to hear and deliver judgment on –

(1) disputes between Contracting Parties;

(2) disputes between Contracting Parties and the Caribbean Community;

(3) referrals from national courts of Contracting Parties; and

(4) applications by nationals in accordance with Article XXIV of the Agreement, concerning the interpretation and application of the Treaty.

pplications efore the ourt

7. Matters pertaining to the exercise of the original jurisdiction of the Court shall be brought before the Court by written application, in the manner prescribed by the Rules of Court.

8A. Appeals shall lie to the Court from decisions of the Court of Appeal of a Contracting Party as of right in the following cases:

(a) final decisions in civil proceedings where the matter in dispute on appeal to the Court is of the value of not less than twenty-five thousand dollars Eastern Caribbean currency (EC$25,000) or where the appeal involves directly or indirectly a claim or a question respecting property or a right of the aforesaid value;

(b) final decisions in proceedings for dissolution or nullity of marriage;

(c) final decisions in any civil or other proceedings which involve a question as to the interpretation of the Constitution of the Contracting Party;

(d) final decisions given in the exercise of the jurisdiction conferred upon a superior court of a Contracting Party relating to the determination of any question for which a right of access to the superior court of a Contracting Party is expressly provided by its Constitution;

(e) such other cases as may be prescribed by any law of the Contracting Party.

8B. An appeal shall lie to the Court with the leave of the Court of Appeal of a Contracting Party from the decisions of the Court of Appeal in the following cases:

(a) final decisions in any civil proceedings where, in the opinion of the Court of Appeal, the question is one that by reason of its great general or public importance or otherwise, ought to be submitted to the Court; and

(b) such other cases as may be prescribed by any law of the Contracting Party.

8. An appeal shall lie to the Court with the leave of the Court of Appeal from the decisions of the Court of Appeal: Appeals

(1) in respect of final decisions in any civil proceeding where, in the opinion of the Court of Appeal, the question involved in the appeal is one that by reason of its great general or public importance or otherwise, ought to be submitted to the Court;

(2) in such other cases as may be prescribed by any law (of the Contracting Party).

9. An appeal shall lie to the Court with the special leave of the Court from any decision of the Court of Appeal from any civil or criminal matter. *(Appeal as of right)*

10. Nothing in this Act shall confer jurisdiction on the Court to hear matters in relation to any decision of the Court of Appeal which at the time of entry into force of the Agreement was, pursuant to the Constitution or any other law, declared to be final. Exemption from Jurisdiction

11. Applications to the Court of Appeal for leave to appeal shall be made by motion or petition within [*FORTY-FIVE*] days from the date of the relevant judgment, and the applicant shall give all parties directly affected by the appeal, notice of the application for leave to appeal. Application for leave to appeal

12. Notwithstanding any other provision of this Act, an application forextension of time within which an application may be made: Extension of time for appealing

(1) to the Court, for special leave to appeal;

(2) to the Court of Appeal, for leave to appeal,

shall be supported by affidavit stating good and substantial reasons for the application.

onditional ave to ppeal

13. Leave to appeal shall be granted only in accordance with paragraph 3 of Article XXV of the Agreement:

(1) upon condition of the appellant, within a period to be fixed by the Court of Appeal *or the Court* , but not exceeding ninety days from the date of the hearing of the application for leave to appeal, entering into good and sufficient security, to the satisfaction of the Court of Appeal (or the Court), in a sum not exceeding [$], for the due prosecution of the appeal, and the payment of all such costs as may become payable to the respondent in the event of:

(i) the appellant not obtaining an order granting final leave to appeal;

(ii) the appeal being dismissed for non prosecution; or

(iii) the Court ordering the appellant to pay the respondent's costs of the appeal; and

(2) upon such other conditions as the Court of Appeal, having regard to all the circumstances of the case, may consider reasonable as the time necessary for the appellant to procure the preparation of the record and the dispatch thereof to the Court.

xecution stay of xecution

14. (1) Where the relevant judgment requires the appellant to pay money or money or perform a duty, the Court of Appeal may, when granting leave to appeal, direct that the judgment or any part thereof be executed or that the execution be suspended pending the appeal, as the Court of Appeal thinks just.

(2) Where the Court of Appeal directs that the relevant judgment be executed, the person in whose favour the judgment is given shall, before the execution thereof, enter into good and sufficient security, to the satisfaction

of the Court of Appeal for the due performance of such order as the Court shall think fit to make.

15. (1) The preparation of the record shall be in accordance with *(the Rules of)* the Rules of Court and shall be subject to the supervision of the Court of Appeal.

Preparation of record

(2) The parties may submit any disputed question arising in connection with the preparation of the record for the decision of the Court of Appeal which shall give such directions thereon as the justice of the case may require.

16. The reasons given by the judge, or any of the judges, for or against any judgment pronounced in the course of the proceedings out of which the appeal arises shall be incorporated in the record.

Judges' reasons

17. The Court of Appeal may grant final leave to appeal to an appellant who has complied with section *(13)* and the appellant shall thereupon prosecute his appeal in accordance with the Rules of Court.

Final leave to appeal

18. (1) Where the Court directs a party to bear the costs of an appeal, such costs shall be taxed by the proper officer of the Court of Appeal in accordance with the rules for the time being regulating taxation in the Court of Appeal.

Taxation of costs of appeal

(2) In any proceedings to which the [Crown] / [State] is a party, either as represented by the Attorney-General or otherwise, costs adjudged to the [Crown] / [State] shall not be disallowed or reduced on taxation merely because the proceedings are conducted on behalf of the [Crown] / [State].

19. Any *judgment or order* which the Court may think fit to make on an appeal from a relevant judgment shall be enforced in like manner as any Court original judgment of [a superior court of .....] would be enforced.

Enforcement of Order of Court

20. (1) A Judge of the Court may exercise all of the powers and functions of [a superior court of .....], except

Powers of Court

that he may not make a determination under paragraph 3(a) of Article XXV of the Agreement.

(2) Without affecting subsection (1), any judgment of a Judge under this section may be varied, discharged or reversed by the Court consisting of five Judges.

ayment rom onsolidated und

21. Monies payable in respect of the Court and the Commission pursuant to Article XXVIII of the Agreement shall be charged on and paid from the Consolidated Fund.

22. (1) The Registrar of the Supreme Court shall be a Deputy Registrar of the Court, within the meaning of Article 12 of the Agreement.

(2) The Registry of the Supreme Court shall be designated a sub-Registry of the Court pursuant to the Rules of Court.

ppointment f Registrar s Deputy egistrar

23. The Rules of Court made by the President in accordance with Articles XXI and XXVI of the Agreement shall be published in the Gazette.

24. (1) The provisions of Section 4 shall not affect any proceedings pending *before* the Judicial Committee of the Privy Council immediately before the commencement of this Act.

(2) For the purposes of this section, proceedings shall be treated as pending where leave to appeal to [Her Majesty in Council] has been granted.

(3) Any *judgment of {Her Majesty in Council}* which at the date of commencement of this Act has been given, but has not been satisfied, may be enforced after the commencement of this Act as if it had been a judgment of the Court.

APPENDIX V

AGREEMENT ESTABLISHING THE SEAT OF THE CARIBBEAN COURT OF JUSTICE AND THE OFFICES OF THE REGIONAL JUDICIAL AND LEGAL SERVICES COMMISSION BETWEEN THE GOVERNMENT OF TRINIDAD AND TOBAGO AND THE CARIBBEAN COURT OF JUSTICE

Preamble

Whereas paragraph 2 of Article III of the Agreement Establishing the Caribbean Court of Justice (hereinafter called 'The Agreement') provides that the Seat of the Court shall be in the territory of a Contracting Party as determined from time to time by unanimous agreement of the Contracting Parties;

Whereas the Contracting Parties to the Agreement have determined that the Seat of the Court shall be in Trinidad and Tobago; and

Whereas Article XV of the Agreement provides for the grant of privileges and immunities to Judges and Officers of the Court necessary to protect their independence and impartiality,

The Parties hereto have agreed as follows:

Article I
Use of Terms

In this Agreement, unless the context otherwise requires:

'*Archives of the Court or Commission*' includes the records, correspondence, documents, manuscripts, photographs, slides, films, sound recordings and electronic storage devices belonging to or held by the Court or Commission;

'*Commission*' means the Regional judicial and Legal Services Commission established by Article V of the Agreement;

'*Competent Authorities*' means national, regional or local authorities of Trinidad and Tobago as may be appropriate in the context and in the laws of Trinidad and Tobago;

'*Conference*' means the Conference of Heads of Government of Member States of the Caribbean Community;

'*Counsel*' means a person qualified to conduct proceedings before the Court on behalf of another;

'*Court*' means the Caribbean Court of Justice established by Article III of the Agreement;

'*the Government*' means the Government of Trinidad and Tobago;

'*offices of the Commission*' means the offices provided by the Government in accordance with paragraph 3 of Article III and occupied by the Commission for its official use;

'*officers of the Court*' means the Registrar of the Court and the Deputy Registrar or other officer for the time being performing the duties of the Registrar or Deputy Registrar;

'*President*' means the President of the Court;

'*Property*' means all forms of property including funds and assets belonging to or held or administered by the Court or the Commission and all income accruing to the Court or the Commission;

'*Seat of the Court*' means the premises provided by the Government in accordance with paragraph 3 of Article III of the Agreement and occupied by the Court for its official use.

Article II
Status of the Court and Commission

1. The Court and the Commission shall possess full juridical personality and, in particular, full capacity to:

(a) contract;

(b) acquire and dispose of immovable and movable property;

(c) institute legal proceedings.

2. In all legal proceedings, the Court and the Commission shall be represented by the Registrar.

Article III
The Seat of the Court and Offices of the Commission

1. The Seat of the Court and offices of the Commission shall be the premises defined in Article I of this Agreement.

2. The President shall have the power to make regulations operative within the Seat of the Court and offices of the Commission for the purpose of establishing therein conditions necessary for the full execution of their functions which shall be carried out through the Registrar.

3. The Seat of the Court and offices of the Commission shall be inviolable and shall be under the authority of the President as provided for in this Agreement.

4. Officials of the Government, whether administrative, judicial, military or police, shall not enter the Seat of the Court or the offices of the Commission to perform any official duties therein except with the consent of and under conditions agreed by the Registrar. However, in the case of fire or other emergency requiring prompt protective action, or in the event that officials of the Government have reasonable cause to believe that such

an emergency has occurred, the consent of the Registrar to entry in the Seat of the Court and offices of the Commission by the officials of the Government shall be presumed if the Registrar cannot be reached in time.

5. The service of legal process, including the seizure of private property, may take place within the Seat of the Court or the offices of the Commission only with the consent of and under the conditions approved by the Registrar.

6. The President shall not permit the Seat of the Court or the offices of the Commission to become a refuge either for fugitives from justice or for persons who are endeavouring to avoid service of legal process or judicial proceedings under the laws of Trinidad and Tobago or against whom an order of extradition or deportation has been made by the competent authorities.

7. The Registrar may expel or exclude persons from the Seat of the Court or the offices of the Commission for violation of its regulations or for any other reasonable cause.

Article IV
Property, Funds and Assets of the Court and Commission

1. The Court, Commission and their property, wherever located and by whomsoever held, shall enjoy immunity from every form of legal process except in cases arising out of or in connection with the borrowing of money or the acquisition or disposal of immovable property or in so far as in any particular case the President has expressly waived their immunity. No waiver of immunity shall extend to any measure of execution.

2. Save as otherwise provided in paragraph 1 of this Article, the property of the Court and the Commission, wherever located or by whomsoever held, shall be immune from search, acquisition, confiscation, expropriation and any other form of interference, whether by executive, administrative or judicial action.

3. Nothing in this Article shall be construed as preventing the Government from taking appropriate action in connection with the investigation into accidents involving motor vehicles belonging to or operated on behalf of the Court or the Commission.

Article V
Archives of the Court and Commission

The archives of the Court and the Commission and in general all documents held by them shall be inviolable wherever located.

Article VI
Exemption from Foreign Exchange Controls

1. Without being restricted by financial controls, regulations or moratoria of any kind, the Court shall be entitled for its official use only:

(a) to purchase from authorised dealers, hold and make use of negotiable currencies, operate foreign currency and external accounts and purchase through authorised dealers, hold and make use of funds and securities;

(b) freely transfer its funds, securities and foreign currencies to or from Trinidad and Tobago or within Trinidad and Tobago and to convert any currency held by it into other currency.

2. The Court, in executing its rights under paragraph 1 of this Article, shall pay due regard to any representations made by the Government and shall give effect to such representation to the extent that such representation may be taken into account without detriment to the interests of the Court.

Article VII
Exemption from Taxes, Customs Duties and Import or Export Duties

1. The property of the Court and the Commission shall be exempt from:

(a) any form of direct or indirect taxation but the Court and Commission will not claim exemption from taxes which are, in fact, no more than charges for public utility services;

(b) customs duties and from prohibitions and restrictions on imports in respect of articles imported or exported for their official use, subject to the condition that articles imported under such exemption shall not be sold within Trinidad and Tobago except under conditions agreed to between the President and the Government;

(c) customs duties and other levies and prohibitions and restrictions in respect of the import, sale and export of their publications.

(2) For the purpose of this Article, indirect taxation means airport departure tax or travel tax, travel ticket tax, hotel and restaurant tax, customs and excise duties, consumption tax, stamp duties, withholding tax on interest, value added tax, finance charges and imports with equivalent effect.

Article VIII
Facilities in Respect of Communications

1. The Court and Commission shall enjoy in the territory of Trinidad and Tobago, freedom of communication for their official communications.

2. The official correspondence and all other forms of official communications shall be inviolable.

3. The Court and Commission shall have the right to use codes and to despatch and receive correspondence by courier in sealed bags, which shall not be searched or detained unless the competent authorities have serious reason to believe that the sealed bags contain other than correspondence, documents or articles for the official use of the Court or the Commission exclusively, in which case the bag shall be opened only in the presence of an officer of the Court.

4. Nothing in this Article shall be construed so as to preclude the adoption of appropriate security measures in the interest of the Government.

Article IX
Judges and Officers of the Court

Judges and officers of the Court and members of the Commission, when engaged on the business of the Court or Commission, as the case may be, in Trinidad and Tobago, shall enjoy:

(a) immunity from legal process in respect of words spoken or written and all acts done by them in their official capacity; such immunity shall continue notwithstanding that the persons concerned have ceased to exercise their functions with the Court or the Commission;

(b) immunity from personal arrest or detention in relation to acts performed by them in their official capacity;

(c) inviolability of all papers, documents and materials related to the work of the Court or the Commission;

(d) exemption from immunisation restrictions, alien registration requirements and national service obligations;

(e) the same protection and repatriation facilities in times of international crisis as are accorded representatives of foreign governments on temporary official missions;

(f) the right, for the purpose of all communications with the Court or the Commission, to use codes to despatch or receive papers, correspondence or other official materials by courier or in sealed bags;

(g) the same privileges and facilities in respect of currency and exchange restrictions as are accorded to representatives of foreign governments on temporary official missions;

(h) immunity from inspection and seizure of personal and official baggage, except in cases of *flagrante delicto*. In such cases, the competent authorities shall immediately inform the

Registrar or other appropriate officer of the Court. Inspection of personal baggage shall be conducted in the presence of the person concerned or his authorised representative and, in the case of official baggage, in the presence of a duly authorised representative of the Registrar;

(i) exemption from any form of direct taxation on salaries, remuneration and allowances paid by the Court or the Commission and from customs duties on imports in respect of articles imported for personal use, subject to the condition that articles imported under such exemption shall not be sold within Trinidad and Tobago except under conditions determined by the Government.

Article X

Counsel Appearing in Proceedings Before the Court

1. Counsel appearing in proceedings before the Court while present in Trinidad and Tobago shall, in the performance of their functions connected with such proceedings, enjoy:

(a) inviolability of all papers, documents and materials relating to the proceedings before the Court;

(b) immunity from personal arrest or detention in relation to words spoken or written or acts performed by them in relation to proceedings before the Court;

(c) exemption from immigration restrictions, alien registration requirements and national service obligations;

(d) the same privileges and facilities in respect of currency and exchange restrictions in relation to proceedings before the Court as are accorded to representatives of Government on temporary official missions.

2. Counsel mentioned in paragraph 1 of this Article shall enjoy, in respect of words written or spoken and all acts done by them in the conduct of proceedings before the Court, immunity from legal process. The immunity shall continue although the person entitled is no longer conducting proceedings before the Court.

3. The privileges, immunities and facilities mentioned in this Article are only intended to assist counsel in the efficient representation of clients in proceedings before the Court and shall not be employed to circumvent applicable laws and regulations of Trinidad and Tobago.

Article XI
Co-operation with Competent Authorities

1. Privileges and immunities are recognised and granted by this Agreement in the interest of the Court and Commission and not for the personal benefit of persons entitled thereto. The Conference, in the case of the President, and the President, in the case of other persons entitled thereto, shall have the right to waive such privileges and immunities whenever in their opinion the enjoyment of the privileges and immunities would impede the course of justice and could be waived without prejudice to the interests of the Court or Commission.

2. The President and the Registrar, as the case may be, shall co-operate at all times with the competent authorities to facilitate the proper administration of justice, secure the observance of the laws and regulations of Trinidad and Tobago and to avoid the occurrence of any abuse in connection with the privileges, immunities and facilities mentioned in this Agreement.

3. Without prejudice to the privileges and immunities accorded by this Agreement, it is the duty of all persons enjoying such privileges and immunities to respect the laws and regulations of Trinidad and Tobago.

4. If the Government considers that an abuse has occurred in the enjoyment of any privilege or immunity conferred by this Agreement, the Registrar shall, at the request of the Government, consult with the competent authorities to determine whether such an abuse has occurred. If such consultations fail to achieve results satisfactory to the Registrar and the Government, the issues shall be settled in accordance with the procedure laid down in Article XIII.

Article XII
Facilitation of Travel

1. Subject to the laws or regulations restricting entry or movement for reasons of national security, the Government shall extend all facilities for the uninterrupted passage within Trinidad and Tobago as well as for the entry and departure therefrom of the categories of persons indicated below:

(a) judges of the Court and members of their families forming part of their household;

(b) officers of the Court and members of their families forming part of their household;

(c) members of the Commission;

(d) counsel and their clients appearing in proceedings before this Court;

(e) persons other than officers of the Court performing missions for the Court and members of their families forming part of their household; and

(f) other persons invited to the Seat of the Court or offices of the Commission on official business.

2. The Registrar shall communicate to the Government the names of the persons mentioned in paragraph 1 of this Article.]

3. This Article shall not be applicable in case of a general interruption of transportation and shall not impede the effective application of laws in force nor waive reasonable application of quarantine and health regulations.

4. Visas required by persons referred to in paragraph 1 of this Article shall be granted expeditiously and free of charge.

Article XIII
Settlement of Disputes

1. The President shall make appropriate provisions for the settlement of:

(a) disputes arising out of contracts and other disputes of a private law character to which the Court or Commission is a party;

(b) disputes involving any judge or officer of the Court or Counsel conducting proceedings before the Court enjoying immunity if such immunity has not been waived by the persons empowered in that behalf.

2. Any difference between the Government and the Court or the Commission arising out of the interpretation or application of this Agreement and which is not settled by negotiation or other agreed mode of settlement shall be referred for final decision to or Tribunal of three arbitrators at the instance of either party: one to be appointed by the Government, one to be appointed by the Registrar, and the third, who shall be the Chairman of the Tribunal, to be chosen by the first two arbitrators. If either of the parties fails to appoint an arbitrator within six weeks of the decision to resort to arbitration, an arbitrator or arbitrators, as the case may be, shall be appointed for such purposes by the Secretary General. If the first two arbitrators within three weeks of their appointment fail to agree upon the third, the Government or the Registrar shall request the Secretary General to choose the third arbitrator. The arbitral Tribunal shall make a determination within six months from the date of its constitution. A majority vote of the arbitrators shall be sufficient to reach a decision, which shall be final and binding. The Chairman shall be empowered to settle all questions of procedure in any case where there is disagreement between the other arbitrators in respect thereto.

Article XIV
Entry into Force

1. This Agreement and any agreement supplementary thereto shall enter into force immediately upon signature.

2. Consultations in respect of any amendment to this Agreement may be initiated by either the Government or the Registrar.

Article XV
Termination

This Agreement and any amendment thereto shall cease to have effect five years after either of the Contracting Parties has given notice in writing to the other of its decision to terminate this Agreement.

IN WITNESS WHEREOF the representative of the Government and the Caribbean Court of Justice being duly authorised in that behalf have executed this Agreement.

Done at .... on the........... day of........................ 199..

For the Caribbean Court of Justice	For the Government of Trinidad and Tobago
....	....

APPENDIX VI

AGREEMENT ESTABLISHING THE CARIBBEAN COURT OF JUSTICE TRUST FUND

The Parties to the Agreement Establishing the Caribbean Court of Justice:

Cognisant that the Court is indispensable for the good governance of the Caribbean Community;

Recognising the critical role of the Court in the efficient administration of Justice in the territories of the Contracting Parties to the Agreement establishing the Court;

Recognising further that the Court is vital for the structured and efficient functioning of the CARICOM Single Market and Economy;

Noting the provisions of Article XXVIII of the Agreement establishing the Court which requires the expenses of the Court and the Commission to be borne by the Contracting Parties to the Agreement establishing the Court;

Conscious that the financial viability of the Court is essential for its efficiency, effectiveness and independence in the performance of its functions;

Bearing in mind the decision of the Twenty-Third Meeting of the Conference of Heads of Government of the Caribbean

Community concerning the capital and recurrent expenditures of the Court;

Determined to promote and safeguard the independence, integrity and credibility of the Court,

Have agreed as follows:

Article I
Interpretation

1. In this Agreement unless the context otherwise requires:

'*Board*' means the Board of Trustees of the Fund;

'*Commission*' means the Regional Judicial and Legal Services Commission established under Article V of the Agreement Establishing the Caribbean Court of Justice;

'*Court*' means the Caribbean Court of Justice established under Article III of the Agreement Establishing the Caribbean Court of Justice;

'*Fund*' means the Caribbean Court of Justice Trust Fund established by Article II of this Agreement;

'*Member*' means a Contracting Party to the Agreement Establishing the Caribbean Court of Justice and in relation to which this Agreement is in force; and

'*Secretary-General*' means the Secretary-General of the Caribbean Community.

Article II
Establishment of the Caribbean Court of Justice Trust Fund

The Caribbean Court of Justice Trust Fund is hereby established.

Article III
Purpose of Fund

The purposes of the Fund shall be to provide the resources necessary to finance the biennial capital and operating budget of the Court and the Commission in perpetuity.

Article IV
Resources of the Fund

1. The resources of the Fund shall consist of:

(a) the contributions of Members;

(b) income derived from operations of the Fund or otherwise accruing to the Fund, and

(c) contributions of third parties being contributions which are not likely to prejudice the independence or integrity of the Court.

2. The Fund shall not solicit nor accept any grant, gift or other material benefit from any source except with the consent of all the Members.

3. Each original Member shall, upon the entry into force of this Agreement, contribute or cause to be contributed to the Fund the amount expressed in the scale of contributions set out in the Annex to this Agreement.

4. Each Member acceding to this Agreement shall make contributions to the Fund in accordance with the provisions set out in its instrument of accession.

5. The Board shall review the adequacy of the resources of the Fund, not later than two years after the entry into force of this Agreement and thereafter at least once within every succeeding biennium.

6. The Board shall communicate the results of the review to the Members.

7. Where upon such a review an inadequacy in resources is found to exist, the Members shall make additional contributions in the proportions reflected in the Annex to this Agreement.

8. Contributions of Members shall be made for the purpose of the Fund without restriction as to use.

9. Financing from the Fund shall be governed by considerations of economy, efficiency and cost effectiveness and the need to safeguard the independence and sustainability of the Court and the Commission.

10. For the purpose of this Article 'original Member' means a State or territory of the Caribbean Community which was a Member on the date this Agreement entered into force.

Article V
Structure of the Fund

The Fund shall have a Board of Trustees.

Article VI
Composition of the Board of Trustees

1. Subject to the provisions of this Article, the Board of Trustees shall consist of the following or their nominees:

(a) The Secretary-General;

(b) The Vice-Chancellor of the University of the West Indies;

(c) The President of the Insurance Association of the Caribbean;

(d) The Chairman of the Association of Indigenous Banks of the Caribbean;

(e) The President of the Caribbean Institute of Chartered Accountants;

(f) The President of the Organisation of Commonwealth Caribbean Bar Associations;

(g) The Chairman of the Conference of Heads of the Judiciary of Member States of the Caribbean Community;

(h) The President of the Caribbean Association of Industry and Commerce; and

(i) The President of the Caribbean Congress of Labour.

2. There shall be a Chairman and Vice-Chairman of the Board elected by the Board from among its members. The Chairman and Vice-Chairman shall hold office for a period of three years.

3. Where a trustee -

(a) resigns or dies;

(b) becomes bankrupt or otherwise insolvent;

(c) becomes unwilling or refuses to serve as a trustee;

(d) is convicted of an offence involving dishonesty; or

(e) in the unanimous opinion of the other members of the Board, becomes unfit or incapable to act as such,

the competent institution shall nominate a person of comparable status or experience to act in place of that trustee.

4. Where an institution fails to nominate a trustee in accordance with paragraph 3 or an institution mentioned in paragraph 1 ceases to exist, the Secretary-General may designate a person or persons, as the case may require, to act as a trustee.

5. Where more than three designations by the Secretary-General are required to make up the full complement of the Board of Trustees, the Members may, by consensus, propose an amendment to the Agreement in accordance with Article XIII.

6. A trustee may resign by transmitting a written notice in that behalf to the Chairman of the Board.

7. Where the Chairman wishes to resign from the office of Chairman or Trustee, such notice shall be transmitted to the Vice-Chairman of the Board.

Article VII

Functions of the Board

1. The Board shall be responsible for directing the operations of the Fund, and, for this purpose shall, in particular, exercise the following functions:

(a) evaluate the performance of the Fund;

(b) establish with the approval of the Members guidelines for prudential investment of the resources of the Fund;

(c) establish with the approval of the Members the financial regulations of the Fund;

(d) appoint the Executive Officer of the Fund;

(e) authorise the provision of resources required for the biennial capital and operating budget of the Court and the Commission submitted by the Executive Officer;

(f) appoint an investment manager or managers to manage the investments of the Fund in accordance with the investment guidelines for the Fund;

(g) approve the annual report on the performance of the Fund for transmission to the Members;

(h) approve the capital and operating annual budget of the Fund;

(i) appoint an external Auditor of the Fund;

(j) submit an annual report to the Members, and

(k) perform such other functions as may be necessary or appropriate for the operations of the Fund.

2. The Board may exercise such powers and establish such rules as may be necessary or appropriate in furtherance of its purpose and functions consistent with this Agreement.

Article VIII
Procedures of the Board

1. The Board shall hold two regular meetings each year and may hold such other meetings as the Board considers necessary.

2. The Board shall elect a Chairman and one Vice-Chairman at its first regular annual meeting.

3. Each member of the Board shall have one vote.

4. A simple majority of the members of the Board shall constitute the quorum for any meeting of the Board.

5. Subject to paragraph 6 of this Article the Board shall take decisions by consensus. A proposal shall be deemed to have been adopted by consensus if no member of the Board raised a formal objection against it during the meeting.

6. Where the Chairman of the Board determines that a decision cannot be reached by consensus, the Chairman shall

submit the matter to a vote. In such a case the Board shall take its decision by a majority of two-thirds of its members.

7. Subject to this Agreement, the Board may adopt its own rules of procedure.

Article IX
The Seal of the Fund

1. The Fund shall have and use as occasion may require, a Seal having a device or impression with the inscription 'Caribbean Court of Justice Trust Fund.'

2. The Seal of the Fund shall be kept in the custody of the Executive Officer and shall be affixed to documents pursuant to a resolution of the Board in the presence of the Chairman of the Board and the Executive Officer.

3. The Seal shall be authenticated by the signatures of the Chairman of the Board and the Executive Officer.

Article X
Functions of the Executive Officer

The Executive Officer shall report to the Board and shall be invited to participate in all its meetings, except where the Board considers it inexpedient, having regard to the matters on the agenda for any meeting. The Executive Officer shall:

(a) prepare and submit to the Board the capital and operating annual budget of the Fund;

(b) manage the day-to-day operations of the Fund;

(c) employ staff and engage the services of consultants;

(d) prepare and submit to the Board for submission to the Members:

 (i) a quarterly report on the performance of the Fund;

 (ii) an annual report on the operations of the Fund.

(e) submit to the Board a statement of receipts and expenditures relating to the Fund during the preceding fiscal year as audited by the External Auditor;

(f) represent the Fund in relation to third parties; and

(g) perform any other functions as may be assigned by the Board from time to time.

Article XI
Juridical Personality and Legal Capacity

1. The Fund shall possess full juridical personality and in particular capacity to:

(a) contract;

(b) acquire and dispose of immovable and moveable property; and

(c) institute legal proceedings.

2. The principal office of the Fund shall be located in Trinidad and Tobago.

3. The Fund shall conclude an agreement with the Government of Trinidad and Tobago on the status, privileges and immunities of the Fund. The agreement shall be approved by the Board, and signed by the Chairman.

Article XII
Privileges and Immunities

1. To enable the Board and Officers of the Fund to fulfill the functions with which it is entrusted, the status, immunities and privileges provided in this Article shall be accorded to the Fund in the territories of each Member.

2. The Fund shall enjoy immunity from every form of legal process. Its property and assets, wheresoever located and by whomsoever held, shall be immune from all forms of seizure, attachment or execution.

3. The archives of the Fund shall be inviolable.

4. To the extent necessary to carry out the operations provided for in this Agreement and subject to the provisions of this Agreement, all property and assets of the Fund shall be free from restrictions, regulations, controls and moratoria of any nature.

5. The official communications of the Fund shall be accorded by each Member the same treatment that it accords to the official communications of other Members.

6. The Fund, its assets, property, income and its operations and transactions, shall be exempt from all taxation, all customs duties on goods imported for its official use and all other imposts.

7. Notwithstanding the provisions of paragraph 6 of this Article, the Fund will not claim exemption from imposts that are no more than charges for public utility services.

8. Where the Fund has paid any duties, taxes or other imposts, the Members shall make appropriate administrative arrangements for the remission or return of the amount of duty, tax or imposts paid.

9. Articles imported under an exemption from customs duties as provided by paragraph 6 of this Article, or in respect of which a remission or return of duty or tax has been made under paragraph 8, shall not be sold in the territory of the Member which granted the exemption, remission or return except under conditions agreed with that Member.

10. No tax shall be levied on or in respect of salaries and emoluments paid by the Fund to members of the Board or other officers, but Members reserve the right to tax their own citizens or nationals or persons permanently resident in the territories of such Members.

11. All officers of the Fund:

(a) shall be exempt from the payment of income taxes except where that officer is a citizen, permanent resident or national of the State granting the exemption;

(b) shall be accorded such immunities from immigration restrictions, alien registration requirements and national service obligations, and such facilities as regards exchange control restrictions, as are not less favourable than those accorded by the Member concerned to the representatives, officials and employees of comparable rank of any other Member;

(c) shall be given such repatriation facilities in time of international crisis as are not less favourable than those accorded by the Member concerned to the representatives, officials and employees of comparable rank of any other Member.

12. The Trustees:

(a) shall be immune from all legal process in respect of the lawful discharge of their responsibilities under this Agreement;

(b) shall be accorded immunities from immigration restrictions and such facilities as would ensure the proper discharge of their functions.

13. The immunities, exemptions and privileges provided in this Article are granted in the interests of the Fund. The Board may waive to such extent and upon such conditions as it may determine, the immunities, exemptions and privileges provided in this Article in cases where such action would, in its opinion, be appropriate in the best interests of the Fund.

14. The Executive Officer shall have the right and the duty to waive any immunity, exemption or privilege in respect of any other officer where, in his opinion, the immunity, exemption or privilege would impede the course of justice and can be waived without prejudice to the interests of the Fund. In similar circumstances and under the same conditions, the Board shall have the right and duty to waive any immunity, exemption or privilege respecting the Executive Officer, and in the case of members of the Board, the Members shall waive such immunity.

15. The Members shall take such action as is necessary in their own territories for the purpose of making effective in terms of their law the principles set forth in this Article and shall inform the Fund of the detailed action which they have taken.

Article XIII
Amendment

Any Member may submit to the Board a proposal to amend a provision of this Agreement. The Board shall promptly submit the proposal to all other Members. The amendment shall take effect on the thirtieth day following the date on which the Secretary-General (hereinafter referred to as 'the Depositary') has received the approval of three-quarters of the Members.

Article XIV
Signature

This Agreement shall be open for signature until 31st March 2004, by the States mentioned in the Annex hereto.

Article XV
Entry Into Force

This Agreement shall enter into force on signature by any ten (10) of the States or Territories listed in the Annex hereto.

Article XVI
Reservations

No reservations may be entered in respect of any provision of this Agreement.

Article XVII
Annex

The Annex to this Agreement shall constitute an integral part of this Agreement.

Article XVIII
Accession

1. Any Member State of the Caribbean Community or any State or territory invited by the Conference of Heads of Government of the Caribbean Community to participate in the Court may become a State or Territory by acceding to this Agreement on terms and conditions agreed between it and the Fund. Accession shall be effected by the deposit of an instrument of accession approved by the Board. This Agreement shall enter into force for the acceding Member on the thirtieth day following

the date on which its instrument of accession was deposited with the Depositary.

2. Where any State ot Territory, other than a State ot Territory to which paragraph 3(b) of Article IV applies, accedes to this Agreement and undertakes to discharge its financial obligations to the Trust Fund, the Annex shall be amended accordingly.

Article XIX
Withdrawal

1. Where a Member withdraws from the Agreement Establishing the Caribbean Court of Justice, such a Member shall be deemed to have withdrawn from this Agreement with effect from the date of that Member's withdrawal from the Agreement establishing the Caribbean Court of Justice.

2. A Member withdrawing from this Agreement shall honour all obligations assumed by it before the effective date of its withdrawal.

Article XX
Depositary and Registration

1. This Agreement shall be deposited with the Depositary.

2. This Agreement shall be registered in accordance with the provisions of Article 102 of the Charter of the United Nations.

DONE at this day of two thousand and three, in a single copy, in the English Language.

Signed by for the Government of Antigua and Barbuda on the day of 2003 at

Signed by for the Government of Barbados on the day of 2003 at

Signed by for the Government of Belize on the day of 2003 at

Signed by for the Government of the Commonwealth of Dominica on the day of 2003 at

Signed by for the Government of Grenada on the day of 2003 at

Signed by for the Government of the Co-operative Republic of Guyana on the day of 2003 at

Signed by for the Government of the Republic of Haiti on the day of 2003 at

Signed by for the Government of Jamaica on the day of 2003 at

Signed by for the Government of Montserrat on the day of 2003 at

Signed by for the Government of St. Kitts and Nevis on the day of 2003 at

Signed by for the Government of Saint Lucia on the day of 2003 at

Signed by for the Government of St. Vincent and the Grenadines on the day of 2003 at

Signed by for the Government of the Republic of Suriname on the day of 2003 at

Signed by for the Government of the Republic of Trinidad and Tobago on the day of 2003 at

ANNEX

CONTRIBUTION OF THE MEMBERS OF THE TRUST FUND

Members	*Per cent share*
Antigua and Barbuda	2.11
Barbados	12.77
Belize	3.44
Dominica	2.11
Grenada	2.11
Guyana	8.33
Haiti	1.68
Jamaica	27.09
Montserrat	0.42
St. Kitts and Nevis	2.11
Saint Lucia	2.11
St. Vincent and the Grenadines	2.11
Suriname	3.92
Trinidad and Tobago	29.73
Total	100.00

APPENDIX VII

STATUTE OF THE INTERNATIONAL COURT OF JUSTICE

June 26, 1945

Article 1

The International Court of Justice established by the *Charter of the United Nations* as the principal judicial organ of the United Nations shall be constituted and shall function in accordance with the provisions of the present Statute.

Chapter I

Organization of the Court

Article 2

The Court shall be composed of a body of independent judges, elected regardless of their nationality from among persons of high moral character, who possess the qualifications required in their respective countries for appointment to the highest judicial offices, or are juris-consults of recognized competence in international law.

Article 3

1. The Court shall consist of fifteen members, no two of whom may be nationals of the same state.

2. A person who for the purposes of membership in the Court could be regarded as a national of more than one state shall be deemed to be a national of the one in which he ordinarily exercises civil and political rights.

Article 4

1. The members of the Court shall be elected by the General Assembly and by the Security Council from a list of persons nominated by the national groups in the Permanent Court of Arbitration, in accordance with the following provisions.

2. In the case of Members of the United Nations not represented in the Permanent Court of Arbitration, candidates shall be nominated by national groups appointed for this purpose by their governments under the same conditions as those prescribed for members of the Permanent Court of Arbitration by Article 44 of the Convention of The Hague of 1907 for the pacific settlement of international disputes.

3. The conditions under which a state which is a party to the present Statute but is not a Member of the United Nations may participate in electing the members of the Court shall, in the absence of a special agreement, be laid down by the General Assembly upon recommendation of the Security Council.

Article 5

1. At least three months before the date of the election, the Secretary-General of the United Nations shall address a written request to the members of the Permanent Court of Arbitration belonging to the states which are parties to the present Statute, and to the members of the national groups appointed under Article 4, paragraph 2, inviting them to undertake, within a given time, by national groups, the nomination of persons in a position to accept the duties of a member of the Court.

2. No group may nominate more than four persons, not more than two of whom shall be of their own nationality. In no case may the number of candidates nominated by a group be more than double the number of seats to be filled.

Article 6

Before making these nominations, each national group is recommended to consult its highest court of justice, its legal faculties and schools of law, and its national academies and national sections of international academies devoted to the study of law.

Article 7

1. The Secretary-General shall prepare a list in alphabetical order of all the persons thus nominated. Save as provided in *Article 12*, paragraph 2, these shall be the only persons eligible.

2. The Secretary-General shall submit this list to the General Assembly and to the Security Council.

Article 8

The General Assembly and the Security Council shall proceed independently of one another to elect the members of the Court.

Article 9

At every election, the electors shall bear in mind not only that the persons to be elected should individually possess the qualifications required, but also that in the body as a whole the representation of the main forms of civilization and of the principal legal systems of the world should be assured.

Article 10

1. Those candidates who obtain an absolute majority of votes in the General Assembly and in the Security Council shall be considered as elected.

2. Any vote of the Security Council, whether for the election of judges or for the appointment of members of the conference envisaged in *Article 12*, shall be taken without any distinction between permanent and non-permanent members of the Security Council.

3. In the event of more than one national of the same state obtaining an absolute majority of the votes both of the General

Assembly and of the Security Council, the eldest of these only shall be considered as elected.

Article 11

If, after the first meeting held for the purpose of the election, one or more seats remain to be filled, a second and, if necessary, a third meeting shall take place.

Article 12

1. If, after the third meeting, one or more seats still remain unfilled, a joint conference consisting of six members, three appointed by the General Assembly and three by the Security Council, may be formed at any time at the request of either the General Assembly or the Security Council, for the purpose of choosing by the vote of an absolute majority one name for each seat still vacant, to submit to the General Assembly and the Security Council for their respective acceptance.

2. If the joint conference is unanimously agreed upon any person who fulfils the required conditions, he may be included in its list, even though he was not included in the list of nominations referred to in *Article 7*.

3. If the joint conference is satisfied that it will not be successful in procuring an election, those members of the Court who have already been elected shall, within a period to be fixed by the Security Council, proceed to fill the vacant seats by selection from among those candidates who have obtained votes either in the General Assembly or in the Security Council.

4. In the event of an equality of votes among the judges, the eldest judge shall have a casting vote.

Article 13

1. The members of the Court shall be elected for nine years and may be reselected; however, that of the judges elected at the first election, the terms of five judges shall expire at the end of three years and the terms of five more judges shall expire at the end of six years.

2. The judges whose terms are to expire at the end of the abovementioned initial periods of three and six years shall be chosen by lot to be drawn by the Secretary-General immediately after the first election has been completed.

3. The members of the Court shall continue to discharge their duties until their places have been filled. Though replaced, they shall finish any cases which they may have begun.

4. In the case of the resignation of a member of the Court, the resignation shall be addressed to the President of the Court for transmission to the Secretary-General. This last notification makes the place vacant.

Article 14

Vacancies shall be filled by the same method as that laid down for the first election, subject to the following provision: the Secretary-General shall, within one month of the occurrence of the vacancy, proceed to issue the invitations provided for in *Article 5*, and the date of the election shall be fixed by the Security Council.

Article 15

A member of the Court elected to replace a member whose term of office has not expired shall hold office for the remainder of his predecessor's term.

Article 16

1. No member of the Court may exercise any political or administrative function, or engage in any other occupation of a professional nature.

2. Any doubt on this point shall be settled by the decision of the Court.

Article 17

1. No member of the Court may act as agent, counsel, or advocate in any case.

2. No member may participate in the decision of any case in which he has previously taken part as agent, counsel, or advocate for one of the parties, or as a member of a national or international court, or of a commission of enquiry, or in any other capacity.

3. Any doubt on this point shall be settled by the decision of the Court.

Article 18

1. No member of the Court can be dismissed unless, in the unanimous opinion of the other members, he has ceased to fulfill the required conditions.

2. Formal notification thereof shall be made to the Secretary-General by the Registrar.

3. This notification makes the place vacant.

Article 19

The members of the Court, when engaged on the business of the Court, shall enjoy diplomatic privileges and immunities.

Article 20

Every member of the Court shall, before taking up his duties, make a solemn declaration in open court that he will exercise his powers impartially and conscientiously.

Article 21

1. The Court shall elect its President and Vice-President for three years; they may be reselected.

2. The Court shall appoint its Registrar and may provide for the appointment of such other officers as may be necessary.

Article 22

1. The seat of the Court shall be established at The Hague. This however, shall not prevent the Court from sitting and exercising its functions elsewhere whenever the Court considers it desirable.

2. The President and the Registrar shall reside at the seat of the Court.

Article 23

1. The Court shall remain permanently in session, except during the judicial vacations, the dates and duration of which shall be fixed by the Court.

2. Members of the Court are entitled to periodic leave, the dates and duration of which shall be fixed by the Court, having in mind the distance between The Hague and the home of each judge.

3. Members of the Court shall be bound, unless they are on leave or prevented from attending by illness or other serious reasons duly explained to the President, to hold themselves permanently at the disposal of the Court.

Article 24

1. If, for some special reason, a member of the Court considers that he should not take part in the decision of a particular case, he shall so inform the President.

2. If the President considers that for some special reason one of the members of the Court should not sit in a particular case, he shall give him notice accordingly.

3. If in any such case the member of the Court and the President disagree, the matter shall be settled by the decision of the Court.

Article 25

1. The full Court shall sit except when it is expressly provided otherwise in the present Statute.

2. Subject to the condition that the number of judges available to constitute the Court is not thereby reduced below eleven, the Rules of the Court may provide for allowing one or more judges, according to circumstances and in rotation, to be dispensed from sitting.

3. A quorum of nine judges shall suffice to constitute the Court.

Article 26

1. The Court may from time to time form one or more chambers, composed of three or more judges as the Court may determine, for dealing with particular categories of cases; for example, labor cases and cases relating to transit and communications.

2. The Court may at any time form a chamber for dealing with a particular case. The number of judges to constitute such a chamber shall be determined by the Court with the approval of the parties

3. Cases shall be heard and determined by the chambers provided for in this Article if the parties so request.

Article 27

A judgment given by any of the chambers provided for in Articles 26 and 29 shall be considered as rendered by the Court.

Article 28

The chambers provided for in Articles 26 and 29 may, with the consent of the parties, sit and exercise their functions elsewhere than at The Hague.

Article 29

With a view to the speedy despatch of business, the Court shall form annually a chamber composed of five judges which, at the request of the parties, may hear and determine cases by summary procedure. In addition, two judges shall be selected for the purpose of replacing judges who find it impossible to sit.

Article 30

1. The Court shall frame rules for carrying out its functions. In particular, it shall lay down rules of procedure.

2. The Rules of the Court may provide for assessors to sit with the Court or with any of its chambers, without the right to vote.

Article 31

1. Judges of the nationality of each of the parties shall retain their right to sit in the case before the Court.

2. If the Court includes upon the Bench a judge of the nationality of one of the parties, any other party may choose a person to sit as judge. Such person shall be chosen preferably from among those persons who have been nominated as candidates as provided in *Articles 4* and *5*.

3. If the Court includes upon the Bench no judge of the nationality of the parties, each of these parties may proceed to choose a judge as provided in paragraph 2 of this Article.

4. The provisions of this Article shall apply to the case of *Articles 26* and *29*. In such cases, the President shall request one or, if necessary, two of the members of the Court forming the chamber to give place to the members of the Court of the nationality of the parties concerned, and, failing such, or if they are unable to be present, to the judges specially chosen by the parties.

5. Should there be several parties in the same interest, they shall, for the purpose of the preceding provisions, be reckoned as one party only. Any doubt upon this point shall be settled by the decision of the Court.

6. Judges chosen as laid down in paragraphs 2, 3, and 4 of this Article shall fulfill the conditions required by Articles 2, 17 (paragraph 2), 20 and 24 of the present Statute. They shall take part in the decision on terms of complete equality with their colleagues.

Article 32

1. Each member of the Court shall receive an annual salary.

2. The President shall receive a special annual allowance.

3. The Vice-President shall receive a special allowance for every day on which he acts as President.

4. The judges chosen under Article 31, other than members of the Court, shall receive compensation for each day on which they exercise their functions.

5. Their salaries, allowances, and compensation shall be fixed by the General Assembly. They may not be decreased during the term of office.

6. The salary of the Registrar shall be fixed by the General Assembly on the proposal of the Court.

7. Regulations made by the General Assembly shall fix the conditions under which retirement pensions may be given to members of the Court and to the Registrar, and the conditions under which members of the Court and the Registrar shall have their travelling expenses refunded.

8. The above salaries, allowances, and compensation shall be free of all taxation.

Article 33

The expenses of the Court shall be borne by the United Nations in such a manner as shall be decided by the General Assembly.

CHAPTER II
COMPETENCE OF THE COURT

Article 34

1. Only states may be parties in cases before the Court.

2. The Court, subject to and in conformity with its Rules, may request of public international organizations information relevant to cases before it, and shall receive such information presented by such organizations on their own initiative.

3. Wherever the construction of the constituent instrument of a public international organization or of an international convention adopted thereunder is in question in a case before the

Court, the Registrar shall so notify the public international organization concerned and shall communicate to it copies of all the written proceedings.

Article 35

1. The Court shall be open to the states parties to the present Statute.

2. The conditions under which the Court shall be open to other states shall, subject to the special provisions contained in treaties in force, be laid down by the Security Council, but in no case shall such conditions place the parties in a position of inequality before the Court.

3. When a state which is not a Member of the United Nations is a party to a case, the Court shall fix the amount which that party is to contribute towards the expenses of the Court. This provision shall not apply if such state is bearing a share of the expenses of the Court.

Article 36

1. The jurisdiction of the Court comprises all cases which the parties refer to it and all matters specially provided for in the Charter of the United Nations or in treaties and conventions in force.

2. The states parties to the present Statute may at any time declare that they recognize as compulsory *ipso facto* and without special agreement, in relation to any other state accepting the same obligation, the jurisdiction of the Court in all legal disputes concerning:

a. the interpretation of a treaty;

b. any question of international law;

c. the existence of any fact which, if established, would constitute a breach of an international obligation;

d. the nature or extent of the reparation to be made for the breach of an international obligation.

3. The declarations referred to above may be made unconditionally or on condition of reciprocity on the part of several or certain states, or for a certain time.

4. Such declarations shall be deposited with the Secretary-General of the United Nations, who shall transmit copies thereof to the parties to the Statute and to the Registrar of the Court.

5. Declarations made under Article 36 of the Statute of the Permanent Court of International Justice and which are still in force shall be deemed, as between the parties to the present Statute, to be acceptances of the compulsory jurisdiction of the International Court of Justice for the period which they still have to run and in accordance with their terms.

6. In the event of a dispute as to whether the Court has jurisdiction, the matter shall be settled by the decision of the Court.

Article 37

Whenever a treaty or convention in force provides for reference of a matter to a tribunal to have been instituted by the League of Nations, or to the Permanent Court of International Justice, the matter shall, as between the parties to the present Statute, be referred to the International Court of Justice.

Article 38

1. The Court, whose function is to decide in accordance with international law such disputes as are submitted to it, shall apply:

a. international conventions, whether general or particular, establishing rules expressly recognized by the contesting states;

b. international custom, as evidence of a general practice accepted as law;

c. the general principles of law recognized by civilized nations;

d. subject to the provisions of Article 5, judicial decisions and the teachings of the most highly qualified publicists of the various nations, as subsidiary means for the determination of rules of law.

2. This provision shall not prejudice the power of the Court to decide a case *ex aequo et bono*, if the parties agree thereto.

CHAPTER III

Procedure

Article 39

1. The official languages of the Court shall be French and English. If the parties agree that the case shall be conducted in French, the judgment shall be delivered in French. If the parties agree that the case shall be conducted in English, the judgment shall be delivered in English.

2. In the absence of an agreement as to which language shall be employed, each party may, in the pleadings, use the language which it prefers; the decision of the Court shall be given in French and English. In this case the Court shall at the same time determine which of the two texts shall be considered as authoritative.

3. The Court shall, at the request of any party, authorize a language other than French or English to be used by that party.

Article 40

1. Cases are brought before the Court, as the case may be, either by the notification of the special agreement or by a written application addressed to the Registrar. In either case the subject of the dispute and the parties shall be indicated.

2. The Registrar shall forthwith communicate the application to all concerned.

3. He shall also notify the Members of the United Nations through the Secretary-General, and also any other states entitled to appear before the Court.

Article 41

1. The Court shall have the power to indicate, if it considers that circumstances so require, any provisional measures which ought to be taken to preserve the respective rights of either party.

2. Pending the final decision, notice of the measures suggested shall forthwith be given to the parties and to the Security Council.

Article 42

1. The parties shall be represented by agents.

2. They may have the assistance of counsel or advocates before the Court.

3. The agents, counsel, and advocates of parties before the Court shall enjoy the privileges and immunities necessary for the independent exercise of their duties.

Article 43

1. The procedure shall consist of two parts: written and oral.

2. The written proceedings shall consist of the communication to the Court and to the parties of memorials, counter-memorials and, if necessary, replies; also all papers and documents in support.

3. These communications shall be made through the Registrar, in the order and within the time fixed by the Court.

4. A certified copy of every document produced by one party shall be communicated to the other party.

5. The oral proceedings shall consist of the hearing by the Court of witnesses, experts, agents, counsel, and advocates.

Article 44

1. For the service of all notices upon persons other than the agents, counsel, and advocates, the Court shall apply direct to the government of the state upon whose territory the notice has to be served.

2. The same provision shall apply whenever steps are to be taken to procure evidence on the spot.

Article 45

The hearing shall be under the control of the President or, if he is unable to preside, of the Vice-President; if neither is able to preside' the senior judge present shall preside.

Article 46

The hearing in Court shall be public, unless the Court shall decide otherwise, or unless the parties demand that the public be not admitted.

Article 47

1. Minutes shall be made at each hearing and signed by the Registrar and the President.

2. These minutes alone shall be authentic.

Article 48

The Court shall make orders for the conduct of the case, shall decide the form and time in which each party must conclude its arguments and make all arrangements connected with the taking of evidence.

Article 49

The Court may, even before the hearing begins, call upon the agents to produce any document or to supply any explanations. Formal note shall be taken of any refusal.

Article 50

The Court may, at any time, entrust any individual, body, bureau, commission, or other organization that it may select, with the task of carrying out an enquiry or giving an expert opinion.

Article 51

During the hearing any relevant questions are to be put to the witnesses and experts under thc conditions laid down by the Court in the rules of procedure referred to in *Article 30*.

Article 52

After the Court has received the proofs and evidence within the time specified for the purpose, it may refuse to accept any further oral or written evidence that one party may desire to present unless the other side consents.

Article 53

1. Whenever one of the parties does not appear before the Court, or fails to defend its case, the other party may call upon the Court to decide in favor of its claim.

2. The Court must, before doing so, satisfy itself, not only that it has jurisdiction in accordance with Articles 36 and 37, but also that the claim is well founded In fact and law.

Article 54

1. When, subject to the control of the Court, the agents, counsel, and advocates have completed their presentation of the case, the President shall declare the hearing closed.

2. The Court shall withdraw to consider the judgment.

3. The deliberations of the Court shall take place in private and remain secret.

Article 55

1. All questions shall be decided by a majority of the judges present.

2. In the event of an equality of votes, the President or the judge who acts in his place shall have a casting vote.

Article 56

1. The judgment shall state the reasons on which it is based.

2. It shall contain the names of the judges who have taken part in the decision.

Article 57

If the judgment does not represent in whole or in part the unanimous opinion of the judges, any judge shall be entitled to deliver a separate opinion.

Article 58

The judgment shall be signed by the President and by the Registrar. It shall be read in open court, due notice having been given to the agents.

Article 59

The decision of the Court has no binding force except between the parties and in respect of that particular case.

Article 60

The judgment is final and without appeal. In the event of dispute as to the meaning or scope of the judgment, the Court shall construe it upon the request of any party.

Article 61

1. An application for revision of a judgment may be made only when it is based upon the discovery of some fact of such a nature as to be a decisive factor, which fact was, when the judgment was given, unknown to the Court and also to the party claiming revision, always provided that such ignorance was not due to negligence.

2. The proceedings for revision shall be opened by a judgment of the Court expressly recording the existence of the new fact, recognizing that it has such a character as to lay the case open to revision, and declaring the application admissible on this ground.

3. The Court may require previous compliance with the terms of the judgment before it admits proceedings in revision.

4. The application for revision must be made at latest within six months of the discovery of the new fact.

5. No application for revision may be made after the lapse of ten years from the date of the judgment.

Article 62

1. Should a state consider that it has an interest of a legal nature which may be affected by the decision in the case, it may submit a request to the Court to be permitted to intervene.

2. It shall be for the Court to decide upon this request.

Article 63

1. Whenever the construction of a convention to which states other than those concerned in the case are parties is in question, the Registrar shall notify all such states forthwith.

2. Every state so notified has the right to intervene in the proceedings; but if it uses this right, the construction given by the judgment will be equally binding upon it.

Article 64

Unless otherwise decided by the Court, each party shall bear its own costs.

CHAPTER IV

Advisory Opinions

Article 65

1. The Court may give an advisory opinion on any legal question at the request of whatever body may be authorized by or in accordance with the Charter of the United Nations to make such a request.

2. Questions upon which the advisory opinion of the Court is asked shall be laid before the Court by means of a written

request containing an exact statement of the question upon which an opinion is required, and accompanied by all documents likely to throw light upon the question.

Article 66

1. The Registrar shall forthwith give notice of the request for an advisory opinion to all states entitled to appear before the Court.

2. The Registrar shall also, by means of a special and direct communication, notify any state entitled to appear before the Court or international organization considered by the Court, or, should it not be sitting, by the President, as likely to be able to furnish information on the question, that the Court will be prepared to receive, within a time limit to be fixed by the President, written statements, or to hear, at a public sitting to be held for the purpose, oral statements relating to the question.

3. Should any such state entitled to appear before the Court have failed to receive the special communication referred to in paragraph 2 of this Article, such state may express a desire to submit a written statement or to be heard; and the Court will decide.

4. States and organizations having presented written or oral statements or both shall be permitted to comment on the statements made by other states or organizations in the form, to the extent, and within the time limits which the Court, or, should it not be sitting, the President, shall decide in each particular case. Accordingly, the Registrar shall in due time communicate any such written statements to states and organizations having submitted similar statements.

Article 67

The Court shall deliver its advisory opinions in open court, notice having been given to the Secretary-General and to the representatives of Members of the United Nations, of other states and of international organizations immediately concerned.

Article 68

In the exercise of its advisory functions the Court shall further be guided by the provisions of the present Statute which apply in contentious cases to the extent to which it recognizes them to be applicable.

CHAPTER V

AMENDMENTS

Article 69

Amendments to the present Statute shall be effected by the same procedure as is provided by the Charter of the United Nations for amendments to that Charter, subject however to any provisions which the General Assembly upon recommendation of the Security Council may adopt concerning the participation of states which are parties to the present Statute but are not Members of the United Nations.

Article 70

The Court shall have power to propose such amendments to the present Statute as it may deem necessary, through written communications to the Secretary-General, for consideration in conformity with the provisions of *Article 69*.

INDEX

www.ingramcontent.com/pod-product-compliance
Lightning Source LLC
Chambersburg PA
CBHW021548210326
41599CB00010B/355

* 9 7 8 9 7 6 8 1 6 7 4 1 5 *